IMPROVED WOOD, WASTE AND CHARCOAL BURNING STOVES

Improved Wood, Waste and Charcoal Burning Stoves

A practitioners' manual

BILL STEWART and others

INTERMEDIATE TECHNOLOGY PUBLICATIONS 1987

A NOTE ON THE AUTHORS

This book began life in 1983 when the ITDG Stoves Team decided that a manual on stoves aimed specifically at the field practitioner was vitally needed to enable stove projects at the community level to set themselves up effectively and to expand within their locality. Bill Stewart wrote the first draft during 1984. Incorporating comments, changes and additions from Stephen Joseph, Yvonne Shanahan, Pete Young, Jon Loose, Ian Grant and others too numerous to mention, a second draft was produced with the invaluable assistance of Sandra Conn in 1985.

At this point, it was felt that the book was very light on dissemination, on moving the project beyond a community to the surrounding areas. Additional chapters were written by Vivienne Abbott on training, and Simon Burne on economics and marketing, and the whole book went through a final edit and update co-ordinated by Simon Burne. The stove design chapter was completely rewritten by Vivienne Abbott and substantial changes were made throughout Sections One and Two, by a number of people. The text illustrations were done by Frances Stuart; the technical drawings are by Pete Young.

In such a massive and long-term project as this, many players inevitably become involved. This genuine team effort, with positive contributions from many different people with diverse perspectives, has led to a book which, it is hoped, will be valuable to fieldworkers around the world.

ACKNOWLEDGEMENTS

The authors and publishers would like to thank the Overseas Development Administration of the British Government for its assistance in the production of this publication, and for reviewing initial drafts.

This publication would not have been possible without the extensive assistance of the following organizations in particular: Dian Desa in Indonesia; RECAST in Nepal; the Gandhi-niketan in South India; the Samodaya Shramadana and the Ceylon Electricity Board in Sri Lanka; KENGO in Kenya; the Department of Community Development in the Gambia; and the National Energy Administration, and the FAO Regional Office, in Thailand. And of course many others too numerous to mention.

Intermediate Technology Publications
9 King Street, Covent Garden
London WC2E 8HW, UK

ISBN 0 946688 65 6

Typeset by Inforum Ltd, Portsmouth
Printed by Short Run Press, Exeter

Contents

Preface

This book is based on the experiences of the ITDG Stoves Project since 1979. During this time the Group has been involved with a wide variety of grass roots, national and international stove activities. It concentrates on the practical operational aspects of a stove project – assessing users' needs; choosing, testing, and adapting stove designs; producing stoves with local resources.

For a number of reasons the book is designed as a reference manual rather than as a stove programme guide. Firstly, the manual is designed for the 'stove practitioner': the person working in a stove project who has responsibility for many different aspects of the project but who doesn't have the time or inclination to sit down and read a learned and weighty tome. As a stove programme develops the need for specific information will be stretched over a period of time, and much of the data on certain stove types or materials will not be appropriate to individual programmes. Also, as the programme progresses and evolves, there will often be a need to develop new options which means approaching the situation again from a different angle. Finally, the organization and implementation of stove programmes, which can be more important than the technical aspects, is covered in the companion ITDG publication on 'Planning and Implementation'.

The manual has been deliberately kept simple. Stove practitioners come from a variety of backgrounds – engineers, teachers, community workers – and this manual aims at providing basic information on all aspects of running a stove project. It is not definitive. Stove experts may find the technical detail too brief: it is deliberately so. Stove practitioners seldom have the luxury of laboratory equipment or computers. Theories of stove design and testing are deliberately aimed at enabling people without high qualification in chemical engineering or combustion dynamics to be able to optimize a stove within their own capabilities.

Structure of the manual

This manual is divided into three sections. The first chapter in Part I outlines the critical issues and steps involved in assessing the situation, especially from the users' point of view. Other publications, in addition to the companion ITDG volume mentioned above, are cited that cover this topic in much greater detail, to which reference should be made when planning and implementing large programmes.

The following three chapters are technical – one covering some scientific background that is useful in designing stoves, another on practical stove-testing procedures, and a final chapter on choosing stove designs appropriate to a particular situation.

Part II covers the basic components of four different stove types – chimney stoves, multi-pot chimneyless stoves, one-pot chimney stoves, and one-pot chimneyless stoves (wood- and waste-burning), and charcoal-burning stoves. Twenty-six different stoves that are being used in on-going dissemination programmes are described. The stoves were chosen to illustrate the diversity of designs and experiences from programmes that have adapted to different user needs and local resources.

Part III takes the stove practitioner from the proven design phase, where limited numbers of stoves have been successfully field tested, to the dissemination phase where stoves become widespread within the area of operation of the project. The first chapter looks at training, often the key to successful dissemination. The following two chapters look at some simple tools for costing stoves effectively and for marketing. Finally, we take a look at production systems and the wide range of options available for producing stoves, from relatively capital-intensive factory production to artisanal production on an individual or family basis.

Note. Except where otherwise stated, all dimensions given in this manual are in centimetres.

PART I
GETTING IT RIGHT

No programme of any sort will succeed unless time is spent at the beginning ensuring that what is 'on offer' is what people really want. In stoves projects, the mistake has been made so often of assuming that an existing stove will be popular in an area simply because it 'saves fuel', or because it performs well in a laboratory.

This section aims to provide you with an understanding of the principles of stove design, both in practice and in theory, and also of the advantages and limitations of different methods of stove testing.

Any successful stove project must put the users first. Unless you find out from people what their own needs and priorities are for an improved stove, you could waste your time designing something which is totally inappropriate. Similarly, designing a stove which cannot be manufactured using local skills and resources will be a fruitless task. Finally, of course, if people cannot afford the stove, then it will not succeed however good it is.

The theory of combustion and heat transfer is complex and not entirely understood by advanced chemists and physicists. While there are complex formulae for calculating 'view factors' and the like, they are only of relevance for high-technology furnaces. For the stove practitioner, some basic ground rules exist which will enable you to optimize more easily the performance of a stove.

Stove testing has been subject to a fairly intense debate over the last few years and is still to be resolved clearly. This manual aims to set out accepted methodologies with their advantages and disadvantages, for practitioners to make their own choice. Ultimately, the only meaningful test is if people use the stove and actually save fuel in practice.

Part I finishes with an examination of different stove materials, and their particular properties and suitabilities to different stove designs and user requirements.

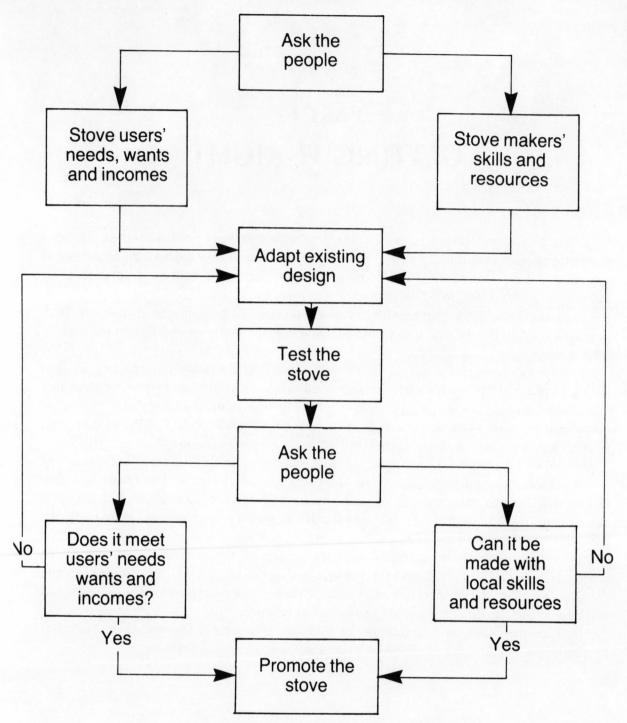

Figure 1: Developing an Appropriate Stove Design

CHAPTER 1

Assessing the situation

The open fires and traditional stoves used throughout much of the world are usually easy to build and to use but there are many cases where improvements could alleviate some of the associated problems. These problems can be grouped into three main categories:

- high fuel consumption, especially where fuel is already, or is becoming, expensive or difficult to collect
- health dangers from smoke particles, poisonous gases, or burns
- general inconvenience, such as being difficult to light, difficult to control heat output, requiring constant attention, etc.

There are many traditional solutions that have been used by people around the world that do not involve changing the open fire or traditional stove. These include more careful fire tending, improving the smoke removal with large chimneys or better ventilation, raising the fire onto a table, changing to other fuels such as kerosene, electricity or natural gas, etc.

Another, often complementary, approach is to introduce an improved stove design. While this often promises to mitigate more of the problems at a lower cost than a collection of simpler traditional improvements, the achievement of considerable positive results requires a thorough assessment of the situation and a systematic strategy to develop appropriate stove designs and dissemination schemes.

One of the first steps should be an assessment of the situation. The following simple guidelines are orientated towards small projects where there has already been a decision to pursue some type of activity to relieve some of the problems associated with the use of open fires or traditional stoves. The analysis of the results of the assessment should influence the pattern of project implementation. Assessment of the community, its range of households, and traditional stoves, in regard to the questions listed will help to prevent unsuitable decisions being made during implementation of the project (for example, in the choice of stove design, the selection of households for field testing and the extension method used). While fieldworkers can rarely change the overall approach of the project, they will be more effective in the field if they take into account the specific local situation when matching a new technology to the users' needs and local resources.

A major reason for obtaining a thorough understanding of the existing situation is that it is easier to promote a new (improved) stove that accommodates as many as possible of the traditional and useful functions of the existing fireplace or stove, than to try to introduce a stove which is very different, however efficient and inexpensive it may be.

For small projects the best approach is not to try to collect statistically accurate information, but rather to define the structure of the community and gather information on each group to obtain a composite view. It is always more difficult to gain information about the poorer groups, but it is important to realize that their problems and available resources are usually very different from those of other sections of the community. Larger projects should be more thorough in their assessment stage because more money and resources will be involved, and there will be less flexibility to change later strategies.

Assessment of the factors which will influence the introduction of new stoves

At the community level factors which influence the pattern of a stove programme, from stove design to dissemination of a new stove, can be grouped into four main categories:

(1) *Area profile*
   physical environment; socio-economic factors; community structure; structure and experience of implementing agency/organization

(2) *The household*
   with particular reference to fuel collection or purchase; the kitchen, fireplace or stove; pots, typical meals and their cooking requirements; kitchen economics; variations between households

(3) *Available infrastructure for new stoves*
   traditional skills; local artisans; available materials; possible outside assistance (e.g. training)

(4) *The user-perceived needs* in connection with the fireplace and their reconciliation with the objectives of the people or group promoting the stoves.

Information must be gathered on all these aspects.

The assessment survey

It is assumed that this preliminary assessment will be done not by a trained social scientist, but by a motivated field worker, community organiser, or technical person. The assessment will probably be completed in less than a month of part-time activity. The purpose of the data collection is not to gather quantitative information through a needs assessment / project appraisal study but to provide qualitative information from which design criteria and a programme strategy can be developed. It is assumed that there will be continual collection of data to assist in re-defining objectives and solving problems as they arise.

Information can be obtained from census data, government publications, research, interviews with people from the range of classes or castes that exist in the community, and from observation.

Information to be collected

1. AREA PROFILES

Environment
   - physical position of the community in relation to towns, other villages, roads, mountains, open land, forests
   - altitude
   - rainfall, prevailing winds, seasonal weather pattern
   - land use (arable, grazing, homesteads, wasteland, forests, plantations); estimate of the amount of land in each category
   - population size and density; comparison with other areas.

Environmental conditions influence the availability of fuel to a large extent. Household interviews with a range of community members will be necessary to discover details about access and rights to gather fuel, problems presented by seasonal changes or by increasing population density, etc. Variations between different sectors of the community should be noted. It should be remembered that the time of year the assessment is carried out may affect some of the answers received.

Socio-economic
   - types of employment in the community, and places of work
   - seasonal variations in employment
   - conditions of land ownership and of access to the different community members
   - the community's degree of integration in the regional market system for purchase and sale of food, goods and services.

This will give information on availability of cash, labour, and other goods, which will influence the choice of stove design(s) to meet the resources the community is willing to use.

Community structure
- the different community groups, (high / low caste, large / small landowners, landlords / tenants, political groupings, members of co-operatives or a village communal system, etc), and the factors affecting their interaction (different languages, employment, etc.)
- the influential groups and individuals in the community and their role in local politics, economy, introduction and promotion of new ideas, etc.
- the work and functions of local government officials in the community
- the type and function of community-organized groups

- the nature of contact between the community and non-governmental outside organizations; the functions of such organizations.

The organization of a community is one of the main factors affecting whether and how an innovation spreads through its different groups. Knowledge of community groupings will improve the ability to design special approaches for groups that have limited resources (e.g. in terms of wealth, contact with government or other organizations) and which do not share contact or information with other groups.

Implementing agency or organization
The agency or organization considering implementing a programme to introduce new stoves should be described, stating its role and listing its existing activities, staff and accomplishments. In particular, note should be made of previous in-

Table 1.1: How the situation can affect the design of a stove or stove programme

Kitchens

Small kitchens	will require smaller stoves
Poorly ventilated	a chimney stove might be successfully introduced (although they have certain disadvantages – see Chapter 2)
Thatched roofs	metal chimneys can be a problem
Temporary	people often do not want to invest in a new fixed stove in a temporary kitchen
Site of kitchen changes seasonally	one improved stove will only be used part of the year unless it is portable

Pots and utensils

Great variation in pot sizes and shapes	flat and round bottom pots will fit into a stove differently and may affect the gap around the pot
	where more than two or three sizes of pots are used it is very difficult to design the stove to accommodate this – special adaptations must be made for the largest and smallest pots
Very small pots	a smaller stove than that for the typical household is required
Very large pots	a larger stove than that for the typical household is required
Cooking practice requires that two large pots are used simultaneously	the pot-holes must be far enough apart so that the pots do not touch when on the stove

Stoves

Existing stoves with a diversity of functions	the options open for the new stove to comply with the functions of the old are given in Table 1.2, but it will still be necessary to determine if the household will still wish, or find it necessary, to use the old stove for light, heat, ritual or special cooking purposes
No tradition of regular stove repair or maintenance	the extra work may be considered to be unacceptable by potential users, and in any case users would require careful training in regular stove maintenance (particularly for mud stoves, and more so if mud stoves are a new concept)

Fuels

Wide variety	it is extremely difficult to design a stove to burn all types of fuel efficiently
Plant residues and wet fuel	both require more air to burn properly; it is normal to introduce secondary air intake(s) in the design to achieve this
Wet fuel	provision of drying space near the stove may be necessary (especially when a chimney is used)
Soft wood (eg pine)	these produce more soot and tar than hard woods, requiring chimneys to be cleaned more often; extra care must be taken to avoid tar catching light in the chimney
High ash content/ low charcoal eg rice husks, straw	ash can block the passageway between the firebox and the second pot seat, lowering the draught and the performance. This can be prevented by raising the connecting tunnel above the bottom of the firebox, or alternatively users must be instructed to keep the passageways clean
Fuels that burn with a short flame	relatively few flames will reach the second pot-hole, which will slow cooking of the second pot
Small/short pieces of wood	a door to the firebox could be used to attain more efficient burning (assuming that this would not hinder observation and tending of the fire).

volvement with community-based projects, especially if they deal with women or small artisans, because they are usually the two most important groups that will affect improved stove diffusion.

2. HOUSEHOLD INFORMATION

This is the most important information to obtain, especially at the beginning of a project. The best place to collect it is from the householders through interviews. If possible, it is desirable to see the kitchen after, or during, the questioning to clarify answers and avoid omissions. It is important to reach a range of households and observe the variations that exist. The decision whether or not to build or buy a new stove is made at the household level, and the variations in households may be central to its outcome. The accompanying Table (1.1) gives examples of the ways in which the nature of the information gathered will affect the design of the new stove or the direction of the programme.

Fuel supply
- source of supply
- if collected – by whom, how often and in what quantity, how much time per collection?
- if purchased – by whom, how often, in what quantity, where from?
- some idea of the quantity of fuel obtained each week, or month
- the type(s) and size(s) of fuel in use (examine where possible)
- seasonal variations in fuel type, size or moisture content
- local practices regarding fuel preparation (cutting, drying) and storage.

Kitchen and fireplace
- kitchen type (size, entrances, ventilation, lighting, storage)
- position of fireplace or stove (floor, platform, inside, outside)
- fireplace or stove type, construction and materials (make sketches and take measurements)
- the origin of the existing fireplace or stove (built / purchased, cost, age)
- reason(s) for having or choosing this fireplace or stove, and whether, given the money or time, they would change it, or change the kitchen
- identification of the person (e.g. male or female head of household, or the cook) who would make the decision to build/buy a new stove
- method of smoke removal (if any)
- importance of the fireplace as a source of light and/or heat

- any rituals associated with fireplace / stove construction or use
- repair and cleaning requirements of the stove; done by whom?

Observations of the differences in traditional fireplaces can give important clues to the constraints caused by variations in fuels, utensils used, available construction materials, and local traditions in stove building. An indication will also be given of the importance a new stove might have in comparison with other kitchen improvements, or whether people would spend money on other household improvements first. It is important to identify the decision maker in the household regarding these matters, and to note variations between different community sections or ethnic groups etc.

Pots and utensils
- types of cooking pots used for main dish, side dishes
- special cooking pots, for example, for tea, boiling water, frying, roasting.

Sketches and measurements should be made of the pots.

Fireplace usage
- functions of the fireplace –
  o cooking: number and kind of meals, number of pots, quantity of food
  o boiling water: quantity, time of day/season room heating: time of day / season
  o light: time of day / season, required for what work or activity?
  o space heating: time of day, season.
- lighting the fire: method and frequency, or is the fire left smouldering all day?
- to what degree the fire is tended when alight, and by whom, at different times of day
- special occasions (irregular or seasonal) when the fireplace is used differently
- who does the cooking?
- cultural factors affecting position, usage, and type of stove.

A daily use cycle for the stove can be constructed from this information, and the relative importance of the different functions assessed. It is essential to spend considerable effort to get householders to explain all the functions of the old stoves. The reason(s) for wide variations between households or groups should be identified if possible.

Kitchen economics
- the cost of a kitchen building

- the cost of currently available kitchen improvements
- the cost of traditional fireplaces / stoves, and pots
- the cost of fuel and of food per day or month
- the income of each household surveyed
- the local minimum / average daily wage
- whether women in the community have independent access to cash (which could be spent on kitchen improvements)
- how decisions are made in the household, and who makes them.

Household variations
In summarizing the household survey information, it is again stressed that the variations may be as important as the similarities in directing the design of the stove.

3. AVAILABLE INFRASTRUCTURE FOR NEW STOVES

Local skills
- traditional skills for building fireplaces, houses, household and agricultural tools
- local artisans, their trade and expertise.

Materials
- range, quality and quantity of available materials
- method of supply and transport to the community.

Outside assistance
- availability of resources outside the community with respect to training (for stove builders and users), other non-training assistance, subsidies, promotion.

4. USERS' NEEDS v. PROMOTERS' OBJECTIVES

Users' needs
Historically the most important characteristic of a successful innovation is not that it has an improved technical performance, low initial cost, or good ratio of benefits to costs, but that it meets a need perceived by the potential users (Barnett, 1983). All of the stoves described in this book have certain advantages and disadvantages compared to traditional fireplaces and stoves. One of the more important purposes of the situation assessment is to give a general idea of what will be acceptable, and it is of course essential to have feedback from the users during early laboratory and field testing. It is possible however, at the assessment stage, to discuss with potential users the possible improvements that could be made and to get some idea of how people, or different groups, would rank them. For such an exchange to be both realistic and productive, it is necessary to give some indication to the potential user of what each improvement would involve in terms of cost (labour or money), *and* associated disadvantages (e.g. restrictions in the size of pots). The users are then in a position to rank their needs in the light of what is possible and acceptable to them, which will not necessarily be in the same order of priority as they had initially intended.

Table 1.2 lists the main categories of 'need' which a stove user is likely to identify, and the options available to satisfy this need, together with the associated cost or disadvantage.

Promoters' objectives
The objectives of the people or organization funding the programme and/or promoting the stoves should be listed, ranked and examined in relation to the perceived needs of the users (preferably after these needs have been ranked by potential users in the light of the options available and acceptable to them). If one of the promoters' objectives is to foster local employment this may need to be reconciled with the users' need for a new low-cost stove. Similarly, if a major objective is to save trees on a regional basis, it must be accepted by the promoters that if the user places great importance on a stove that performs other functions apart from cooking (providing room heat and light for instance) then it will not be possible to maximize fuel savings. The gaps between 'needs' and 'objectives' must be recognized and as far as possible reconciled from the outset if the programme is to have a chance of success.

Table 1.2: User requirements of a stove, the options available, and their cost

CRITERIA	OPTION	COST TO THE USER
Significant fuel savings	An artisan-built metal or pottery stove	Cash purchase
	More careful fuel preparation and fuel feeding	More time required by cook before and during meal preparation
	Cooking two pots at once	A large stove that must be built or purchased

CRITERIA	OPTION	COST TO THE USER
	A stove designed for special pots	Special pots must be purchased and cooking restricted to that size of pot
	Any improved stove	High initial cost (compared with traditional stove) and proper maintenance required for new stove
Faster cooking	Cooking two pots at once	A well-built and well-maintained stove, therefore usually initially expensive in building skills and money, and time-consuming to use and maintain
	Insertion of the pot into the stove body	Less versatility in shape and size of pots which can be used
	An efficient stove with high output	A well-built artisan- or factory-made stove (therefore expensive) which must be properly maintained (time-consuming or difficult)
Ease of operation		
– General	Cooking two pots at once	A well built (therefore difficult/expensive) and well-maintained (time-consuming) stove (and note that such a stove will be harder to operate when only one pot requires heating)
	Minimize fire attendance necessary by having a continuously burning fire	Usually requires excessive use of fuel when power inputs required are low
	Have a readily visible fire	Sacrifice higher efficiencies and faster cooking
	Raise stove on table or platform	Cost of table or platform
– With wet fuels	Use a grate or	Cost of grate
	Allow the build-up of charcoal in a high draught stove	Early use of stove is slow
– With a wide variety of fuels	A stove with variable control features	Sacrifice higher efficiency and faster cooking
Ease of maintenance	An artisan-built stove	Higher cost
	A stove with no chimney	No smoke removal
	A stove with no grate	Lower efficiency and slower cooking
Removal of smoke	A chimney stove	Higher cost, lower efficiency, slower cooking and higher maintenance requirement
	Cook outside	Wind reduces efficiency and increases cooking time
	Install hood over stove	Cost (higher than for a small chimney); but note that compared with a chimney, a hood would have a longer lifetime and require much less maintenance
Increased safety	Insulate stove	Increased cost (more materials required). A portable stove would become heavier. Efficiency may be reduced and slower cooking result
	Raise stove on table or platform	Cost of table or platform
Provide light	A stove with an open firebox	Reduced performance
Provide space heat	A metal stove	High cost, artisan-made: potential for burns
	Release the smoke	Smoke problems
	Thin-walled mud stoves, or no insulation on pottery stoves	Reduces strength, lowers lifetime of stove.
Low initial cost	Use cheap raw materials	Short lifetime
	Stove built by owner	Short lifetime, often with poor performance (associated with difficulty of accurate construction)
	Dispense with a chimney	Smoke problems
Long lifetime, and low cost per year	High quality metal or pottery stove	Higher initial cost
Aesthetically pleasing	Use high quality materials and extra finishing	Higher initial cost, possibly high construction skills

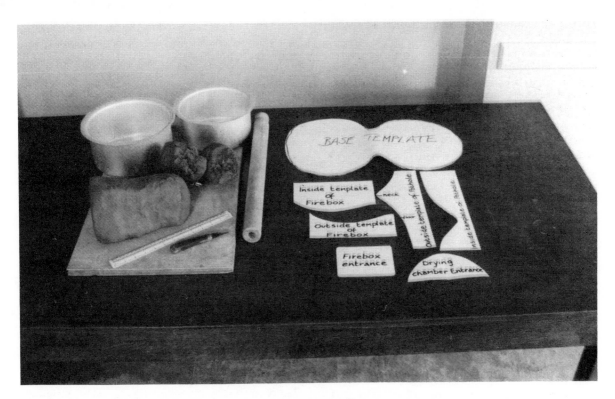

CHAPTER 2

Theory of stove design

Introduction

If a stove programme is to be successful, the stove design (or designs) must achieve certain objectives: it must 'work' i.e., achieve the technical objectives; and it must be widely acceptable to, and eventually used by, the target group.

The main technical objectives of stove design are to:

(1) maximize the efficiency of the fuel combustion process
(2) transfer heat from the source to the food (and possibly to the room) at the required rate as efficiently as possible.

The social objectives are that the resulting stove should:

Table 2.1: Ultimate analysis of some biomass fuels

Fuel	Carbon	Hydrogen	Nitrogen & sulphur	Oxygen (by difference)
Straw	49.4	6.0	0.4	44.2
Bagasse	48.0	6.0	—	46.0
Coconut shell	53.0	5.8	0.2	41.0
Wood (oak)	49.4	6.3	—	44.5
Wood (pine)	49.9	6.3	—	43.8
Peat	60.0	6.0	2.0	32.0

[Taken from Parker and Hurley, *Combustion of vegetable waste in relation to power production*, 1954]

(1) be acceptable to the vast majority of potential users
(2) offer recognizable benefits to those users
(3) be easily produced locally
(4) be cost-effective for the user.

It is unlikely that today's stove practitioner would need to design a stove from basics, since there are enough tried and tested stove designs in use around the world to enable the choice and adaptation of a suitable design.

Over the last few years considerable effort has been put into developing specific design rules from the theory. However the processes of heat transfer and combustion are so complex that the theory has only limited applications to small-scale combustion, such as occurs in a stove. Furthermore, it is impossible for the theory to incorporate the social objectives for any given situation. Despite this, before attempting to produce or choose an effective stove design, you will probably find it useful to have an understanding of the basic principles of combustion and heat transfer.

The fuel

PROPERTIES OF BIOMASS FUELS

Biomass is formed by the process known as photosynthesis – the chemical reaction combining water and carbon dioxide using the sunlight's energy. It is the reverse reaction that we call 'combustion' – the process of breaking down the biomass and releasing heat energy which can be used for cooking, heating and drying etc.

In order to use biomass effectively as a fuel it is worthwhile to have some understanding of its chemical and physical properties because it is these that determine the material's handling, combustion and heat-release characteristics.

CHEMICAL

Most biomass consists of three complex chemical compounds – hemicellulose, cellulose, and lignin. It also contains water, smaller quantities of resins and mineral salts, the latter remaining as ash after combustion. Ash has no heating value.

Table 2.1 (page 9) gives examples of the ultimate analysis of certain biomass fuels, and it can be seen that most fuels have an approximate composition of 50% carbon, 43% oxygen, and 6% hydrogen. The slight differences in chemical composition do not significantly affect the combustion performances of the different biomass fuels. However the way that the biomass structure is broken down into its components during the initial heating-up period prior to combustion often determines the heat release characteristics.

The composition of biomass is often considered in terms of the amount of fixed carbon, of volatile matter, and of ash produced when it is heated in the absence of air. This is known as the proximate analysis (Table 2.2)

TABLE 2.2: Proximate analysis of some biomass fuels

Fuel	Volatile matter	Fixed carbon	Ash	Volatile matter dry ash free
Straw	78.4	16.3	5.3	82.8
Rice husks	60.9	17.4	21.7	77.6
Bagasse	83–87	10–15	2–2.5	84–89
Coconut shells	78.0	21.6	0.4	78.3
Groundnut shells	67.0	32.4	0.6	67.4
Softwood	82.7	14.9	2.4	85.2
Hardwood	78.4	19.8	1.8	79.8
Peat	62.5	33.7	3.8	64.8

[Taken from *Combustion of vegetable waste in relation to power production*, Parker and Hurley, 1954]

PHYSICAL

There are many types of biomass fuels, including trees, grasses, shells, husks, etc. and these have very varied physical properties. Each type of biomass behaves differently when burnt and in order to maximize their effectiveness as fuels the stove design must be appropriate to the fuel.

The four main physical properties which affect combustion and therefore stove design are: size/shape, density, moisture content and calorific value.

Size/shape

The greater the overall surface area of fuel exposed to the required quantities of oxygen and heat, the faster the burning process will occur and hence the greater the power output. For example small wood chips will burn faster than larger logs of the same wood. Many biomass fuels are more useful in a briquetted form, (e.g. husks, sawdust etc.), increasing their size, reducing overall surface area and hence slowing the burning process and enabling them to be more easily handled.

The size and shape of a fuel will always affect the stove door design and the configuration of the combustion chamber.

Density/structure

The density and structure are related in so much as the proportion and size of pores in a biomass fuel affect its density. As the proportion of pores to solid matter increases, so the density decreases. These pores, holding air or moisture, have the effect of facilitating the escape of volatile gases and the breakdown of the structure as the material is burnt.

In a fuel such as wood in its natural state, the plant fibres lie virtually parallel, which promotes better burning and escape of volatiles. In many briquette fuels this structure is partially disrupted, often making such fuels more difficult to burn. However if low density residue is not compacted into pellets or briquettes, much larger combustion chambers are needed for a given heat output. The density of briquetted fuels can be varied to a certain extent.

Moisture content

Most biomass fuels are hygroscopic (they attract water and are therefore rarely 'dry'). Charcoal is the least hygroscopic but its porous structure can hold large quantities of water if it gets wet. Most recently-cut biomass fuels contain a great deal of water (80–90% on a dry-weight basis). Over a period of several months most of this moisture will evaporate, but a point will be reached when no further moisture loss occurs; the wood/biomass is then considered 'air dried', having reached its equilibrium moisture content. The moisture content of air-dried biomass depends on the relative humidity and can vary from 10–26%.

The moisture content of the fuel has a very significant effect upon combustion. After the water content of the fuel has been heated to about 100°C, it evaporates, leaving the stove and the heat energy involved in the process is effectively lost and not recoverable. For example the moisture content of recently cut biomass (80–90% moisture content on dry weight basis) would reduce the net available energy by 50–60% as against the same biomass when it had been dried, and in practice the evaporation of this moisture can cool the fire so much that it cannot burn. This problem can be corrected by seasoning and drying the fuel correctly.

Fuel with a high moisture content burns better in the traditional open fireplace, than in many improved stoves that tend to restrict the air flow.

The moisture content affects the stove design in so much as the higher the moisture content the more excess air-flow through the stove is needed. Hence a stove required to burn a high moisture content fuel will need a larger door opening and/or more air holes.

Calorific value

The calorific value (c.v.) of a fuel is also one of the physical properties that significantly affects the design of the stove.

The calorific value of a biomass fuel depends on its chemical composition and moisture content. Two values are quoted for biomass:

(1) The higher calorific value, or gross calorific value, is the maximum amount of energy that can be liberated when the fuel reacts with air. It is measured in kilojoules per kilogram of oven-dried fuel by the following specific methods as laid down by international standards.

(2) The lower calorific value or net calorific value is expressed as the high heat value less the latent heat of evaporation of the water formed as a by-product of the combustion process per kg. The average hydrogen percentage in wood is 6%; that is, every kilogramme contains 60g of chemically-bonded hydrogen which combines with oxygen during combustion, producing 0.54kg of water.

The latent heat of evaporation per kilogram of dry wood is:

$$0.54kg \times 2.26MJ/kg = 1.2204 \text{ MJ}$$

The lower heat value becomes:

$$= \text{High heat value} - 1.2204MJ/kg$$
for oven-dried fuels

In practice, of course, the fuel is seldom oven dried and the effect of water supported within the fuel has an even greater effect upon the heat released. If 1kg of wood containing 25% moisture dry basis is burnt it would consist of 0.8kg wood + 0.2kg water.

Hence the net calorific value is the gross calorific value less the heat required to evaporate 0.2kg water.

THE HEAT SOURCE – FIRE

The most important thing to remember when designing or adapting a stove is that fire requires three essential ingredients to start and to continue burning:

FUEL + OXYGEN + HEAT

If any of these are not present in sufficient quantity, the fire will not burn.

To start a fire the heat needed is usually supplied from an external source, e.g. a lighted match or perhaps, for a charcoal fire, a piece of glowing charcoal from a neighbour's fire.

Once the fire is lit, the heat needed for it to continue burning is usually supplied by the fire itself.

A fire can be controlled by controlling its supply of FUEL, OXYGEN AND HEAT.

Examples

Many charcoal stoves have a door or air holes that you can close to reduce the air flow (and hence the oxygen supply) to the fire – this causes the fire to

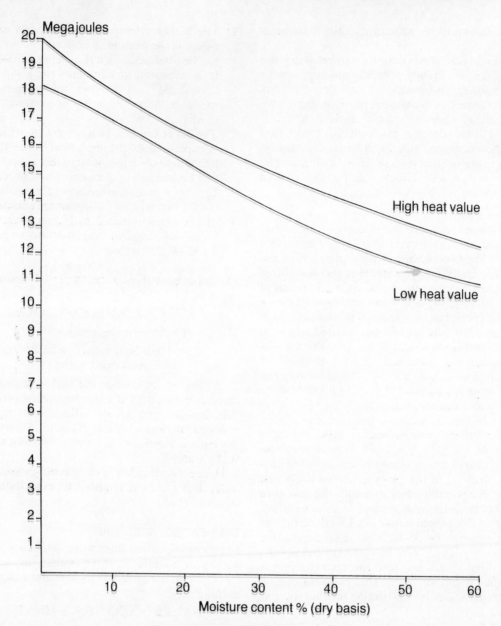

Figure 2.1. The effect of moisture content of fuel on heat value.

burn more slowly. If you want the fire to burn faster and hotter you can fan the hot coals.
– If you add more fuel to a fire (provided the supply of oxygen and heat are sufficient) the fire will burn faster and hotter.
– In a wood fire, if you move the burning logs further apart the fire cools and burns more slowly.
  The relative quantities of FUEL, OXYGEN AND HEAT needed will depend on the type of fuel to be used and on the application.

COMBUSTION
Combustion of biomass can be considered as taking place in four stages. All the stages can, how-

ever, be taking place at the same time. For example, a log of wood does not burn in one go. Similarly, a stove that is re-charged during cooking will be experiencing different phases of combustion simultaneously.

Stage 1.
In lighting the fire, supplying the initial heat source, the water content of the fuel is evaporated off at about 100°C.

Stage 2.
When the fuel temperatures reach between about 200°C and 350°C the volatile gases (compounds of

Table 2.3: Typical combustion heat values for biomass fuels

Fuel	Density kg/m³	Ash %	Combustion heat value MJ.kg
Oak hardwood	832	0.6	18.63
Fir softwood	480	0.6	20.18
Anogeissus latifolia	900	1.5	19.5
Calliandra colothyrus	650	1.8	19.3
Straw	—	—	18.42
Bagasse	—	2.0	19.26
Groundnut shell briquettes	1.2	—	18.58
Rice husks	—	25.0	12.9
Peat	—	3.8	23.3

Data taken from – *Combustion of vegetable waste in relation to power production*, Parker and Hurley, 1954; *European woods*, Brame and King, 1967; *Firewood crops*, National Academy of Sciences, Washington DC, 1980

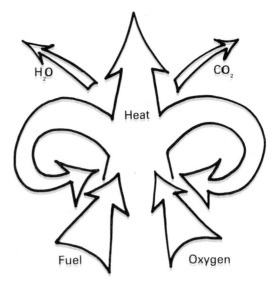

Figure 2.2.   What happens in a fire.

carbon, hydrogen, and oxygen) are released.

Stage 3.
The volatile gases mix with oxygen and ignite at temperatures in excess of about 450°C and burn with a yellowish flame radiating heat. Some of this heat is reabsorbed by the fuel releasing more volatiles. This process should become self-sustaining until all the volatiles have been released.

The volatiles need sufficient heat, oxygen, space and time to ignite. If any of these are lacking the volatiles may leave the combustion chamber without igniting; the combustion will then be incomplete and inefficient; the fire will be smoky and may die altogether.

- o The volatiles and oxygen will mix more thoroughly if the air flow through the combustion chamber is slightly turbulent.
- o When all the volatiles have been released, charcoal remains. (Charcoal is mostly fixed carbon).

Stage 4.
The charcoal burns (oxidizes), provided there is sufficient oxygen at the fire-bed, at temperatures around 800°C. The carbon monoxide produced reacts with oxygen (again provided oxygen is available) just above the fire bed, to give carbon dioxide. The charcoal will usually continue to burn long after the volatiles have been used up.

A charcoal fire requires oxygen both at the fire bed (primary air) and just above the coals (secondary air). If there is insufficient secondary air, the fire will give off carbon monoxide which can be dangerous to the stove user especially in enclosed spaces.

Note
In a charcoal-burning stove only stage 4 occurs and hence the pot can be much closer to the fire bed than in a wood burning stove where the volatiles need space to mix and react with the oxygen. In a wood fire, if large quantities of charcoal remain after the fire has burnt out it indicates insufficient oxygen or heat at the fire bed.

HEAT TRANSFER
Heat is energy. At 'absolute zero' (-273°C or 0°K) there is no molecular movement, but above this temperature the molecules of every substance vibrate. As the substance is 'heated' the molecules vibrate more. 'Heat transfer' is the transfer of this energy from one location to another: in the case of a cooking stove from the fire to the food; or in the case of space heating from the stove to the room.

There are three main modes of heat transfer:
- o CONDUCTION
- o RADIATION
- o CONVECTION

Conduction
Conduction is the passage of heat through a solid, from a hot area to a cold area.

$$\text{Conducted heat flow} = \frac{kA(T_1 - T_2)}{L}$$

where k = thermal conductivity of material
A = contact area
T_1 = higher temperature

13

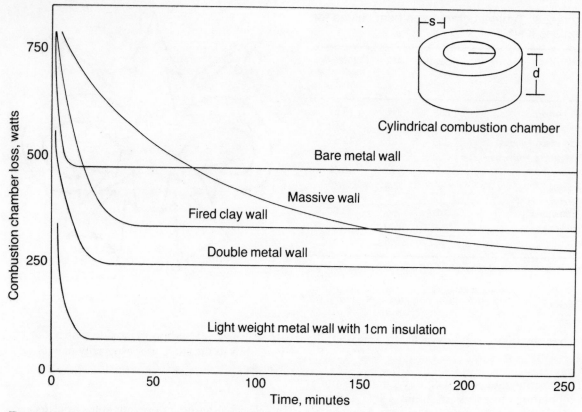

Figure 2.3 Rate of heat loss (From Baldwin, *Biomass stoves: Engineering design, development and dissemination*, VITA, 1986)

T2 = lower temperature
L = distance between hot area and cold area.

In other words the rate at which heat is conducted increases with:
 - increased contact area
 - increased temperature difference
 - increased thermal conductivity
 - reduced distance between hot and cold area.

Conductive heat transfer to the pot is relatively minimal but it is a major cause of heat loss through the stove walls. Materials such as clay and mud have much lower thermal conductivities than steel or aluminium. Therefore aluminium cooking pots increase the rate of conducted heat transfer from the outer surface of the pot into the food when they replace clay pots. However, the opposite is true when a clay or mud stove is replaced by a metal one. Then, more of the heat of the fire is carried away through the walls of the metal stove than through poorer conductive materials like mud or clay. An insulating material (i.e. material with very low thermal conductivity) can be used to reduce heat losses.

Radiation
All bodies radiate heat and the hotter they are the more they radiate. When radiated heat, which requires no medium to travel through, comes into contact with a surface it is either reflected or absorbed. The amount of radiated heat received by a body from a source is proportional to:

a) $(T_1^4 - T_2^4)$ where T_1 is the absolute temperature of the source and T_2 that of the body.
b) The projected area of the body at right angles to the radiation. Since radiation travels in straight lines like light this factor is really an expression of the extent to which the source can 'see' the body.
c) $1/L^2$ where L is the distance between the body and the source.

The amount of heat which the body actually absorbs is determined by the nature of its surface. Light coloured and shiny surfaces absorb a smaller fraction of the received radiation than dark coloured and matt surfaces.

Therefore radiated heat transfer is increased by:
 - increasing the temperature of the source

14

- reducing the distance between the receiving body and the source
- increasing the receiving area exposed
- darkening the exposed surfaces.

The yellow flame produced by the burning volatiles radiates heat as do the red-hot coals in a wood or charcoal fire. Radiation is the principal means by which heat is transferred from the fire to the pot.

Convection

Convection is the process of heat transfer by the flow of a fluid (such as air or water). There are two forms of convective heat transfer:
(1) Natural or free convection – if a hot object is placed in a stationary cooler fluid, a movement of that fluid will result due to the reduction of density of the warmed fluid close to the hot object. This fluid will rise and be replaced by cooler fluid.
(2) Forced convection relies on a source of motion (external) to the fluid. This is a more efficient method of convective heat transfer.

Convective heat transfer rate $= aA (Ts - Tf)$
where a = heat transfer coefficient
   A = area of surface receiving heat
   Ts = temperature of surface
   Tf = temperature of fluid

Convective heat transfer is increased by:
- increasing the area of contact with the fluid
- increasing the temperature difference between the fluid and the surface
- increasing the flow of the fluid with an external source of motion.

The hot waste gases carry convected heat to the cooking pot but heat is also convected away from the outside hot stove walls and the sides of the pot. In windy conditions this heat loss increases considerably.

CHIMNEYS – TO HAVE OR NOT?

Many people assume that an 'improved stove' should have a chimney. There exists the idea that a smoke-free 'kitchen' is a major advantage of having an improved stove and that a chimney is the only way to achieve this.

A well-designed chimney has two main effects: it removes smoke from the 'kitchen' and it draws air into the stove, because the hot gases in the chimney rise due to their reduced density, and cold air is drawn into the fire through the door/air holes. The rate at which it draws depends on the chimney height and diameter and on the restrictions to the passage of air.

There exist guidelines for chimney design but usually much experimentation and testing is required.

Effective working chimneys are difficult to build as the dimensions are critical and wind direction etc. can drastically change their characteristics. Chimneys need regular cleaning, too.

Chimney stoves are rarely more efficient than chimneyless stoves because the hot waste gases do not circulate and leave the stove around the pot, so the convected heat transfer from these gases to the pot is greatly reduced.

A simple efficient form of 'chimney', used in a number of the stove designs illustrated in Chapters 5 and 6, is to leave a gap around the pot (or in the case of two-pot stoves, a gap around the second pot). This gap has two functions, firstly, in enabling the hot waste gases to leave the combustion chamber, drawing air into the stove through the door/air holes, and secondly, as the hot gases leave the stove they are forced to circulate close to the cooling pot, increasing heat transfer from the gases to the pot. (Optimum gap dimensions for particular stoves are given in Part 2). This method does not remove smoke from the kitchen; however, it should also be remembered that an efficient combustion process greatly reduces the smoke in the kitchen and this may be sufficient to meet the demand for less smoky kitchens.

CHOOSING OR DESIGNING THE STOVE

However technically efficient a chosen stove design is, if that design is not acceptable to the users – if it does not offer recognizable benefits and if it is not cost effective – the stove programme will be doomed to failure. So before designing or adapting a stove there is a lot of information to be collected by talking with the target group and observing existing cooking methods.

The sorts of questions to be asked are listed in Chapter 1. The 'social' design of a stove is every bit as important as the 'technical' design and the two should be combined at all times.

It is unlikely that you will be designing a stove from scratch. What is more likely is that you will adapt features from one or more existing stove designs to meet your technical and social criteria.

Adapting a stove design may involve some of the following:
- altering stove dimensions to fit the size of pots used locally
- altering pot supports to accommodate local pots
- altering door dimensions to accommodate larger fuel
- increasing stove stability for safety or local cooking practises
- changing the materials depending on local availability

– minor design changes to make manufacture easier.

The adapted stove should be laboratory tested to ensure that the combustion and heat transfer characteristics are good, and the following critical dimensions should be optimized:

- grate diameter
- combustion chamber height
- door size
- air inlet position/size
- exhaust outlet size.

When you are confident that the stove 'works' i.e. achieves the technical objectives, the next step is to field test the design.

Organize the local manufacture of the test stoves and then distribute them to users who are prepared to try out the new design. Qualitative and quantitative data should then be collected to enable your to decide if the stove is acceptable or not, and if any further improvements can be made.

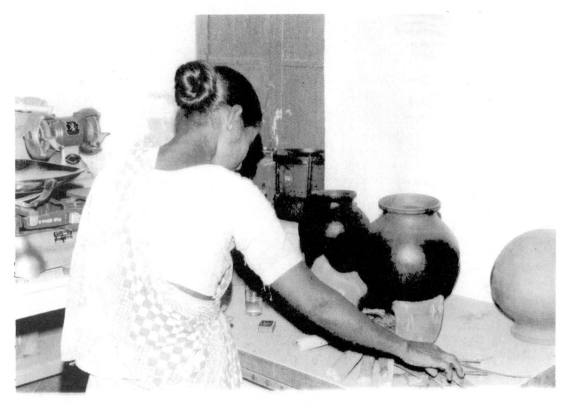

CHAPTER 3

Stove testing

Introduction

HOW TESTING FITS INTO THE OVERALL PROGRAMME PLAN

Before promoting any new type of stove it is important to have a good understanding of how its performance will compare to that of the traditional stove, or stoves, in the area.

The first step, outlined previously, is to collect information on the designs of traditional stoves, their method of operation, cooking practices, pots, and types of fuel used. This information is the essential basis of any test programme.

The next step is to review other alternative designs (such as the ones in this book) in the light of the information gathered in the situation assessment, and decide which may be suitable for the conditions in the area under consideration. This process of choosing another design or designs for testing is considered at greater length in Chapter 4, 'Choosing appropriate stove designs'. Comparative tests should then be carried out between the different stove types under local conditions. There are three types of tests, that can be carried out:

- Field Tests (carried out in kitchens to determine actual fuel use)
- Controlled Cooking Tests
- Water Boiling Tests.

Before describing these three types of test in detail, it is appropriate to make some general observations on the testing of stoves, and on the information that is derived from the tests.

REASONS FOR TESTING

The three main purposes of testing are:
(1) To determine the comparative performance of improved and traditional stoves
(2) To determine the potential and expected fuel savings offered by a new stove
(3) To obtain the data necessary for optimization of stoves.

The purpose of particular types of tests are discussed under the appropriate headings.

Basic rules in stove testing

A great deal of experience has been accumulated on this subject, coupled with considerable debate. In December 1982 a provisional standard was drafted by a group of scientists and stove practitioners, and published in 1983 by VITA. This has since been revised and finally published as *Testing the efficiency of wood-burning cookstoves*, VITA 1985. These standards are now generally accepted as the test procedure that can be applied universally. The descriptions of several of the tests which follow are based largely on the stove-testing guidelines produced by VITA.

Based on experience gathered over seven years, the ITDG Stoves Project has reached the following conclusions about the design of a test procedure or test programme.

1. *The information required from the test must be carefully defined.*

    This is neccessary is order to make the most appropriate selection from the types of test which can be carried out.

2. *The simplest test possible to meet that objective should be developed.*

    Accuracy and repeatability are much more important than the experiment's sophistication – the tester can be the greatest source of error.

3. *If resources are limited the most important piece of equipment is an accurate balance.*

    This should weigh accurately to within 1% of the smallest quantities weighed.

4. *The results and other necessary data for every*

test *in each series of tests should be methodically recorded.*

A recording form for each type of test should be carefully designed, ideally on one sheet of paper, to allow quick and logical entry of data as the test proceeds. Incorrect results occurring from careless recording and consequent miscalculation can be more misleading than those caused by inaccurate equipment or slight variations in procedures. Examples of Test Recording forms are given at the end of this chapter.

5. *Careful observation and questioning of users can reveal as much vital data on performance as can detailed laboratory and field tests.*

    The involvement of potential owners of a new stove, whether by trying out the stove in everyday use, or actually carrying out formal tests, should be a deliberate and integral part of any test programme.

In addition, it should be appreciated that accurate measurement of fuel consumption in a kitchen is extremely difficult. It can really only be undertaken in a well funded programme, where experienced research workers are available, although indirect measures have been developed that allow reasonable approximation of fuel savings to be made.

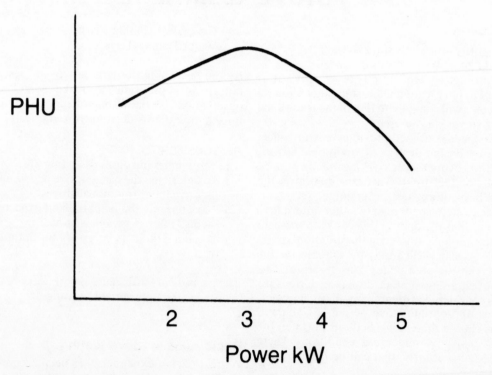

Figure 3.1. Typical PHU: power output curve for a stove.

Definitions

Performance

The tests designed to examine a stove will reveal quantitative and qualitative information about its performance, embracing the following of its characteristics:

(1) The amount of fuel required to cook a given quantity of food
(2) The thermal efficiency (or Percentage Heat Utilized – PHU) for different rates of boiling water i.e. high or low power
(3) The range of power output (also expressed as 'turn down ratio')
(4) The ease of operation
(5) Level of pollution
(6) Maintenance requirements
(7) Lifetime.

We will now clarify some of these attributes.

Efficiency

There has been much controversy over the definition of the concept of efficiency. Many workers consider it to be a valid concept for use in laboratory work, and the formula in general use is given below. It is essentially expressing the ratio of the energy transferred to the water, divided by the energy liberated by the burning fuel.

$$PHU = \frac{M_n \, C_p \, (T_b - T_o) + M_e \, L \times 100}{M_f \, E_f}$$

where –

PHU	=	Percentage Heat Utilized (Thermal Efficiency)
M_n	=	Mass of water in the pot(s) (kg)
C_p	=	Specific heat of water (kJ/kg/°C)
T_o	=	Starting temperature of the water (°C)
T_b	=	Boiling temperature of the water (°C)
M_e	=	Mass of water evaporated (kg)
L	=	Latent heat of evaporation (kJ/kg)
M	=	Weight of fuel burnt (kg)
E_f	=	Calorific value of the fuel (kJ/kg)

If charcoal is left at the end of the test (i.e. the fuel does not completely burn to ashes), then a correction can be made to allow for the energy retained in the charcoal. The weight of fuel burnt is then given by –

M_f = Weight of wood left – Weight of charcoal × 1.4

Power Output

The Power Output is the amount of energy released from the fuel in a given time, for example, a power output of 3kW equals 3 kilojoules per second, which is equivalent to about 0.6kg of dry wood per hour.

The power (P) of a stove is given by

$$P = \frac{M_f \times E_f}{t}$$

where

M_f = Weight of fuel burnt
E_f = Calorific value of the fuel
t = time

Quoting a single efficiency does not help in defining the performance of a stove as cooking usually involves a high power phase as well as intermediate (boiling) and lower (simmering) power phases. Efficiency should always be quoted in relation to a specific power output for a given pan:stove combination. Thus the graph in Figure 3.1 indicates that the maximum efficiency is gained at an output of 3kW but the stove can be used at lower or higher outputs with a consequent loss in thermal efficiency. The curve will vary with the type of wood, moisture content, etc. The curve may also shift if the operating conditions change.

Once the Power:PHU is known for a certain set of conditions (i.e. pot and wood types, and moisture content), then the aggregate efficiency for any cooking operation can be calculated.

Let us assume that the local cooking practice involves bringing one pot of water to the boil in 14 minutes. This is found to require an output from the fire of 5 kilowatts, and the PHU is 20%. The water is then simmered for 30 minutes at a power output of 2 kW (PHU = 25%). The average PHU is:

$$= 20 \times \frac{14}{14 + 30} + 25 \times \frac{30}{14 + 30}$$

$$= 6.4 + 17$$

$$= 23.4\%$$

Specific Fuel Consumption

The use of Specific Fuel Consumption (SFC) as a means for expressing the efficiency of a stove when cooking a controlled meal is extremely useful and is becoming increasingly more popular amongst the stove-testing agencies. However, the calculation of the specific fuel consumption for water boiling tests can be very misleading and needs careful definition. In water boiling tests the SFC is defined as the amount of dry wood equivalent used achieving a defined task divided by the weight of the task, for example:

The task is to boil 5 kg of water and it requires 3.5 kg of dry wood to achieve the required time of boiling.

The SFC becomes $\dfrac{\text{wood required to achieve task}}{\text{weight of water}}$

$$= \frac{3.5 \text{ kg}}{5 \text{ kg}} = 0.7$$

There are a number of other ways to calculate the SFC, particularly related to water boiling procedures, and these are described in the section on International Testing Standards.

Water Boiling Tests

INTRODUCTION

The first stage in a test programme is to carry out Water Boiling Tests. At least three different procedures have been developed, each with its advantages and disadvantages. A joint programme between Eindoven University and ITDG has indicated that at least two of these procedures give comparable results (procedures 2 and 3 below). The first procedure described can be used to make a quick assessment of a stove, without the need for any laboratory equipment.

Water Boiling Tests can be carried out in a laboratory or a field station, by scientists or field workers, at the initial assessment and development stage. They can be used for assessment of stove designs and optimization of stoves. Most frequently they are used for comparisons between stoves, or between a stove and an open fire. They can also be used to help determine the effect of deterioration or poor installation of a stove in household situations. In some cases, where cooking tests or kitchen field tests cannot be undertaken, Water Boiling Tests can be used to give a rough approximation of relative fuel savings.

Procedure I Quick assessment, with minimum equipment [detailed in the panel opposite]
Use of the Test:
To make a quick assessment of the difference in performance between two stoves.

Advantages
This test requires minimal equipment – a watch, a bottle to measure equal volumes of water, and, if no scales are available, a simple pivot balance can be constructed to make measurements of equal quantities of wood (see Figures 3.2).

= The procedure is not complicated and no special preparation of fuel is needed.

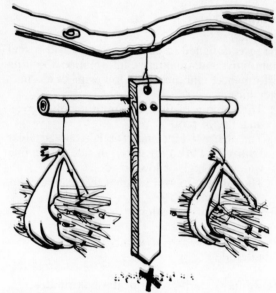

Figure 3.2.   Simple pivot balance.

= The results provide a quick indication of the relative performance between stoves.
= The results provide a clear indication if modifications to a stove significantly change its performance.
= The procedure allows one set of tests to be compared with tests done under similar conditions.
= The procedure enables designers to determine whether the performance of the stove is affected by the type, size and moisture content of the fuel, by the size and type of pots, weather conditions, etc.

Disadvantages
= The test does not indicate the range of power output of the stove, or how easily the output could be controlled.
= The test does not indicate if the performance is a function of cooking time; the warm-up time is the least efficient period, and in this type of lengthy test is considerably reduced as a proportion of the whole.
= In particular, the test does not adequately account for heat which does not actually boil the water.
= The test does not provide data for optimization.

Procedure 1
(To make a quick assessment of the difference in performance between two stoves.)

Method
(1) PREPARE THE FUEL

Take approximately 2kg of wood and divide it into two equal portions, by weight.

(2) PREPARE THE POTS

Take at least 8 pots, (4 for each stove), of the same size and weight, and fill to three quarters full with water (from the same supply – i.e. same temperature).

(3) LIGHT THE FIRE AND BRING THE POTS TO BOIL SEQUENTIALLY

Light the fire, place one of the pots over the fire, and when it comes to the boil replace it with a second pot. Note the time when the pot came to the boil. NOTE – If the stove has a second pot-hole, start with a pot on both pot-holes, and when each comes to the boil replace it with a new pot of water. Repeat this until all the wood is used up.

(4) END OF TEST

At the end of the test note down the number of pots of water that each stove has brought to the boil. Calculate the time each pot took to come to the boil.

(5) REPEAT THE TEST

Each stove should be tested at least 4 times.

stove as related to actual operating conditions and procedures (i.e. fuel type, moisture content, wind, etc.).
To determine the operating characteristics of a stove (e.g. ease of ignition, ability to change the power output).
To determine levels of pollution (given the necessary measuring instruments).
(It should be pointed out that the test is not suitable for accurate determination of a heat balance).

Advantages
– This procedure very quickly gives an accurate picture of the relative fuel efficiency, range of power output, and cooking times of two stoves (e.g. the existing stove, and a new stove) under the operating conditions observed in the field.
– The test allows a rating of relative ease of ignition between the stoves, and the number of times the fuel must be pushed into the stove to prevent burning outside the firebox.
– The procedure is very similar to that used for cooking, and it has been observed that senior extension workers can learn how to carry out the test in a few hours.

Disadvantages
– The stove must be operated in the same way for each test to obtain repeatable results.
– Discrepancies can occur between test results due to significantly different amounts of charcoal building up, as some field workers have problems in recovering the charcoal for its accurate weighing at the end of a test.

Procedure 2 Simulated cooking test * [detailed in the panel opposite]
* This water boiling test is described thus as it is based on actual cooking procedures, although only water is used in the cooking pots.

To develop the test it is necessary to draw on the household information obtained during the assessment survey. In order to design the test to simulate local cooking practices it is necessary to know such things as: the quantity of food cooked in each pot; the average time taken to cook each dish; whether pots are interchanged during cooking, and the timing involved; the most commonly used fuels, and typical moisture content(s); the method of igniting the fuel and controlling the fire.

Use of the Test
To determine the efficiency and power range of a

Procedure 2
(Simulated cooking test)

General
The following example summarizes the pattern of the test to simulate the cooking of rice and lentils. The detailed method then follows.

TYPICAL COOKING PROCEDURE	TEST PROCEDURE
(1) Bring 3kg rice + water to the boil on the 1st pot-seat.	Place 3 litres of water to boil on the 1st pot-seat. Heat 1 litre of water
(2) Heat 1kg lentils + water on the back pot-seat.	on the 2nd pot-seat. When the first pot is boiling lower the out-
(3) When the rice is almost cooked (requiring about	put to simmer (vigorously) for 10 minutes,

TYPICAL COOKING PROCEDURE	TEST PROCEDURE
10 minutes boiling), inter-change with the pot of lentils, and continue steaming the rice on the 2nd pot-seat.	then inter-change this pot with the back pot. Continue to simmer the front pot for 20 minutes.

(4) Continue to cook the lentils on the 1st pot-seat (for another 20 minutes).

Equipment required
- Stove
- Pots with lids
- A balance accurate to 10g and with the capacity to weigh the largest pot holding the predetermined amount of water
- A device to measure or estimate the moisture content of the fuel
- The locally dominant fuel at a uniform and known moisture content
- Water, for the pots, within 2°C of the ambient temperature
- A timing device
- A mercury or digital thermometer for measuring temperatures up to 105°C. (A larger scale thermometer will be needed if stack temperatures are to be measured)
- Tongs, gloves, for removing the embers at the end of the test (for weighing)
- A Test Record Sheet (for each test) designed to allow simple and logical recording of all the data needed to carry out the final calculations.

Detailed method (See Appendix 2 for Data Record Form)
Note: the figures in square brackets refer to the appropriate technical note given in Appendix 1.

(1) RECORD THE TEST CONDITIONS
Draw the stove to be tested (see Appendix 6), including all relevant stove dimensions, and showing how the pots fit into the stove [1].
Note the capacity, material, and relevant dimensions of the pots to be used.
Note weather conditions [2].

(2) PREPARE THE FUEL
Weigh the fuel to be used (taking not more than twice that estimated necessary for the test) and record the weight on the test record sheet (examples in Appendix, pages 00–00).
Record the moisture content [3].

(3) PREPARE THE POTS
Weigh the pots, with their lids, and record the weight (on Test Record Sheet). Fill each pot with the predetermined amount of water (see Test Summary above) and record the total weights.

(4) MEASURE INITIAL WATER TEMPERATURE
This should be measured about 1cm above the bottom of the pot, and recorded on the Test Record Sheet [4].

(5) LIGHT THE FIRE AND BRING THE POTS TO THE BOIL
After a final check that all is ready for the test, light the fire in a standard manner [5] and record the lighting time.
When the fuel (not just the kindling) is burning, place the pots on the stove and record the starting time.
Bring the first pot to the boil as rapidly as possible using the method commonly used locally (e.g. fanning, blowing etc.)

(6) RECORDING OF DATA AS THE TEST PROCEEDS
Weigh and record each charge of fuel before it is added to the fire.
Make notes of any actions taken to control the fire (e.g. fanning), and the time.
Make notes of fire behaviour (smoke, etc.).
Continually monitor water temperatures and record the times at which each pot comes to (a brisk) boil, and any other data itemized on the Test Record Sheet (e.g. the temperature of pot 2 when 1 boils) that is required for the final calculations.

(7) AT COMPLETION OF THE TEST
Record stack temperature.
Remove and weigh the remaining wood and any charcoal formed; record weights [6].
Weight the pots (with remaining water) and record the weights on the Test Sheet.

(8) CALCULATIONS
Carry out the calculations for the information sought from the test (e.g. PHU, Specific Consumption – see page 19, power output) and record them on the Test Record Sheet.

(9) REPEAT THE TEST
The test should be carried out at least four times. The stove should also be tested in the same way for a range of fuel types at different moisture contents.

Procedure 3 International Standards Method based on specific fuel consumption analysis.

Use of the Test

To determine the specific fuel consumption of a stove in a way that enables the potential fuel savings to be more accurately calculated.

Advantages

– Results are more comparable between different stove types and between different projects.
– The SFC method of analysis predicts potential fuel savings more accurately.
– The procedure follows cooking procedures much more closely.
– Only basic equipment necessary.
– Easier to compare one- and two-pot stoves.

Disadvantages

– The efficiency or PHU is more widely understood and accepted as a way of expressing a stove's performance.

This Water Boiling Test uses water to simulate food; the standard quantity is two-thirds the full pot capacity.

The test includes 'high power' and 'low power' phases. The high power phase involves heating the standard quantity of water from the ambient temperature to boiling as rapidly as possible (see Technical Note 1). The low power phase follows. The power is reduced to the lowest level needed to keep the water simmering over a one-hour period.

Each test should be repeated at least four times. Results may be averaged and analysed statistically.

Equipment

– Stove
– Pots without lids (see Procedural Note 1)
– A balance accurate to 10g with a recommended capacity of 5kg (Technical Note 2)
– Locally-dominant wood species, air dried (Technical Notes 3, 4), preferably pieces of uniform size
– Water, within 2°C of ambient temperature
– Timing device
– Mercury or digital thermometer for measuring temperatures up to 105°C (Technical Note 6)
– Device to measure/estimate the moisture content of wood (Technical Note 4)
– Forms for recording data and calculations
– Optional: wire tongs for handling hot charcoal and wood; insulated gloves.

Procedure 3 (See Appendix 3 for Data Record Forms)

(1) Determine and record moisture content for wood to be used in test (see Technical Notes 3 and 4).
(Note: this is generally done for a series of tests, rather than for each individual test.)

(2) Note and record the test conditions. Prepare a drawing of the pots and stove to be tested. (Note: in any test series be sure to use the same pots for all tests.) Include all relevant stove dimensions and show how the pots fit into the stove (Technical Note 9). Note climatic conditions (Technical Note 8).

(3) Weigh the empty, dry pots, and record this weight on the Data and Calculation Form. Fill each pot with water to two-thirds capacity and record the new weight.

(4) Take a quantity of wood not more than twice the estimated needed amount, weigh it, and record the weight on the Data and Calculation Form.

(5) Place a thermometer in each pot so that the water temperature may be measured in the centre, about 1cm from the bottom. Record water temperatures and confirm that they vary no more than 2°C from ambient.

(6) After a final check of the preparations, light the fire as in Technical Note 10. Record the exact starting time. Throughout the following 'high power' phase of the test, control the fire with the means commonly used locally to bring the first pot to a boil as rapidly as possible.

(7) Regularly record the following on the Data and Calculation Form:
– the water temperature in each pot;
– the weight of any wood added to the fire;
– any action taken to control the fire (dampers, blowing, etc.); and
– the fire reaction (smoke, etc.).

(8) Record the time at which the water in the first pot comes to a full boil.

(9) At this time rapidly do the following:
Remove all wood from the stove and knock off any charcoal. Weigh the wood, together with the unused wood from the previously weighed supply
– Weigh all charcoal separately (Procedural Note 2)
– Record the water temperature from each pot
– Weigh each pot, with its water

Procedure 3 continued

> – Return charcoal, burning wood, and pots to the stove to begin the 'low power' phase of the test

Record all measurements on the Data and Calculation Form.

With practice a single tester can complete this step within 2 to 4 minutes and move on to Step 10 without introducing significant error to the data. If, however, this interruption is judged too difficult or disruptive, an alternate procedure is suggested in Procedural Note 3.

(10) For the next 30 minutes maintain the fire at a level just sufficient to keep the water simmering. Use the least amount of wood possible, and avoid vigorous boiling. Continue to monitor all conditions noted in Step 7. If the temperature of the water in the first pot drops more than 5°C below boiling, the test must be considered invalid.

(11) Recover and weigh separately the charcoal and all remaining wood. Record the weights.

(12) Weigh each pot with its remaining water. Record the weight.

(13) Calculate the amount of wood consumed, the amount of water remaining, the test duration, the Specific Fuel Consumption, and, for multipot stoves, the Consumption Ratio (Procedural Note 5). Minimum and Maximum power levels may also be calculated (Technical Note 11).

(14) Interpret test results (see Procedural Note 4), and fill out a Test Series Reporting Form.

Procedural notes for Procedure 3

(1) Stove tests are often conducted with lidded pots to reduce the effect of draughts on the evaporation rate from the pot. However, if the testing site is properly protected from draughts, lids should be left off, thus reducing the error caused by condensed water dripping from the lid back into the pot.

(2) With lightweight stove models, often the stove and its contents can be weighed together as a unit, and the weight of the empty stove subtracted later. It is not necessary to separate charcoal and ashes, since ash weight is usually insignificant.

(3) 'High power' and 'low power' tests may be conducted separately. The fire is extinguished at the end of Step 7, and the stove is allowed to cool. The entire test is then repeated in exactly the same way, except that the fire is reduced the moment the first pot comes to a boil. There is no interruption to weigh water or fuel as described in Steps 8–13.

The test is ended 30 minutes after boiling, and all measurements are recorded. The weight of the fuel used during the high power phase is subtracted from the total amount used in the low power phase. A separate or modified data sheet is needed for recording test results. Final calculations remain unchanged.

(4) It is important to know how to interpret the results of the WBT, and to remember that a low specific fuel consumption indicates a high efficiency. As efficiency declines, Specific Fuel Consumption (SFC) rises. It is possible to use WBT results to judge the suitability of a stove for various cooking tasks. For example, for high power cooking (rapid frying and boiling), a stove with the greatest high power efficiency might be best; for simmering, however, the best stove might be the one that shows low SFC for both high and low power. (See also pages 19 and 20 which explain concepts of efficiency).

(5) The Consumption Ratio may be useful when testing stoves that accommodate more than one pot. It expresses the amount of water evaporated from the main pot as a fraction of the total evaporated from all pots.

The consumption ratio is always less than 1.0. The lower its value, the lower the proportion of heat used by the main pot.

There are at least two ways in which the Consumption Ratio may be useful to the stove tester:

a) It serves as a check on consistent stove operation. With multipot stoves the user determines how heat from the fire is apportioned to the various pots. In a series of Water Boiling Tests it is essential that this is done in a consistent manner. By comparing the Consumption Ratios in a test series one can detect variations in stove operation.

b) It may help to show whether enough heat reaches all the pots to be useful for cooking.

As a rule, the Consumption Ratio should *not* be used as a correction factor for comparison of multipot and single pot stoves. Such comparisons are never valid in Water Boiling Tests because of the many interfering variables.

Constraints and limitations of Water Boiling Tests

The introduction of a standard by which all stoves should be tested and reported has created considerable controversy, primarily because cooking requires skill and is often a matter of personal taste and choice. This introduces insurmountable constraints and limitations when assessing one stove against another at a finite level of accuracy. The following worked example comparing two stoves highlights the significance of the user and suggests that creating fuel conservation awareness alongside the introduction of improved stoves will have greater significance when assessing fuel consumption at the national level.

WORKED EXAMPLE

Consider two stoves with the following performances:

Stove A   No.2.3

	Power Phase		
	Up to boiling point	*15 mins rapid boil*	*30 mins simmer*
SEC	0.11	0.394	0.315
PHU	21.2%	28.7%	35.8%
Burning rate (kg/min)	0.0254	0.0194	0.0073
Evap. rate (kg/min)	—	0.0490	0.0230
Time to boil	12 mins	4 kg = 3 mins/kg	

Stove B

SFC	0.094	0.400	0.342
PHU	22.3%	28.3%	33.0%
Burning rate (kg/min)	0.0269	0.0162	0.0064
Evap. rate (kg/min)	—	0.0407	0.0187
Time to boil	11 mins	4 kg = 2.75 mins/kg	

At first glance the two stoves appear very similar. However, as we apply this data to cooking procedures, major differences soon appear.

Consider a meal that requires 3kg of food to be brought to the boil as quickly as possible, and then simmered for 2 hours.

Most woodstoves cannot be turned down, unlike many charcoal stoves, unless fuel is actually removed from the fire. This habit is quite rare amongst most users, therefore we shall consider an interim period of 15 minutes to allow initial quantities of wood put into the fire necessary to give high power (so that water is brought to the boil as quickly as possible) to die away to give a much reduced power output for simmering.

The power/time diagram looks thus:

Calculations

1. The expected water evaporation losses need to be added to the initial food quantities and are represented by time × evaporation rate.

Expected water loses

Power phase	Stove A	Stove B
Up to boiling point	0	0
High	15 × 0.049 = 0.735	15 × 0.0407 = 0.611
Simmer	120 × 0.023 = 2.760	120 × 0.0187 = 2.244
Initial Food	3 kg	3 kg
Total food + water	6.495	5.855

2. Now that we known what quantities of food and water are required to give us 3kg of food at the end of the test, we can now also calculate the fuel requirements to complete the cooking procedure.

The fuel requirements are simply represented by time × burning rate.

Fuel requirements

Power phase	Stove A	Stove B
Time to boil	6.495 × 3 = 19.5 mins	5.855 × 2.75 = 16.1 mins
Up to Boiling Point	19.5 × 0.0254 = 0.495	16.1 × 0.0269 = 0.433
High	15 × 0.0194 = 0.291	15 × 0.0162 = 0.243
Simmer	120 × 0.0073 = 0.876	120 × 0.0064 = 0.768
Total wood requirement	1.662 kg	1.444 kg

3. The potential fuel savings of stove B over stove A can be simply calculated based upon the test fuel consumption

$$\text{Savings} = \frac{1.662 - 1.444}{1.662} \times 100$$

$$= 13\%$$

Looking back at the analysis, stove B is clearly best in terms of saving fuel as well as time. This is not due to greater efficiencies, because, on the contrary, A was marginally more efficient than B

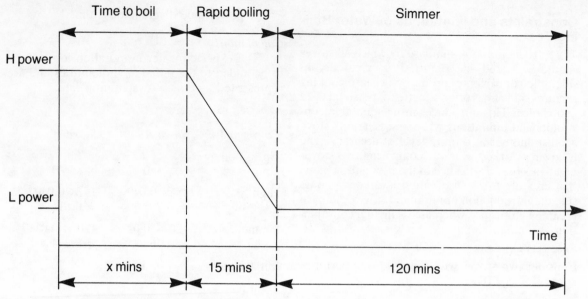

Figure 3.3. Power/time curve for a typical stove.

in the rapid boiling phase and considerably more in the simmering phase, although stove B was marginally more efficient during the heating phase. Undoubtedly, stove B used less fuel because less water was evaporated as a result of much lower burning rates and evaporation rates after reaching boiling point, therefore less water was needed from the start. This had also benefitted the time taken to bring the pot to the boil.

If these two stoves were being tested in the field, most users would of course not know that each stove requires different quantities of water to start with and would probably start with the quantities traditionally used. Let us assume initial water quantities were 6.75kg. Extra quantities of water need to be evaporated. There are two options to achieve this, either:

a) increase power output; or
b) retain minimum power levels but increase the simmering period.

If it is assumed cooks would tend to increase power levels, burning rates would become:

	Stove A	Stove B
Initial water	6.75	6.75
Loss of water (high power)	0.735	0.611
Food	3kg	3kg
To be lost in simmering =	3.015	3.139
Evap. rate required	3.015/120 = 0.025	3.139/120 = 0.026

	Stove A	Stove B
Burning rate required	0.025/0.023 × 0.0073 = 0.0079	0.026/0.0187 × 0.0064 = 0.0089

The fuel requirements (assuming that the power levels are only increased during simmering) then become:

Power phase	Stove A	Stove B
Up to boiling point	6.75 × 3 × 0.0254 = 0.495	6.75 × 2.75 × 0.0269 = 0.433
High	15 × 0.0194 = 0.291	15 × 0.0162 = 0.243
Simmer	120 × 0.0079 = 0.948	120 × 0.0089 = 1.068
	1.734	*1.744*

Comparing the total fuel requirements for stoves A and B, it is seen that stove A is marginally better.

Savings represented by
$$\frac{1.744 - 1.734}{1.744} \times 100$$
$$= 0.6\%$$

although stove B was still slightly faster because of the higher burning rates during the bring to boil phase.

Time taken to boil Stove A = 20.3 minutes
Stove B = 18.6 minutes

Comparing these fuel consumptions with the previous worked example, we find

Stove A	Stove B
$\dfrac{1.734 - 1.662}{1.662}$	$\dfrac{1.744 - 1.444}{1.444}$
= 4% more fuel	= 21% more fuel

This clearly shows that choosing the appropriate quantities of water to mix with the food is particularly important if overall savings are to be achieved. The fuel efficiency of improved models can easily be lost if greater amounts of water are added to the food than is generally required, if the stove is to be operated at its maximum and minimum power levels at the appropriate times.

These calculations show the importance of cooking skills; the most important issues are clearly:
a) selecting the least amount of water to achieve the desired amount of cooking
b) regulating the power levels to achieve the greatest efficiency and lowest evaporation rates.

If expertly handled even the open fire can be more efficient by applying these two most important issues. However, there are usually two main disadvantages that occur and prevent the adoption of fuel-saving techniques:
a) increased cooking times
b) increased fire attendance.

Most stove research programmes around the world recognize the importance of local cooking techniques and realize the difficulties involved in initiating changes. Primarily based on this argument, the simplest and easiest way to achieve fuel savings is to build stoves with greater PHU values because this has the greatest effect upon fuel consumption levels when cooking methods remain the same. This explains to some extent why the calculation of the PHU value has remained a favourite way of expressing stove performance amongst some researchers, rather than adopting the provisional set of standards which promotes the use of SEC values. For completeness it is suggested that it would be useful to express both PHU values and the SFC for various power levels and respective cooking tasks.

Controlled Cooking Test

The Controlled Cooking Test (CCT) is intended to be an intermediate step between the Water Boiling Test(s) and the Kitchen Performance Test. From analysis of the results of the Water Boiling Tests, the best stove or stoves can then be selected for comparison with the traditional stove, using Controlled Cooking Tests.

The test involves the cooking of a 'standard meal' and the results are most simply reported as the amount of fuel needed to cook the meal in the ratio of

$$\left(\frac{\text{fuel used}}{\text{food cooked}} \right)$$

This is known as the Specific Fuel Consumption.

These tests are normally conducted in a laboratory or field demonstration centre by trained stove testers, extension workers or potential users. In addition, it is useful to do controlled cooking tests with women outside the project, such as through women's groups, or in their houses if they are willing. This requires particularly careful organization, and the results are often more variable because of changes from place to place, and the greater differences between cooks' techniques.

Use of the Test
To compare the fuel consumed and the time taken to cook a particular meal on different stoves.

To determine whether a stove can effectively cook a range of meals normally prepared in the area where it is to be introduced.

To compare different cooking practices on the same stove.

To subject a stove to more realistic, whilst still controlled, conditions (as compared to the Water Boiling Tests).

To give a cook the opportunity to try out a stove and to learn how to operate it correctly.

DESIGN OF THE TEST
The CCT must be tailored to specific local cooking practices, for which the same information used to design the simulated Water Boiling Test is required (gathered as part of the household information during the assessment survey). Where several types of meals are prepared in the region, no more than two should be chosen for the test – one requiring a long cooking time, the other short.

Alternatively, a team of say, three to five, experienced local cooks could be asked to define the one or two standard meals to be used for the test, and to establish the specific way the food should be prepared and cooked.

The cooks carrying out the tests, ideally women, should be experienced in traditional cooking techniques. All the cooks should run tests on all the stoves, to eliminate any bias caused by the inevitable variation between cooks. The quantities of food and water to be used, and an agreed end-point in the cooking process, must be set before the tests are commenced (see Appendix 1, Technical Note 11).

Advantages
- The test results are more compariable to the way people judge the fuel consumption of stoves.
- The tests give a better prediction of actual fuel savings than do Water Boiling Tests.
- Much information can be obtained on the suitability of the stove for the local cooking techniques and its appropriateness when used in a variety of ways.
- The subjective opinions of testing staff and potential users can be very valuable.

Disadvantages
- The tests are more expensive to carry out than Water Boiling Tests.
- In order to design the test it may be necessary to conduct a more thorough survey of local cooking practices than was carried out as part of the assessment survey.
- Cooking tests are more difficult to organize than Water Boiling Tests.
- The variation between different cooks and the quality of the raw food on different days must be taken into account (although these may yield useful information about the stove's performance).
- It is difficult to determine the end point of the test (see Technical Note 11).
- More tests need to be carried out than with Water Boiling Tests.

Details of the equipment required, and the outline of a cooking test procedure, are given in the panel opposite.

Equipment
- A homogenous mix of fuelwood, as it is normally supplied locally, sufficient for at least 20 tests (see Technical Note 3).
- Sufficient ingredients, of a uniform quality, as set down by the 'standard meal' definition, for 20 tests.
- Weighing scales accurate to 10g, with a capacity of 5 to 10kg (depending on the amount of food prepared in each test, see also Technical Note 7).
- Timing device.
- Pots, lids, and other cooking untensils (to be used throughout the test, and its repeats).
- Test Record, and Calculation Sheets (see Appendix 4).

Procedure (See Appendix 4 for Record Forms)
(1) ESTABLISH THE TEST DETAILS
 See text on Controlled Cooking Tests.
(2) PREPARE THE STOVE
 Remove any ash and charcoal from the stove to be tested.
 (The stove should not be warm from a previous fire.)
(3) INITIAL RECORDING OF DATA
 Complete all the data required on the Test Record Sheets, concerning the stove, pots, weather conditions, etc.
(4) PREPARE THE FUEL
 Take a quantity of wood, not more than twice the estimated amount needed. Weigh it and record the weight on the Test Record Sheet.
(5) PREPARE THE POTS
 Weigh the pots to be used, with their lids, and record their weight.
(6) PREPARE THE FOOD TO BE COOKED
 Weigh and have ready the food (and water) to be cooked, placing the ingredients in the pots (depending on the standard cooking method designed for the test).
(7) LIGHT THE FIRE
 Record the time of ignition. (See Appendix 1, Technical Note 5).
(8) PERFORM THE DEFINED COOKING TASK
 See step 1.
(9) END OF TEST
 At the predetermined 'meal now cooked' point, record the time. (See Technical Note 11).
 Weight (separately) the remaining wood and charcoal (see Appendix 1, Technical Note 6).
 Weigh the food in its pot(s), including any lids.
(10) SPEDIAL TEST NOTES
 Record comments from the cook on any problems encountered during the test, including qualitative differences between the tested stove and other stoves.
(11) REPEAT THE SAME TEST
 The same test should be carried out five times for each type of standard meal selected for testing. The same test (including repeats) should then be carried out *using a different stove, or the traditional stove or fireplace* for comparison.
(12) CALCULATIONS
 For each test calculate the total test time, and the Specific Fuel Consumption.

continued

28

continued

For each set of repeat tests, calculate the standard deviation of results; record these on the Test Series Report Form (see page 40) and carry out a Student t-Test to compare statistically the two types of stove tested.

(13) TEST REPORTS

Write a test report for each series of tests (using, for example, the Test Record Sheets, etc, shown on pages 39–41). The report should include details of:
- stove and pans used in the test
- standard meal prepared for the test
- standard procedure used to cook the test meal.

Field tests

INTRODUCTION

Water Boiling and Controlled Cooking tests will indicate whether a new (or redesigned) stove is more fuel efficient. If potential users involved in the stove testing respond favourably to the stove, that is, in terms of finding its operation and performance satisfactory, the next testing stage is to carry out field tests. These require considerably greater resources and unfortunately are not even attempted in many projects. When resources are scarce the most effective solution is to co-ordinate the field tests with the monitoring process, after new stoves have been introduced or stove dissemination has commenced.

Although very little work has been carried out to measure changes in fuel consumption in the kitchen following introduction of a new stove, experience to date indicates that it is an extremely difficult process and that many factors can lead to the collection of data that may be totally inaccurate. It is apparent that, if a major objective of the programme is to collect accurate data on fuel consumption, then a range of methods must be used and extensive resources allocated to the task.

Three procedures which can be used to collect data on household fuel consumption are described below.

All the tests are carried out in households which are actually using the new stove, and should also be run parallel with tests in a control group of households having only the traditional stove. The tests involve the active co-operation of households over a period of one to two weeks soon after acquiring the new stove, and again about six months later. It is necessary to repeat the tests when the stoves have been in use for some time as this will reveal changes due to many possible factors – seasonal effects (on weather, fuel type, etc.); stove degradation; the fading of the 'novelty value' of the new stove – resulting in less careful operation and maintenance, which may lower its efficiency.

Procedure 1 User perception of fuel consumption

This procedure essentially allows users to quantify how much fuel they feel they have saved. The number of households (the sample) that will be required to participate in the study will depend on the variance in the sample (see also Appendix 1, Technical Note 12). For example, in a study carried out in Nepal, there were so many different types of kitchen and cooking practice that, to obtain sufficient data for valid statistical analysis of the results, it was necessary to survey 600 households.

It is necessary to ask particular questions of participants, and to make certain observations when carrying out the field survey, in order to compare the outcome with the consumption figures obtained. For example, people with both new and traditional stoves should be asked how often they use the new one – if they claim it is only used half the time, yet the fuel consumption is apparently reduced by 50%, then the information is obviously invalid. Whenever data is collected from participants observation should be made, where possible, of whether the stove (new or traditional) is in use, warm, or cold.

Use of the Test

To investigate the (approximate) fuel consumption levels in households using the new stove, and to compare the results with those of households using only the traditional stove.

Advantages
- Relatively inexpensive to implement, therefore a large sample can be taken so that statistical variation in perceived performance can be ascertained.
  - Household routines are not disturbed and privacy is not invaded.
  - Problems with the stove not discovered or foreseen in the earlier testing stages can be dealt with before embarking on a more elaborate field test (see Procedures 2 and 3 following), or large-scale dissemination.

Disadvantages

- People's perception may not correlate with the actual savings (if any): they may not tell the truth out of politeness, or fear of losing a stove which was installed free; they may not remember or be able to calculate exact figures.
- Very little detailed information can be gained on how cooking practices may have been changed by acquisition of the new stove, and why any variation in perceived savings occurs in the test group.
- A large number of new stoves may have to be installed to obtain reliable results.
- It is possible that making the survey itself will induce a reduction in fuel consumption. Although it may be possible to assess this by statistical analysis of the two sets of results from the test group and the control group, Wood (1982) reported a 25% decrease in fuel use by a control group cooking with open fires in Upper Volta when they were involved in a detailed field test.

To investigate the approximate fuel consumption levels of households with a new stove:

Procedure 1

(1) SELECT HOUSEHOLD SAMPLE

Select a random sample of households, sufficiently large for statistically valid results to be obtained, and visit each one to explain the nature and purpose of the test survey. (Refer to Table 3.1 for details of estimation of sample size. It may be necessary to obtain advice from a statistician before commencing this step.)

Obtain data on the number of 'UN standard' adults and children (see Appendix 1, Technical Note 13) normally cooked for in each household, and note the type of traditional stove used.

If fuel is regularly obtained in the same container or same-sized bundles, note the average weight of each fuel load (for each household, if applicable).

(2) FIRST HOUSEHOLD VISITS

Make 2 to 4 visits to each household during a two-week period.

Ask how much fuel has been collected or purchased since the last visit and whether the number of people cooked for has changed during that time.

(3) INSTALL NEW STOVES

Install a new stove in half of the sample. Note whether the traditional stove remains, or is removed.

continued

---

(4) SECOND HOUSEHOLD VISITS

Make daily visits to the 'new stove' households during a 2 to 4 week period. Ask how much fuel has been obtained since the last visit and whether the number of people cooked for changed during that time.

(5) THIRD HOUSEHOLD VISITS

Repeat step 4 six months after the new stove has been introduced, but for the whole sample (i.e. including the control group having only the traditional stove). Observe, as far as possible, to what extent the new stoves are being used.

Ask people to themselves assess any difference in the amount of fuel obtained (each day or week) since acquiring the new stove.

(6) CALCULATIONS

From the records of fuel quantities obtained, determine whether there has been any change in fuel consumption (as a weight per standard UN person) between the start of the test survey, the introduction of the new stove, and six months later. Statistical techniques can be used to accommodate the variations of fuel use with family size. Compare the results to any change observed for the control group during the same period. If there is a change, statistical analysis can be used to determine whether the perceived savings are due to the introduction of the new stoves in the other half of the sample, or simply due to the fact that people were conscious of the observations being made.

Table 3.1: Minimum number of households necessary for the Kitchen Performance Test relative to expected differences in fuel use for different stoves

Expected difference in fuel use (%)	10	20	30	40
Minimum number of households*	54	14	7	5

*Corresponds to a Coefficient of Variation of 0.4; 10% level of significance

From *Testing efficiency of wood-burning stoves, international standards*, VITA, 1985

Procedure 2 Kitchen performance test

Most of this procedural description is based on that for the Kitchen Performance Test detailed in the VITA publication mentioned at the beginning of this chapter.

The Kitchen Performance Test measures the rate of fuelwood consumed by a stove, expressed in terms of Specific Daily Consumption (Total Fuel Consumed/ Standard Adult / Day). The mean values for different households using the same type of stove can then be compared statistically with results of the same test carried out in other households using a different type of stove

It is a prolonged test that can only be carried out with the willing co-operation of, and some discipline by, the individual families. The tester must be well motivated, trained to follow instructions, and have certain basic numerical skills.

The introduction of a new stove may alter the amount and type of cooking done in a household, and this may mean that the fuel savings expected from the results of controlled tests are not attained. For example, money saved on fuel may be spent on extra food (increasing cooking time) or better quality food which requires shorter cooking. Having the fire more enclosed within the new stove may necessitate the purchase of a kerosene lamp for lighting. This test therefore will give a real indication of the fuel savings from the stove in actual use.

The results of the KPT as described should not be used to estimate the potential fuel saving of a new stove before it is widely accepted and used. This would require considerable expansion of the test to include:
- a large sample, representative of the locality
- test periods that cover all seasons
- recordings of stove repairs, and adjustments for stove deterioration rates.

However, when collecting household data for the situation assessment, the Kitchen Performance Test could be carried out in a suitable selection of households as an accurate method of determining fuel consumption, rather than simply by interviewing and check-weighing. Later, if new stoves are built or bought by these households, the Kitchen Performance Test can be repeated in these same households when they are familiar with the new stove.

Use of the Test
To study the impact of a new stove on overall household energy use.

To demonstrate to potential users the fuel-saving quality of a new stove in the household (having given instruction on the correct operating procedure).

KP Tests can be repeated at later intervals to check fuel consumption levels, which will change as the stove deteriorates.

User surveys carried out at the same time as the KP Tests will provide information on how well the stoves are being received, and if other factors have influenced the stove's long term acceptability.

Advantages
- This test can provide detailed information of fuel consumption in kitchens under reasonably controlled conditions.
- This test provides the most reliable indication of stove performance under actual household conditions, compared with other tests.

Disadvantages
- In practice it has proved very difficult to account for all fuel leaving and entering a defined store area (e.g. relatives may take fuel without the household being aware of it).
- The test causes disruption to people's everyday cooking procedures.
- Complications for the test recorder occur in households where:
- more than one stove is used
- people are away from their homes from early morning to late night (e.g. during harvest)
- Changes in cooking patterns are not observed.

To study the impact of a new stove on overall household energy consumption. (NOTE: The figures in brackets refer to the corresponding Technical Note):

Procedure 2
(1) SELECTION OF HOUSEHOLDS
    Select the appropriate type and number of households (Appendix 1, Technical Note 12).
    Explain to all members of the family the purpose of the test, and arrange to measure fuelwood each day. Where there is more than one stove in the household, encourage the family to use only the stove to be tested.
(2) INITIAL DATA RECORDINGS
    Establish and record the sex and age of each person served meals, and calculate the number of 'standard adults' (13).
    Determine the approximate cost of fuel (in time or money) to each household and record the information on the Data Record Sheet (example on page 42). Collect and note any other information which may help interpret final results (e.g. details of any other stove(s) used in the house, and for what purposes; uses made of fuelwood other than for cooking
    continued

food; the main employment of the head of the household (indication of economic level); tribal or cultural affiliation, etc.).

(3) DEFINE THE TEST PERIOD

Discuss with the household the time at which the test period (normally of seven days) will commence (e.g. to avoid any ususual family events which would disrupt the normal household routine) (15). If it is not possible to measure for seven days, measure for at least five.

Arrange to visit the household (to make measurements) at the same time each day.

(4) SETTING UP THE FUEL STORAGE AREA

Agree and define with the household the fuel inventory area for wood to be used during the test (14); make sure that the household members understand that all fuel entering or leaving this area must be accounted for during the test.

Weigh all wood and other fuels in the inventory area on Day 0, and record the data on the Record Sheet.

Estimate the moisture content of the wood, or remove a sample for measurement (3), and record the value on the Data Record Sheet.

(5) TAKING DAILY MEASUREMENTS

Visit the household each day (if possible) at the arranged time, without being intrusive.

Weigh the wood remaining in the inventory area, and add to it if necessary, recording weights on the Data Record Sheet.

Enquire about the number of people being served meals each day.

Confirm that the stove is operating properly.

(6) CALCULATIONS

Compile the results at the end of the test period. Calculate the Specific Daily Consumption for each household and the mean and standard deviation.

Compare the results with those from households using other stoves (but which were recorded during a similar period).

(7) THANKING PARTICIPANTS

Use of the Test
To gain detailed measurements of the amount of fuel used for cooking.

To determine whether cooking practices have changed and to observe any other alteration which can be attributed to the introduction of the new stove.

Advantages
- An in-depth understanding is obtained of why use of the stove does, or does not, save fuel.
- Figures obtained are very accurate and there is little of the 'researcher' effect on the results – the study is carried out over a long period of time which will tend to eliminate any bias by the researcher.
- Valuable data can be obtained that can be used to improve the design and extension strategy of the stove programme.

Disadvantages
- The researcher must be experienced in both participative observation and quantitative measurement.
- If kitchen systems are different a number of researchers will be needed in a range of representative households/villages, making the exercise expensive.
- considerable time can elapse before results are known.

To gain detailed measurements of fuel used for cooking, and to observe any changes in cooking practices, and other household routines as a result of introduction of a new stove:

Procedure 3

(1) INTRODUCTION TO TEST AREA, AND SELECTION OF SAMPLE

The researcher (a trained social scientist) should explain the nature of the exercise by way of meetings, etc, and list those households, not yet having a new stove, willing to participate.

An initial assessment of fuel consumption and cooking practices should be made as a check against people later altering habits due to the presence of the researcher.

The researcher should then randomly select the households to be sampled.

(2) HOUSEHOLD VISITS

The researcher should visit the selected households at random, and spend a day with the women of the household, taking detailed measurements of food cooked, fuel used, number of people sharing each meal, etc.

Observations should also be made of cooking procedures, alternative uses of the stove and other kitchen chores.

---

continued

(3) INSTALLATION OF NEW STOVES

After carrying out household visits for several weeks new stoves should be introduced to about twenty households from the original sample.

(4) CONTINUATION OF HOUSEHOLD VISITS

Step 2 should then be continued for another period of several weeks in the household with the new stove.

(5) CALCULATIONS

The results should be analysed in a similar manner to those obtained using Procedure 2 (Kitchen Performance Test).

Appendix 1: technical notes

To be read in conjunction with the test procedures given in Chapter 3

TECHNICAL
NOTE NO.

1. Description of the cooking unit (stove and pots) used in test

The size and shape of a pot will affect the way it sits on or into a stove, and thus will alter the internal dimensions of the stove, and consequently may alter the stove's performance. Therefore the particular stove:pot(s) combination being tested must be carefully described as part of the test record. Sheet iii of the Controlled Cooking Test Record Sheets shows an example of a suitable form for this purpose.

If, when in the field, a tape measure is not available, improvized measures can be used, for example, the sides of the pages of a notebook. The diameter (D) of a spheroid pot, or chamber, can be derived from its circumference (C) measured with a length of string (D=C/Pi, where Pi= 22/7).

The stove. The diagrams (Figure 3.4) show the type of sketches of the stove that are required. It should be remembered that it is the internal dimensions of the stove (firebox, flues, etc) which are the most important.

The pots. Details such as size, shape, weight, etc. can be noted on the Test Record Sheet, but it is also important to report on how the pot(s) fits into the stove. This can be done in the sketches of the stove. Stove pot measurements which cannot be made directly, e.g. the distance between the firebox floor and the bottom of the pot, should be calculated from external measurements (see cutaway view below), or can be made using the soft clay method described on page

2. Weather conditions

The most important weather conditions on which

to report are air temperature, wind, and relative humidity.

Air temperature. This affects the rate of heat loss from stove and pots.

Wind Wind will affect the stove's draught and can have considerable influence on stove performance. Stove testing should ideally be carried out in calm conditions, or a windbreak should be erected around the test area to reduce air movement. A simple description of wind conditions is sufficient for all but the most rigorous experiments.

Relative humidity. This factor can provide an indication of the moisture content of air-dried fuelwood (see Technical Note 3). It is a useful parameter to measure and can be done simply with, for example, a small sling psychrometer (wet-and-dry bulb thermometer), or a hair hygrometer. The latter should be recalibrated frequently by wrapping in a wet cloth, leaving for 5 minutes, and adjusting it to 100% RH.

3. Moisture content of fuel

Different types, sizes, and conditions of fuelwood are a potential source of great variation in all the tests described. If the moisture content of the fuelwood used varies, then the energy value per unit weight will also vary. The following precautions can help minimize this variation.

Air drying. Use only wood that has been thoroughly air dried. For sticks 3–4cm diameter drying time may be 3–8 months depending on temperature, relative humidity, protection from rain and mist, air circulation through the wood pile, and the wood species. Air-dried wood is generally lightweight and brittle. Hot water and steam should not escape from the wood as it is burned. [NB: In countries where only damp wood is available all year or during the wet season, for some tests it may be more relevant to use moist wood].

Cut wood. Use only wood cut to a uniform cross-section. It may then be difficult to ignite and maintain a fire without smaller or tapered places.

Wood storage. When a series of tests is planned, prepare in advance a stack of fuelwood to be used for each test. Stacks should be similar in terms of wood type and sizes, and should be bound up to prevent loss of pieces. Sealing each wood stack in a large plastic bag will protect from outside moisture.

Insect damage. Protect fuelwood from insects.

Determination of moisture content. Moisture content (MC) should be calculated on a dry basis.

$$MC = \frac{\text{Weight of water}}{\text{Weight of oven dry wood}} \times 100$$

When there is no access to an oven with a thermostat, the oven sketched below can be made from a cheap commercial sheet metal oven, three light bulbs and fittings, some wire, and wood.

In a small oven (35cm × 35cm × 40cm) it is possible to keep the internal temperature around 100°C with about 210 watts of lighting. The internal temperature should be checked with a thermometer, as different designs of ovens, or ambient temperatures, can change the results. The power output can be altered by changing the light bulbs or lifting the oven off the ground. It is best to keep the fuel to be dried at least 7cm away from the bare light bulbs, as the temperature will be considerably higher right next to them.

4. Temperature measurement

Inside pots. Temperaure gradients may occur in the water, or food, when it is not boiling. A representative position at which to take an 'average' temperature seems to be in the centre of the pot, about 1cm above the bottom. It is a good practice to have one thermometer or temperature probe in each pot, for example by the use of special lids with a support in the centre to keep the thermometer in place at a suitable level (see diagram below).

Stack temperatures. Mercury thermometers reading up to 250°C can be used with care to measure the stack (chimney) temperatures, but many two-pot stoves will reach stack temperatures well above this. Digital thermometers are more accurate, and cover a much wider range, but are relatively more expensive.

5. Ignition

For Water Boiling Tests and Controlled Cooking Tests it is important to light the fire in the way it is normally done in that locality. This may be done, for example, using kerosene as the ignition material.

To standarize this method of ignition, either a measured amount of kerosene (less than 10g) can simply be poured over the wood, or three pieces of wood can be dipped vertically into kerosene (about 8cm deep) for about five seconds, and the excess kerosene tapped off. The dipped wood should contain about 10g of kerosene (this can be checked by weighing the wood before and after dipping). The test's starting time coincides with the lighting of the kerosene-soaked wood pieces.

One gram of kerosene is equivalent to about 2g of wood, so the kerosene used can be considered as consumed fuel: however, the energy involved is so small that it may be safely ignored in the calculations.

Another method of ignition used for tests is with kindling, especially where this is the local method employed to light fires. Throughout a series of tests the same kind and weight of kindling should be used to light each fire.

6. Recovery of charcoal at end of test

Recovering and weighing hot coals from a stove can be simplified by using a removable metal ash tray on the floor of the combustion chamber. The tray and contents can then be weighed together, and the weight of the empty tray subtracted. It is not necessary to separate charcoal and ashes, since ash weight is usually insignificant. Wire tongs may be used to pick up hot pieces of charcoal. Heat resistant, insulated, or leather gloves are also useful.

7. Balances

A 10g accuracy for good laboratory tests is recommended, but even this can still have an error of ± 7% on tests using 4 litres of water, due to the small but significant amounts of charcoal, and of evaporation. 25g accuracy scales are sufficient for field tests.

For accuracy and convenience it is desirable to have the capacity to weigh pots both empty and with water (or water plus food) at the start and end of the test. This would require the use of spring balances (with hooks, for weighing pots with handles), or platform scales with platforms large enough to accommodate the pots.

Scales for weighing wood in moisture content analysis should be accurate to 1% of the total sample weight – e.g. to 1g for a 100g wood sample.

8. Timing devices

Wristwatches, stop watches and large clocks should display seconds as well as minutes, and should keep good time.

9. Test area

The stoves should not be affected by wind, there should be a ready exit for smoke, and there should be sufficient room for testing a few stoves at one time and storing all the equipment and fuel needed for the tests.

10. Calculations

Several examples of Test Record Sheets, with room (space permitting) for recording the results of calculations, are supplied. See pages   to

These show the data that must be recorded for each test and the calculations which can be made from that data.

11. Controlled Cooking Tests — determination of 'end of test'

It is important to consider the criteria by which the food will be considered 'done', since this determines the end of the test. Some objective criterion must be selected – such as 'the skins come off the beans', or 'the porridge loses all traces of graininess'. However, even if very subjective criteria are involved in the test design, e.g. 'the sauce tastes just right', they should still be mentioned. Whatever the criteria used, the cook must be encouraged to be very consistent in judgement.

12. Kitchen Performance Tests — sample selection

1. Households from approximately the same economic level should be selected, to reduce variation and permit more reliable interpretation of the results.
2. Participating families should use fuelwood for at least 90% of their household cooking needs.
3. For each stove to be tested a minimum of 5 households each having that type of stove is essential. The smaller the expected difference in fuel use between two stoves, the greater the sample required.

13. Field Tests (to determine fuel consumption) — definition of 'standard adult'

The 'standard adult', for the purposes of these tests, can be defined according to a simplified version of the United Nations formula shown below (taken from *Guidelines for woodfuel surveys*, FAO, Keith Openshaw)

Table 3.2: 'Standard adult' defined in terms of age and sex

Age (years)	Sex	Fraction of standard adult
0–14	child, either	0.5
over 14	female	0.8
15–59	male	1.0
over 59	male	0.8

Equivalence is 1 unit = 3,000 kcal (12.6MJ)

14. Kitchen Performance Tests — household fuel and its storage during the test period

1. Different types and sizes of fuel used by different households may introduce unwanted variation in the test results. To avoid this, uniform fuelwood could be provided for the duration of the test, but it is important to ensure that the household does not significantly change its fuel consumption pattern as a result of this.
2. It is recommended that no more fuel be in the inventory area than is likely to be consumed during the test period. If more is stored than will be used, a smaller inventory area should be defined from which all fuel used during the test should be taken. It must be stressed to the household members that during the test, wood must only be taken from the smaller inventory area, and if it becomes necessary to add to it from the larger pile, then the tester must be present to weigh the fuel added.

15. Kitchen Performance Tests — test period

Seven days is usually the shortest time likely to include market days, work days, and any weekly religious observances in their proper proportion during the test. This will require eight days of measurement (to include Day 0). A 'relief' tester may be required to take measurements on the original tester's day of weekly religious observance.

Appendix 2: Simulated Cooking Test — Data Record Sheet

Test Code: _____

Operator: _____

Date: _____

Total Weight of Wood: _____

Weight of Kerosine Used: _____

Weights of Pots	1	and	2
Empty:			
With Water:			
Temp of Water:			
Temp of Air:			

Start Test

    Time to Boil Pot 1 _____

    Temp of Pot 2 _____

Switch Pots

    Time to Boil Pot 2 _____

    Temp of Pot 1 _____

Simmer

    Time Taken to Simmer _____

    Temp of Pot 1 _____

Stop Test

    Final Weight of Wood _____

    Final Weights of   Pot 1 _____ and Pot 2 _____

    Charcoal Remaining _____

Water Boiling Test
Data and Calculation Form*

Test Number _____ Location _____

Date _____ Test conditions _____

Stove _____ Remarks _____

Tester _____ _____

	Initial Measurement	End of High Power Phase	End of Low Power Phase
Wood moisture content	a) _____		
Dry weight of Pot 1	b) _____		
Dry weight of Pot 2	c) _____		
Weight of wood	d) _____ kg	j) _____ kg	s) _____ kg
Weight of charcoal		k) _____ kg	t) _____ kg
Weight of pot 1 with water	e) _____ kg	m) _____ kg	u) _____ kg
Weight of pot 2 with water	f) _____ kg	n) _____ kg	v) _____ kg
Water temperature, pot 1	g) _____ C	p) _____ °C	w) _____ °C
Water temperature, pot 2	h) _____ °C	q) _____ °C	y) _____ °C
Time	i) _____	r) _____	z) _____

(use the graph outline on reverse side to record changes in water temperature)

Calculations	High Power Phase	Low Power Phase
Wood consumed	A) $d-j =$ _____ kg	J) $j-s =$ _____ kg
Charcoal remaining	B) $k =$ _____ kg	K) $t-k =$ _____ kg
Equivalent dry wood consumed	C) $A/(1+a)-1.5^-B =$ _____ kg	L) $J/(1+a)-1.5\ K =$ _____ kg
Water vaporized, pot 1	D) $e-m =$ _____ kg	M) $m-u =$ _____ kg
Water vaporized, pot 2	E) $f-n =$ _____ kg	N) $n-v =$ _____ kg
Consumption ratio	F) $D/(D+E) =$ _____	P) $M/(M+N) =$ _____
Specific fuel consumption	G) $C/D =$ _____	Q) $L/M =$ _____
Duration of test	H) $r-i =$ _____	R) $z-r =$ _____
Burning rate	I) $C/H =$ _____ kg/min	S) $L/R =$ _____ kg/min

Overall Specific Fuel Consumption (SFC): $(C+L)/(D+M) =$ _____

*This is an example of a form to be completed every time a test is run. It is easily modified for cases where high and high-low power phases are run independently.

Organization conducting tests _____

Mailing address _____

Name of stove tested _____

Test numbers being reported _____ Test supervisor _____

Summary of Test conditions (draft protection, ambient temperature, etc.)

_____

_____

_____

_____

	Species *(Botanic name)*	*Approx % Total* *(by weight)*	*Moisture* *Content*	*Mean* *Dimensions*
	_____	_____ kg	_____ %	_____
	_____	_____ kg	_____ %	_____
	_____	_____ kg	_____ %	_____
	_____	_____ kg	_____ %	_____

		Pot 1	*Pot 2*	*Pot 3*
Weight (empty, dry)		_____ kg	_____ kg	_____ kg
Maximum capacity		_____ litres	_____ litres	_____ litres
Diameter at rim		_____ cm	_____ cm	_____ cm
Composition		_____	_____	_____

		High Power Phase		*Low Power Phase*		
Test *No.*	*Burning Rate* *(kg/min)*		*SFC*	*Burning Rate* *(kg/min)*	*SFC*	*Overall* *SFC*
1	_____		_____	_____	_____	_____
2	_____		_____	_____	_____	_____
3	_____		_____	_____	_____	_____
4	_____		_____	_____	_____	_____
5	_____		_____	_____	_____	_____

(Full description of stove on reverse side)

This is an example of a form to summarize and report results from a series of water boiling tests. It is easily modified for cases where high and high-low power phases are run independently.

Appendix 4
Controlled cooking test
Data and calculation form *

Test Number _____   Location _____

Date _____   Air temp °C _____ Wind _____ Rel. humidity _____

Stove _____   Stove condition _____

Cook _____   Remarks _____

BASIC TEST DATA	*Initial Measurements*	*Final Measurements*	

BASIC TEST DATA

	Initial Measurements	*Final Measurements*	
Weight of wood	(A)_____ kg	(G)_____ kg	
Weight of charcoal		(H)_____ kg	
Wt of pot 1 (empty)	(B)_____ kg	(I)_____ kg	(with cooked food)
Wt of pot 2 (empty)	(C)_____ kg	(J)_____ kg	(with cooked food)
Wt of pot 3 (empty)	(D)_____ kg	(K)_____ kg	(with cooked food)
Time	(E)_____	(L)_____	
Wood moisture content	(F)_____		

CALCULATIONS

(M) Weight of wood used	$A - G =$	
(N) Equivalent dry wood used	$M(1-F) - 1.5\,H =$ _____ kg
(P) Weight food cooked, Pot 1	$I - B =$ _____ kg
(Q) Weight food cooked, Pot 2	$J - C =$ _____ kg
(R) Weight food cooked, Pot 3	$K - D =$ _____ kg
(S) Total weight food cooked	$P + Q + R =$ _____ kg
(T) Specific consumption	$S/N =$ _____
(U) Total testing time	$L - E =$ _____

Cook's comments about stove performance, ease of use, etc:

_____

_____

_____

_____

_____

_____

_____

_____

_____

_____

*This is an example of a form to be completed every time a test is run

Controlled cooking test   **Test series reporting form**

Organization conducting tests _____

Address _____

_____

Names of stoves compared: (1) _____ (2) _____

Testing location _____

Testing period *Months* _____ *Year* _____ Name of test supervisor _____

CLIMATE		Maximum	Minimum	Mean
	Air temperature	_____°C	_____°C	_____°C
	Relative humidity	_____%	_____%	_____%
	Wind conditions	_____m/s	_____m/s	_____m/s

FUELWOOD

Species (Botanic name)	Approx % total (by weight)	Moisture content	Mean Length	Mean Diameter
_____	_____	_____	_____	_____
_____	_____	_____	_____	_____
_____	_____	_____	_____	_____

Calculated overall fuelwood moisture content _____

Method of determining moisture content _____

_____

Fuelwood cost per kg: _____ OR _____ = $ _____

estimated collection time   local currency   US dollars

MEASURING DEVICES

Instrument	Range	Scale Length	Type, manufacturer
Balance #1	_____kg	_____cm	_____
Balance #2	_____kg	_____cm	_____
Thermometer	_____°C	_____cm	_____
R.H. indicator	_____%	_____cm	_____
Anemometer	_____m/s	_____cm	_____
Other	_____	_____cm	_____

STOVE #1

	Mean	Standard Deviation	Coeff. of variation	Standard Error	95% Confidence Interval
Equiv. dry wood consumed per test	_____kg	_____	_____	_____	_____
Total weight food cooked per test	_____kg	_____	_____	_____	_____
Calculated specific consumption	_____	_____	_____	_____	_____
Duration of test	_____hrs	_____	_____	_____	_____

Total number of tests: _____

STOVE #2

	Mean	Standard Deviation	Coeff. of variation	Standard Error	95% Confidence Interval
Equiv. dry wood consumed per test	_____kg	_____	_____	_____	_____
Total weight food cooked per test	_____kg	_____	_____	_____	_____
Calculated specific consumption	_____	_____	_____	_____	_____
Duration of test	_____hrs	_____	_____	_____	_____

Total number of tests: _____

t-Value = _____ at _____% level of significance and _____ degrees of freedom.

* This is an example of a form used to summarize and report from a series of tests of two stoves being compared.

(Continued)...

CCT Series Reporting Form, continued

Description of standard meal. _____

_____

_____

Defined procedures for cooking the meal. _____

_____

_____

_____

_____

_____

_____

Summary of cook's comments, Stove #1 _____

_____

_____

_____

_____

_____

_____

Summary of cook's comments, Stove #2 _____

_____

_____

_____

_____

_____

_____

Appendix 5

Kitchen performance test

Data and calculation form

Household No._____ Family Name_____

Location_____

<table>
<tr><td rowspan="6">HOUSEHOLD</td><td></td><td>Number</td><td>Standard adult equivalents</td><td>Other household information</td></tr>
<tr><td>Children 0-14 years</td><td>_____ x 0.5 =</td><td>_____</td><td>_____</td></tr>
<tr><td>Women over 14 years</td><td>_____ x 0.8 =</td><td>_____</td><td>_____</td></tr>
<tr><td>Men aged 15-59 yrs</td><td>_____ x 1.0 =</td><td>_____</td><td>_____</td></tr>
<tr><td>Men over 59 years</td><td>_____ x 0.8 =</td><td>_____</td><td>_____</td></tr>
<tr><td colspan="2">(A) Total adult equivalents:</td><td>_____</td><td>_____</td></tr>
</table>

<table>
<tr><td rowspan="6">FUELWOOD</td><td>Species (Botanic Name)</td><td>Approx % total (by weight)</td><td>Mean Length</td><td>Mean Diameter</td></tr>
<tr><td>_____</td><td>_____</td><td>_____ cm</td><td>_____ cm</td></tr>
<tr><td>_____</td><td>_____</td><td>_____ cm</td><td>_____ cm</td></tr>
<tr><td>_____</td><td>_____</td><td>_____ cm</td><td>_____ cm</td></tr>
<tr><td colspan="4">Condition of fuelwood: (dry/damp/wet green)_____</td></tr>
<tr><td colspan="4">Fuelwood cost per kg:_____ OR _____ =$_____
    estimated collection time   local currency   US Dollars</td></tr>
</table>

<table>
<tr><td rowspan="3">ALTERNATIVE FUELS/STOVES</td><td>Description</td><td>Function</td></tr>
<tr><td>Other fuels in use: _____</td><td>_____</td></tr>
<tr><td>Other stoves in use: _____</td><td>_____</td></tr>
</table>

	Total wood remaining in inventory area	*Wood added to inventory area*	*Comments*
Day 0	_(None)_ kg	_____ kg	_____
Day 1	_____ kg	_____ kg	_____
Day 2	_____ kg	_____ kg	_____
Day 3	_____ kg	_____ kg	_____
Day 4	_____ kg	_____ kg	_____
Day 5	_____ kg	_____ kg	_____
Day 6	_____ kg	_____ kg	_____
Day 7	(**B**)_____ kg	_(None)_ kg	_____

(**C**) Total wood added to inventory

_____ kg

(**D**) Total wood consumed:

C-B = _____ kg

(**E**) Test duration:_____ days

Specific daily consumption: **D/A/E** = _____

* This is an example of a form to be used for each participating household.

Kitchen performance test
Test series reporting form *

Organization conducting tests_____

Address_____

_____

Names of stoves compared: (1)_____   (2)_____

Testing location_____

Testing period   *Months*_____   *Year*_____   Name of test supervisor_____

		Standard adult equivalents	Specific daily consumption	Fuelwood cost/kg
STOVE #1	Arithmetic mean:	_____	_____	_____
	Standard deviation:	_____	_____	_____
	Coefficient of variation	_____	_____	_____
	Standard error	_____	_____	_____
	95% Confidence Interval:	_____	_____	_____
	(Total number of tests_____)			
STOVE #2	Arithmetic mean:	_____	_____	_____
	Standard deviation:	_____	_____	_____
	Coefficient of variation	_____	_____	_____
	Standard error	_____	_____	_____
	95% Confidence Interval:	_____	_____	_____
	(Total number of tests_____)			

Specific daily consumption:

t-Value= _____ at _____% level of confidence and _____ degrees of freedom.

(Attach a full description of both stove models tested)

* This is an example of a form used to summarize and report results from a series of tests of two stoves being compared.

Appendix 6. Simulated cooking test

CCT Series Reporting Form

Name and origin of stove _____

_____

Name of stove builder(s) _____

Construction date _____ Materials used _____
_____

Stove location and condition _____
_____
_____

TOP VIEW	PERSPECTIVE

CUTAWAY VIEW WITH POTS	FRONT VIEW

	Pot #1	Pot #2	Pot #3
Weight (empty)	_____ kg	_____ kg	_____ kg
Maximum capacity	_____ 1	_____ 1	_____ 1
Diameter at rim	_____ cm	_____ cm	_____ cm
Composition	_____	_____	_____

POTS

Details of stove construction _____
_____
_____
_____
_____

CHAPTER 4

Choosing appropriate stove designs

The situation assessment will provide a preliminary view of the users' needs (see pages 5 and 7 and Tables 1.1 and 1.2), and the diversity among different economic and ethnic groups and areas.

The next major step should be choosing one or a small number of basic designs for further development and testing. Stove designs developed for one situation, and their related production and dissemination systems, will rarely be perfect for another situation, so the modification to meet local needs is critical. In the light of the users' needs, and their order of importance to the user, a systematic appraisal of the different designs is necessary.

The first part of this chapter is a general overview of the basic technical characteristics of the stoves which are presented firstly according to the stove type (number of pot-holes, and use or non-use of a chimney) and secondly by the type of material used for their construction. This is followed by a short summary of the questions that must be considered concerning the resources necessary for stove production and dissemination at the required scale. Finally the basic factors that affect adoption on the part of the user are considered.

Stove characteristics and construction materials

Stove designs can be considered from two aspects:

1. – Stove type
   and the performance for cooking and other functions; and
2. – Construction materials
   and the implications for construction, transport, installation, use and maintenance.

1. STOVE TYPE

One of the simplest ways to classify stoves is by the number of pot-holes and whether or not a chimney is used; this gives four groups:

Multi-pot chimney stoves
Multi-pot chimneyless stoves
One-pot chimney stoves
One-pot chimneyless stoves.

Table 4.1 gives a brief summary of the cooking performance and ancillary functions of the four groups.

2. STOVE MATERIALS

The material of which any design of stove is made will play a very important role in the stove's production, performance, operational lifetime and required maintenance, initial and annual costs, and the extension strategy.

For improved stoves to have a better performance than traditional stoves, they must be designed and made to more exacting specifications which change little over the stove's lifetime. Improved stoves must also be designed to withstand greater thermal and mechanical stresses because the combustion chamber temperatures are higher than those found in the semi-enclosed or enclosed mud and ceramic stoves that have been used for hundreds of years in Africa and Asia.

One of the major conflicts in designing improved stoves is to meet these more stringent requirements and still have a relatively low-cost stove adapted to local conditions. This requires a good understanding of the properties and design limitations of the different materials that can be used to make stoves. The following pages give a general summary of the characteristics of the different materials. More detailed information on stove production systems is given in Chapter 12.

The total costs of new stoves depend on many factors, but simple estimates can be based on the cost per kilogram of other products on the market made from the same materials.

Insulators

The reduction of heat losses into and through the walls of stoves can significantly improve their performance, and the type of insulation used makes a considerable difference to the overall effect. Some insulators, like mud, bricks, and pottery, have a low rate of heat transfer, but because of their relatively high mass (needed for structural strength) and high specific heat, they absorb considerable amounts of heat, which is not very useful for the cooking process or for high temperature radiant room heating. Their density (and therefore heat-holding capacity) can be decreased by the addition of low-density insulators such as grain husks, rice husk ash, sawdust, or air. A 10cm-thick section of mud will absorb approximately three times as much heat as a 10cm-thick section of a 2:1 (by volume) mix of rice husks and mud, because the density will be 0.8g/cu cm compared to 2.4g/cu cm.

Table 4.1: Stove types: cooking performance and ancillary functions

Type of stove	Laboratory efficiency for well-designed models	Characteristics in use	Secondary pot-holes	Smoke	Light	Space heating
Multi-pot chimney	20–25% with pots on top, 25–35% with sunken pots	All pots receive energy input simultaneously and in an essentially constant ratio which can reduce the versatility. All pots must be used to obtain maximum benefit. Chimney must be cleaned regularly to maintain proper operation	Often have low energy input, especially with three or more pot-holes	All pots must fit tight to remove smoke. Need standard pots, metal pot rings, or small pot-holes. All smoke is removed via chimney	Some light can come from open arch in front	Radiant room heat is at a low temperature
Multi-pot chimneyless	20–27% with pots on top. Optimum operation when both pots used simultaneously	Energy input ratio can be altered somewhat. Single pot can be used with reasonable efficiency if pot placement is modified	Second pot-hole gets greater % of total heat than in chimney stoves	Smoke released at back end of stove away from cook, but still in the kitchen	Some light can come from open arch in front	Greater than for chimney stove because of heat from exhaust
One-pot chimneyless	25–29% with pot on top, 25–35% with sunken pot	Power output highly variable, and easily controlled. Incremental pot shielding improves efficiency. Simplest design of all stove types; smallest, requires least material, usually portable		Released from around the pot but is usually less than an open fire	Can be emitted in small or significant amounts	From stove radiation, flames, and exhaust gases

48

Type of stove	Laboratory efficiency for well-designed models	Characteristics in use	Secondary pot-holes	Smoke	Light	Space heating
One-pot chimney	16–19% with pot on top, up to 45% with sunken pot	The performance of stoves with the pot on top decreases with deviations from the optimum pot-to-baffle gap, and always cook considerably slower than chimneyless stoves of the same size. Sunken pot design is most applicable for large pots that are used constantly. High and variable power output is possible. Sunken pot also significantly reduces heat losses from the pot walls. Chimney must be cleaned regularly or it will get blocked and not operate properly. Very few of this type of stove are used for domestic cooking		Removed via chimney	No light	Potential low temperature radiation from stove walls

Table 4.2: Stove materials

Stove material:	MUD MIX	POTTERY	STEEL	FIRED BRICK & MORTAR
LIFETIME	6 months to 5 years	1 to 8 years	1–10 years, depending on steel thickness	3 to 15 years
CONSTRUCTION Raw materials	Clayey soil, sand, fibres, dung, ash. Large amounts required and must be near site. Poor quality of mix of material means poor stove	Clay, sand, rice husk ash, grain husks. Quality varies considerably and local producers are best source of information. Pottery stoves often require additives for thermal strength. Fuel required for firing	Used oil barrels, old cars, scrap sheet steel. All these are cheaper than new steel, but more difficult to work	Fired bricks, mud mortar, steel top plates and supports, exterior cement plaster
Requirements for labour, investment, and organization	Low capital investment per worker, but good training and follow-up are necessary if trainees are to build many quality stoves. Relatively high labour, and high organization cost per stove, with many part-time builders. Rarely becomes a self-sustaining business	Traditional potters usually have necessary skills and equipment for small numbers. Larger scale production requires more skill, investment and organization	Traditional artisans are versatile but additional quality control necessary on complicated stoves. Investment in better tools and working area pays off with continuous production	Mainly built by skilled masons for large kitchens
TRANSPORT	Stoves usually weigh 50–150kg and cannot be transported. Transport of raw materials and builders can be a considerable part of total cost	Bulky. Can be transported by lorries, bicycles, or persons with proper packing, but some breakages will occur. Average weight 3–5kg per pot-hole, and per 30cm of chimney	Very tough and easy to transport and store	Heavy materials must be transported like other building materials. Masons must travel to site
INSTALLATION (excl. chimney)	Must generally be built on site over a few days	Can be used as portable stoves, or surrounded with mud to give added protection	Portable. Steel top plates warp unless thick and welded	Built on site
USE	Little high temperature radiation; little danger of burns. Large stoves are slow to warm up	Radiates more heat than mud-mix stoves because of thinner walls. Portable stoves are more fragile than insulated ones	Hot surfaces and significant radiation. Easy to start and reaches a steady temperature quickly	Usually built for long hours of use per day. Thick walls reduce room radiation. Heavy mass gives high strength
MAINTENANCE	Exterior repairs are simple. Interior repairs are more difficult, but often necessary to maintain original performance	Exterior repairs are simple and do not affect performance. Small cracks can be tolerated but large cracks usually mean stove must be replaced	Portable stoves or removable pieces can be repaired or replaced at an artisan's workshop	Periodic maintenance of mortar and interior bricks important because of heavy use. Steel sections will burn out over time

Stove material:	HEAVY CEMENT	LIGHTWEIGHT CEMENT MIX IN CONCRETE	CAST IRON	CAST ALUMINIUM
LIFETIME	6 years	6 months to 3 years	5–20 years	1–6 years
CONSTRUCTION Raw materials	Cement, sand, gravel, metal, reinforcing wire	Cement, rice husk ash, vermiculite, perlite, spray plaster, wire	Iron scrap. Coke or charcoal	Aluminium scrap. Charcoal
Requirements for labour, investment, and organization	Steel shuttering is initially expensive, but long lasting and gives best product. Space needed for curing pieces if production is at a central location	Usually low	Existing foundries have necessary skills to cast. Mould makers are needed for new moulds. Large or complicated stoves require larger foundries	Very small aluminium foundries are common. Need mould maker for moulds
TRANSPORT	Pre-built stoves are very heavy and must be transported by truck. Stoves built on site require transport of raw materials, shuttering and labour	Relatively robust but can chip	Relatively tough, but can crack	Simple castings can crack if dropped
INSTALLATION (excl. chimney)	Pre-built stoves placed in desired position. Sectional stoves must be assembled after moulding	Portable	Portable, or used as pieces of stoves made from other materials	Portable, or used as top plates of stoves made from other materials
USE	Thick walls best matched with large pots. Relatively low room radiation	Lightweight. Insulation especially appropriate for charcoal stoves	Same as steel	Same as steel
MAINTENANCE	Cracks from heat are difficult to repair and grow with age	Small cracks develop from effects of heat and grow with age. Surface coatings can reduce erosion	Cast iron is more resistant to heat and the corrosives in wood and charcoal fires, and will outlast steel	Corrodes more quickly than steel or cast iron. Will melt at temperatures over 600°C, and solder repairs will melt at lower temperatures

The rice husks also give more binding strength, prevent cracking and allow thinner walls to be made.

A better insulator is one with both a low heat transfer coefficient and a low specific heat. Usually such insulators cannot withstand direct flames and impact, but are very useful around a stronger firebox lining. Rice husk ash (often mixed with a small amount of clay for binding), vermiculite, perlite, diatomite, rockwool, glass wool, and other commercial insulators can often significantly improve performance at a reasonable cost, especially on small stoves.

Resources

To meet the potential users' needs, a considerable amount of planning and resources will be necessary, as with the promotion of any new commercial item, or an improved agricultural technique. Any type of improved stove will require significant resources outside of the household, and an objective analysis must be made to determine if they will be available, and to calculate their cost.

Stove construction
  materials
- types of raw materials available
- cost per stove
- availability: would materials be sufficient if stove became unduly dessimated?
- seasonality of supply
- the need to purchase large stocks of material, and whether this would decrease or increase the cost per stove
- consistency of quality.

  labour
- training required for a stove builder
- follow-up training or supervision necessary
- total cost of training and follow-up per stove built
- payment to builder per month, per stove
- number of stoves built each month by one good builder, one average builder.

Stove production
- cost to set up a simple artisan production system
- whether cost of each successive unit set up will decrease or remain the same

- the project support required to produce a certain number of stoves per month under:
  - simple artisan system
  - more advanced system
  - small factories
- minimum and average stove costs for different levels of production
- working capital required to maintain production levels.

Stove distribution

- transport required per stove for skilled people, raw materials, or finished stoves
- education, promotion, and follow-up necessary for a successful programme
- whether the project needs to provide support for repairs and maintenance.

Factors affecting user adoption

In a review of the Sarvodaya stove project in Sri Lanka, Howes et al (1983) highlight four conditions, applicable to any stove programme, that must be satisfied for a person to adopt a new design of stove.

'They must be aware of its existence and of the functions which it performs; they must be able to obtain access to it; they must regard it as superior both to existing stoves, and to other alternative stoves of which they are aware; and they must regard it as more desirable than other goods or services which could be acquired with the same resources.'

1. AWARENESS
The main potential sources of new information are:

- neighbours
- the market place where new goods can be seen
- village organizations
- visiting government and NGO representatives (directly), and through demonstrations, meetings and training programmes organized by them
- the mass media.

The sources are listed in approximate descending order of the impact and usefulness of the information to the recipient. Neighbours and the market place are probably the two most important sources of new information for poor or rural households, and the information they transmit is often more important than the intended message.

2. ACCESS

Access to the new stove can be through direct or indirect means of acquisition.

Direct:
- cash, and the ability to bring the stove back from market
- home purchase from 'dealers'.

For stoves requiring outright purchase, or hire of labour, access is fairly simple – it depends on the supply of the goods, or the skill and the ease with which a prospective purchaser can make contact. This can however become a constraint when a relatively small programme is spread over a wide area.

Indirect:
- moulds, in the control of someone
- contact with skilled extension workers
- contact to get the specific information necessary to build the stove.

When acquisition of the stove is not by purchase, access is often complicated because it is based on random visits or a rationing system involving personal contacts and political affiliations which can have very little to do with the value of the stove to the potential user.

Poor or rural people rarely, if ever, consider leaflets or drawings to mean 'access'; some form of personal contact is necessary. Where extension workers help build the stove the cost of providing the information through personal contact can be very high.

3. PERCEIVED SUPERIORITY

This is the most important characteristic and the most complex. The consumer can be expected to judge the stove in terms of:
- its efficiency for cooking, heating and lighting
- its other attributes
- costs and benefits.

Cooking, heating and lighting

Traditional stoves have evolved to provide cooking, heating and lighting with inevitable compromises to suit users' total requirements of a stove. New or re-designed stoves usually limit the effectiveness of one or more functions to significantly improve a relatively more important function.

The desired improvement in cooking efficiency is the most important, but is not always the same as the change recorded in the laboratory, or referred to by the promoters of the stove. The exact dimensions of the stove, the size of pots used, the burning procedure, the type and moisture content of the fuel, etc., can all make a considerable difference. The actual efficiency in cooking can only be found out under actual field conditions. The field tests described in the chapter on testing are the best way to get reliable results, but even a limited number of tests, visits, and interviews with a greater number of households can give a useful idea of the actual change.

Improved stoves often entail a loss of effective heating and lighting, and field interviews are the only way to find out how important this is.

Other attributes

The consumer will also make a judgement on the following attributes of the new stove.

Lifetime
- Under a normal use-and-repair regime.

Failure rate
- If 25% of the stoves built are incorrect, the consumer may consider the risk of getting a 'bad' stove too high, even if the other 75% work satisfactorily and last for five years.

Maintenance
- While it is possible to keep mud stoves operational with only monthly repairs, if regular stove maintenance is not an accepted local tradition, then the work will often not be done, or will be considered a burden, especially if there is little spare time for it.

Appearance
- The aesthetic appearance of the stove (especially for urban markets) is important, and mud-mix stoves are often regarded as inferior for this reason.

Environmental
- The kitchen environment may change for better or worse, e.g. there may be smoke removal, reduced burn hazards, an improved appearance, or the stove may take up more room or require to be in an inconvenient position (for chimney placement, for example).

Attendance
- A stove with a grate may require more attention, especially during simmering. It may be necessary to chop wood into smaller pieces, not just to fit into the stove but also to maintain proper burning. Such requirements may be considered unacceptable.

Cost and benefits

How these are valued is difficult to judge in advance. In many cases fuel gathering and cooking are done by members of the household whose time is not highly valued, whereas the new stove will usually require a cash outlay. The risk of short lifetimes and high failure rates for stoves paid for in money or labour will deter many people, especially those with little of these commodities to spare – the very ones for whom the burden is the greatest. Often future benefits are not considered, or are heavily discounted so that the initial cost is too great for the perceived benefits.

If the replacement stove has to be purchased, and the decision on spending is made by men, they will need to be involved in the decision to adopt the stove, and must be shown how it would benefit them – particularly if they do not collect wood.

4. BEST USE OF AVAILABLE FUNDS

The final condition is that buying the stove should be considered more worthwhile than purchasing other goods such as other kitchen equipment, tools, food, etc. While relatively expensive stoves could significantly reduce fuel use, it is probable that many households would prefer to use the cash for the purchase of more immediate needs or more productive investments – which would significantly lower the market demand for the improved, but expensive, stoves.

PART II

STOVES FROM AROUND THE WORLD

Earlier chapters have equipped you with the necessary skills to develop suitable stove designs. These chapters describe the details of stoves that have been developed successfully in different parts of the world. These are meant as useful starting points from which the successful stove designs can be adapted for your stove programme. The stoves are classified according to the four types already designated – multi-pot chimney, multi-pot chimneyless, one-pot chimney, and one-pot chimneyless, with a fifth chapter on charcoal stoves.

Each chapter has a brief introduction followed by a detailed description of that type of stove's components and their functions, as experience has shown that guidelines developed for one type are often not universally applicable. The individual stove descriptions that follow, together with notes on their construction, installation and use, are biased towards stoves that have proved acceptable to a relatively large number of users, and not to stoves which have better efficiencies and performance in the laboratory, but which have yet to be successfully disseminated.

Each chapter includes a table summarizing the results of tests carried out on the individual stoves described. The tests were comparable, and unless otherwise stated they were carried out with covered aluminium pots containing 2kg to 4kg of water, brought to the boil and kept at a vigorous boil for a short period of time (up to 30 minutes). The energy used for evaporation is included in the efficiency calculations. The high heat value of the fuel is used in all calculations with the exception of test results from Eindhoven, the Bellerive Foundation, and VITA (African results), which use the low heat value. Using the low heat value results in a slightly higher (5–10%) efficiency.

Experience has shown that the performance of new stoves often falls short of expectations, and may even be worse than that of the traditional stove it replaces. The optimization of stoves to a specific operating condition, and the correction of serious problems, must be part of any successful stove programme. Although there is a section in each chapter outlining the major symptoms, causes, and recommended solutions for that stove type, these summaries cannot cover all the possible problems that can occur with individual stoves – a more specific list would be required to meet the needs of individual programmes. If the stoves are to give satisfaction to the users, this information, together with instructions on general repair and maintenance, must be readily available to the appropriate personnel, whether they be extension workers, self-employed artisans, or the users themselves.

A NOTE ON PART II

Within each chapter, the descriptions of the individual stoves are presented under the following headings:

1 *Name*
The name by which the stove is described in reports, and known in English. The stoves are often known by other names locally.

2 *Drawing*
All drawings are to scale, but where a range of sizes is made, only one is represented.

3 *Description*
The material(s), size, weight, general shape and other important characteristics are detailed.

4 *History and field experience*
The origin of the stove design, and its later evolution, together with any special characteristics of its production and dissemination.

5 *Construction, installation, and maintenance*

6 *Use of the stove*
Notes on operation of the stove, feeding of fuel, types of cooking commonly carried out, control of power input to pots.

The individual stoves described have been chosen for a number of reasons:

- to cover a range of stove designs and materials within each stove type, as the desired stove for a new area must often draw on characteristics from a variety of stoves;

- for their relative low cost and simplicity (although more complex designs would usually improve the efficiency);

- for their ability to burn a wide variety of fuel sizes, and not to require special pots (in most cases);

- for the potential transferability of the design to other countries, on the basis of suitability of materials and production systems;

- for the availability of test results based on equivalent procedures, enabling comparison of their respective performances.

The most important characteristic that ties all these stoves together is that they are currently being used in expanding field programmes which have gone through adaptations and modifications to meet users' needs and local resources.

CHAPTER 5

Chimney stoves

Introduction

This type of stove gained prominence in the late 1940s in India and was the basis of nearly all stove programmes through to 1980. Most of the stove literature concerns this type, and numerous books have been written on their design and construction: *Lorena stoves* (Evans and Bouttette, 1981) and *Wood conserving cookstoves: a design guide* (VITA, 1980) being two of the better known.

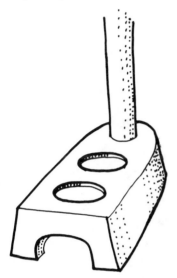

Figure 5.1. Typical chimney stove.

The basic design has a firebox with a door opening at one side and the first pot directly on top. From the firebox the flames and smoke pass through a tunnel and underneath one to three pots before leaving through a chimney. Entrance doors, metal grates, primary air inlets, and draught control dampers are included in some designs. Most of the stoves have thick walls for strength (Figure 5.1). The following stoves in this general category are described:

Magan Chula
Nepali Insert stove
UNICEF/New Nepali Chula
Nada Chula
Lorena stove
Thai moulded stove
Pogbi stove
Community stove (the only single-pot chimney stove).

The earliest multi-pot chimney stoves were usually made of mud mixtures, In India, cow dung or agricultural wastes were added to the clay to reduce cracking and improve the strength. In Central America 'lorena' – literally, a mixture of sand and clay – is the most popular mix. Mud stoves made in moulds are used in Thailand and Africa. Brick and mortar stoves have been promoted in a number of places but have not been used in large numbers. The Gandhiniketan Ashram (South India) programme, and the recent Nepalese programmes, are all based on pottery liners which are surrounded by a mud mixture, for strength.

For this type of stove two characteristics have had considerably more importance than fuel efficiency and cooking speed – the removal of smoke and the ability to use a wide range of pots. Only the Pogbi stove, which has been built in limited numbers, has pots specially designed to fit into the stove to provide more area for heat transfer. All the other designs have pot-holes smaller than the large principal pot so that a wide range of pots can be used on the front pot-hole.

Doors provided to control the air entering the firebox are usually unused, to allow the burning of long pieces of wood, to see the fire, and to let out some room heat. Large door openings are common, so that bulky agricultural wastes can be fed in. Draught control dampers near to or in the chimney are also rarely used except on the larger stoves. To compensate for the non-use of doors and dampers, the most satisfactory way to try to ensure good performance is to place a large baffle beneath the second pot. This delays the flames in their passage to and out of the chimney, enabling more heat to be transferred to the pots.

Grates are used on the T. Kallupatti Magan Chula made at the Gandhiniketan Ashram, and on the Nepalese UNICEF stove, to improve the burning of wet fuels and agricultural wastes, and also to increase the maximum power output.

The use of more than two pot-holes does not reduce fuel consumption because the third and any additional pot-holes increase resistance to flow of the gases, and thus increase heat losses in the stove. These pot-holes are useful only for warming food or water, and may be desirable simply as an added convenience.

The maximum performance of chimney stoves is dependent on the proper draught of the stove,

which will vary with the chimney dimensions and installation (e.g. location), and also with the pot types used. Installers and users must be given the knowledge to adjust the stove, as poor field performance is more common with this type of stove than any other, and the common problems can be readily solved (see the 'problem solving' section at end of chapter).

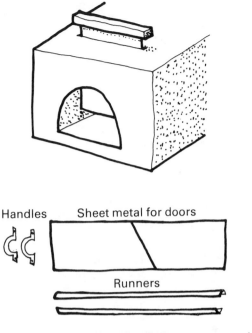

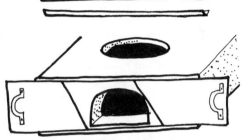

Figure 5.3. Firebox entrances and doors. Doors in slots require a longer entrance way and introduce structural weakness (top drawing, from *Lorena stoves*, 1981). Bottom drawing (from Chiplankar, 1982, and Sarin, 1983) shows sliding doors installed on the front of a stove.

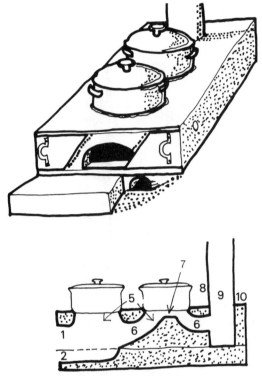

Figure 5.2. Typical multi-pot chimney stove. (Front View, and longitudinal section)

1. Fuel entrance
2. Primary air entrance
3. Firebox floor
4. Firebox
5. Pot-holes
6. Tunnels
7. Baffle
8. Damper
9. Chimney
10. Walls

Firebox entrance

This is where all fuel and all or some of the air enters the firebox. In the simpler designs most of the air enters through the firebox doorway, and doors are not used, as the fire size is controlled by the cook manipulating the wood rather than by controlling the flow of air. The entrance should be big enough to manoeuvre at least three average-sized wood sticks. Doors are more common on large stoves made to be filled with fuel which is then left to burn slowly for a long period, or on stoves where most of the air is to be drawn through a grate.

Extra airholes, commonly called *secondary*

airholes, are added to some designs to get air into parts of the firebox where there would otherwise be poor mixing and insufficient air for the fuel to burn properly. If the size of the firebox entrance and secondary airholes is too great, an excess of air will enter the firebox, lowering the flame temperatures and overall stove performance. Too small a firebox results in poor combustion.

Primary air entrance

When a grate is used the undergrate air can enter through a primary air entrance. If the stove is to be used for slow burning the primary air entrance should also have a door, such as a brick, and it must be designed to allow easy removal of the ash (which will otherwise accumulate and block it). The size of the primary airhole depends on the other dimensions in the stove (these control the total resistance to flow, and thus the amount of air entering the stove); it must be large enough to allow sufficient air for maximum power output to

59

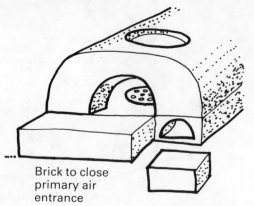

Brick to close primary air entrance

Figure 5.4. Primary air entrace. Having the primary air entrance offset, i.e. not underneath the firebox entrance, allows a platform to be made in front of the firebox.

be obtained (see Figure 5.4).

The use of grates in chimney stoves improves efficiency and power output, but also adds some significant complications in use. The positive effect of a grate is often cancelled out because it can quickly become blocked with ash and may not be regularly cleaned, and unless made of cast iron it can break or burn out in a year. Grates are not suitable for unattended low output fires because the charcoal is consumed rapidly on the grate instead of being buried in the ash to assist slow burning.

The grate can be designed to cover all or part of the firebox base, depending on other factors such as cost, percentage area of holes, and stove design. The grate holes should be from 0.7cm to 2cm in diameter so that they are large enough to allow ash, but not sizeable pieces of charcoal, to fall though. For stoves with tight-fitting doors the percentage of openings should be from 25–35% of the total floor area, but for open door stoves, 10–25% will usually be sufficient.

Figure 5.5. Calculating percentage grate area.

Diameter 20cm	Diameter 20cm
Area $100\pi = 314_2$	Area $100\pi = 314cm_2$
23 holes 2cm diameter	Grate 10.5cm × 10.5cm
area $23\pi = 72cm_2$	6 gaps of 9cm × 1cm = 54cm_2
% grate area = 23%	% grate area = 17%

A grate diameter of 18cm will allow a fire to reach an output of 6 to 8kW (see Figure 5.5).

If grates are critical to the design, it is imperative

that they are made of cast iron, or that the owner can easily obtain replacements. Cheap pottery or sheet metal grates made by local craftsmen may be unobtainable in rural areas, and will often not have the required percentage area of holes.

When a grate is *not* used it is common practice to leave a thick bed of ash on the firebox floor. This is a good insulation for the charcoal and the fire, and makes the stove easier to light and keep going. In many areas this is the practice with traditional stoves and should be considered in the design of the new stove.

Firebox

The height from the top of the fuel bed to the pot is more important than that from the firebox floor to the pot. One rule of thumb is that the fuel bed to pot distance should be equal to half the diameter of the pot-hole (Baldwin, 1984). When pots of 17–25cm diameter are used the firebox should be 15–18cm high for burning large pieces of wood and bulky bundles of fuel; a height of 12–16cm is sufficient for smaller pieces of relatively straight wood. For larger pots, of 25–40cm diameter, the firebox should be slightly taller (16–22cm) to allow for the greater amount of fuel needed.

Where there is no grate the firebox should be partially spherical so that the halfway diameter is 10–15% greater than the pot-hole diameter; this shape allows the flame plume to develop properly. Where there is a grate less combustion volume is required, so the walls can be straight and the total height slightly reduced.

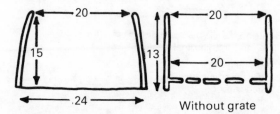

Without grate

Figure 5.6. Firebox cross-sections (with and without grate).

Pot-holes

In all cultures a variety of pot sizes is used, and this is especially important in the design of stoves as the relationship of pot sizes to the pot-hole will significantly affect their efficiency. According to work carried out by the Woodburning Stove Group in Holland on a number of two-pot stoves, the heat transferred in a chimney stove is proportional to the surface area of pots either sitting on top, or partially sunk into the hot gases (Nievergeld et al, 1981). For a limited number of straight-sided pots, the pot-holes can be designed to take sunken pots.

The pot-hole should be designed for the largest

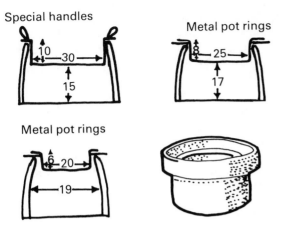

Special handles

Metal pot rings

Metal pot rings

Figure 5.7. Sunken pots. Shallow pots will be further away from the fuel unless concave metal pot rings are used. The lower drawing shows a special pot with raised pot rim for easier handling (Micuta, 1981, and others).

and most commonly used pot, which can rest on its rim. Smaller pots can be used with steel rings, but the larger pots must sit on top of the stove. They may therefore be quite far from the fire, and there will be poor heat transfer, slower cooking, and an overall performance possibly worse than that of an open fire.

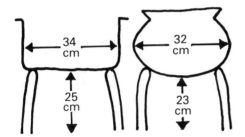

Figure 5.8. Large pots on a stove designed for sunken pots. If pots that do not sink in are used on stoves designed for sunken pots there will be poor heat transfer, slower cooking and an overall performances worse than that of an open fire.

If there is a very wide range of straight-walled pot sizes, or if round–bottomed pots are used, the method of using steel rings is too cumbersome, or not possible at all. The simplest and cheapest approach is to design the pot-holes, especially the first, so that the most commonly used large pots have most of their base exposed to the flame. Small pots and tea kettles can be supported on top of steel rings, and the largest, less often used pots can sit on the pot-hole, but will have a relatively small portion of the base exposed.

If pot-holes are designed to accommodate the smallest to the largest pot, without the use of rings,

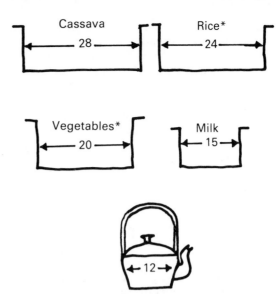

Figure 5.9. Fixing pot-hole size for a wide variety of pots. When different pots are to be used on one stove the most effective solution is to have the front pot-hole as large as the most commonly-used large pot, the second as big as the pot commonly used *with* the largest pot, and to use metal pot rings for the rest. Thus:

good design
23cm front pot hold
19.5cm back pot hole

poor design
15cm front pot hole
15cm back pot hole

The good design will expose twice as much area to the flames as the poor design

the overall performance (time to boil, and efficiency) will be low.

Pot-holes should be spaced so that the two largest pots most commonly used together can fit on the stove without touching.

Tunnels

It is extremely important to achieve an even distribution of flow under the first pot, and this is done by placing the tunnel at the back of the firebox. To reduce turbulence at the tunnel entrance (and therefore reduce heat loss) it is necessary to taper the tunnel at both entrance and exit.

Figure 5.10. Position of firebox exit (top view of fireboxes). From *Lorena Stoves*, 1981.

The area of the tunnel at its narrowest section will, along with the baffle height, determine the amount of heat being transferred to the second pot. For a heat ratio of 2.5:1 for front to rear pot, the cross-section of the tunnel should be around 100–120 sq cm when the baffle to pot height is 2–3cm. In chimney stoves, the diameter of the rear exit also plays an important part in setting the draught. Small changes in the diameter can lead to large variations in flame path.

Tunnels must be easy to clean with a spoon or stick, as clogged tunnels are one of the most common problems with chimney stoves.

Baffles

The role of baffles is to create pressure drops, resulting in turbulence and increased convective heat transfer underneath the pots. Baffles should always be placed under the second and subsequent pots and can be put in the firebox if a very large proportion of the total heat is required on the first pot, with very little on the remaining pot(s).

Recent experimental work carried out by RE-CAST (Nepal) has indicated that baffles should be situated near the front of the second pot to obtain maximum heat input to the pot. Where round-bottomed pots are used the baffle should be curved.

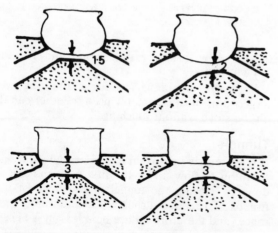

Figure 5.11. Position and shape of baffle. When both round and flat-bottomed pots are used the top of the baffle should not be in the middle of the pot-hole because the average round-bottomed pot will sit deeper in the middle than a flat-bottomed pot. It is better to place the baffle two thirds of the way back or forward than in the middle. Figures indicate pot-to-baffle gap in centimetres.

The size of the pot-to-baffle gap will depend on the stove draught. For a simple two-pot stove with a 1.5 – 3m chimney, gaps of 2–4cm are commonly used. In theory, smaller gaps would increase the heat transfer to the second pot, but in practice the increased resistance to air flow results in poor combustion and decreased heat transfer. For more than two pots, the pot-to-baffle gaps must be larger (4–6cm) to allow for adequate gas flow through the stove.

MEASURING POT-TO-BAFFLE GAP

Put a lump of soft clay approximately 5cm in diameter on the ridge of the baffle about one-third away from the side of the pot-hole (to get an average gap value for round-bottom pots). Place the pot into the hole then remove it. Measure the height of the clay lump.

Dampers

Dampers are used to control the output of the fire. By partially closing a tunnel with a damper the resistance to air flow is increased.

A damper does not increase the efficiency of a stove, but gives the user the chance to control the fire more effectively, which should lead to greater fuel savings.

Dampers can be considered in the design of stoves for areas where variable wind conditions affect the draught, or where a long, slow-burning fire is required. Dampers are also useful to allow regulation of the flow rate of air for different fuels. Straw, for example, requires more air than wood for good combustion; the damper would be opened to burn straw and partially closed to burn wood. Dampers can be placed at the front of the stove, in a tunnel or passageway, or in the chimney.

In practice howeve, dampers tend to be little used, especially in rural areas, and it is often wiser to design the stove to operate under a reasonable range of conditions without requiring careful adjustment of a damper.

Chimneys

The chimney takes all the gases and smoke generated from the fire and releases them away from the occupants, usually outside the kitchen, but sometimes only above head level. The force with which the chimney pulls the smoke is related to the temperature difference between the gas at the chimney base and the outside environment, the chimney height and its diameter, and any constrictions or bends within the stove.

CHIMNEY DESIGN AND DIMENSIONS

The chimney should be tall enough to release the smoke above the heads of the occupants. If smoke is deliberately released underneath a thatched roof (to preserve it) the top of the chimney must be at least one metre away, and preferably more, to reduce the fire hazard. In such a situation users must feel it is more important to preserve the roof, as this chimney arrangement will not remove smoke completely.

The taller the chimney, the greater the draught. Chimneys as short as one metre have been used successfully, but these do not take the smoke very far away from the occupants; two- to three-metre chimneys are more common. Chimneys should be at least 10cm in internal diameter to avoid clogging, and 12cm is preferable. Height should be no less than 1.8 metres. Stoves for pots over 35cm diameter (such as may be used in restaurants and for institutional cooking) often require larger chimneys of 12–15cm diameter.

Bends in a chimney increase the resistance to air flow and reduce the total draught, but this can be compensated for by use of a taller chimney or by reducing the pressure drops created by baffles and tunnels. The draught of chimneys can be controlled by a damper in the chimney, but if the stove has an open firebox entrance it will be difficult to use the damper effectively.

In many parts of the world house roofs are made of flammable materials and sparks coming out of the chimney could be a fire hazard. Resinous fuels and some agricultural wastes will produce a considerable amount of sparks, and the only solution for a capless chimney is to place a wire mesh on top to reduce this danger. This mesh will also trap soot and tar, and will have to be cleaned regularly. A capless chimney should not be installed within one metre above a thatched roof. Metal chimneys should not be in direct contact with thatched roofs, and a metal thimble will reduce the danger of a fire.

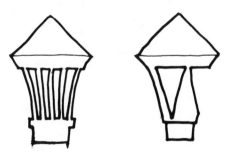

Figure 5.12. Chimney thimble. The openings should be equal to at least 75% of the cross section area of the chimney. If the openings on the thimble are small they are especially susceptible to clogging up. In the chimney pipe most of the soot and tar will collect in the lower half of the chimney. To clean a straight chimney it is necessary to go up on to the roof and run a plunger up and down.

CLEANING OF CHIMNEYS

Lack of chimney maintenance is one of the major reasons for the failure of chimney stoves. Soot and tar from the fire collect and condense in the chimney continuously (mostly in the lower half) and can

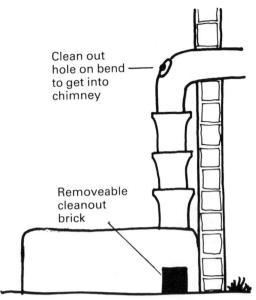

Figure 5.13. Chimney cleaning. (From Joseph, 1982.) (First drawing) A straight chimney can be cleaned from the roof by running a plunger up and down – this can be a stick (long enough to reach the base), with a tin-can lid, or a bundle or twigs, fixed to the end, to scrape the chimney walls.

clog up the stove in only a few months if no cleaning is done.

Soot that naturally falls down the chimney, and is knocked down during cleaning, must not block the funnels. Provision of a collecting well at the chimney base allows for less frequent cleaning. Soot can be removed via the last pot-hole through a cleanout hole with a door or closure brick. This hole can be at the rear, side or on top of the stove – the best position depending on how and where the stove is built. The more accessible the well, the more often cleaning is likely to be carried out.

CHIMNEY CAPS

The openings in the chimney cap should not be so small as to restrict the exit of smoke. It has been found that the most effective form of chimney cap is a T-section.

If the cap is next to a wall, instead of above the roof, special precautions must be taken to ensure effective smoke removal. When wind hits a wall, pressure is built up making it difficult for the smoke to escape. The chimney exit must therefore be positioned away from the wall, where the pressure is lower. The chimney should be at least 10cm from the wall; greater distances often require supports, and the resistance to flow of the horizontal section may make it necessary to increase the total height of the chimney to achieve the same draught.

The best solution is to put the chimney on the

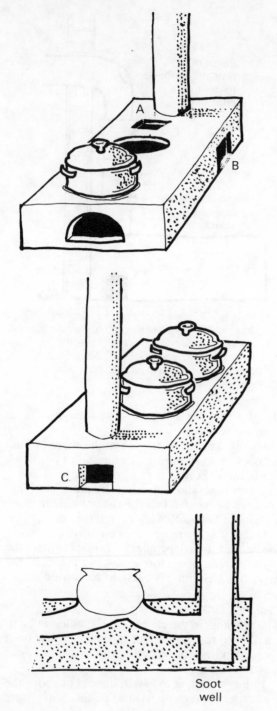

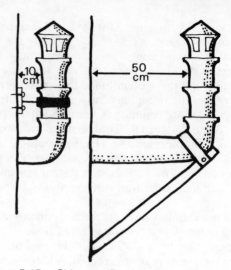

Figure 5.15.   Chimneys fitted next to walls.

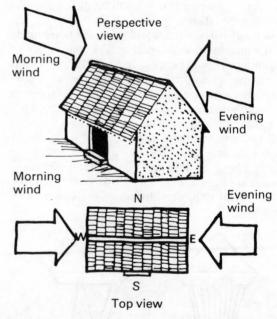

Figure 5.16.   Positioning of chimneys in Kathmandu valley, Nepal.

Figure 5.14.   Soot well at chimney base, showing provision for cleaning out.

side of the house that has the least wind hitting it. Figure 5.16 shows a common situation in Nepal for houses in valleys where the wind goes up the valley in the morning, and down in the evening.

On the west wall the wind will force some smoke down the chimney in the morning; on the east wall this will happen in the evening. Chimneys on the north or south walls will always have the smoke pulled away.

If possible, chimneys should always be placed on walls that the wind does not strike, or strikes only infrequently. The farther away the chimney is from the wall, the less chance there is of the pressure of the wind hitting the wall forcing smoke down the chimney.

Chimney caps can also reduce the possibility of backdraught but cannot overcome direct wind.

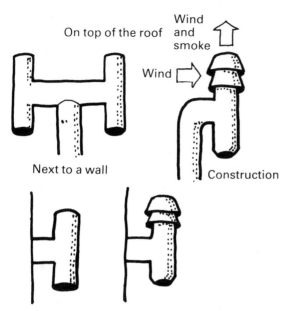

Figure 5.17. Chimney caps to reduce backdraught. The construction (top right-hand drawing, underneath cap and pipe junction) increases the speed of the smoke and reduces backdraught.

The following designs reduce the chance of backdraught by reducing the size of the outlet, which increases the smoke speed and therefore pressure at the outlet.

CHIMNEY MATERIALS AND LIFETIMES

The main requirements are for ease of installation, durability, and reasonably low cost per annum (rather than low initial cost). Where transport is limited, home-made chimneys of thin metal, rein-

forced mud, or mud blocks, seem appropriate because of their low cost, but they have very short lifetimes (often less than a year). Fired pottery and thick metal chimneys cost more but will last much longer – 4 to 10 years; the yearly cost will often be lower, and there is no need to make provision for continual chimney replacement.

Pottery chimneys can be made in a number of ways. In many areas extruded 10cm internal diameter drainage pipes are available on the open market, in 60cm lengths. These are quite heavy.

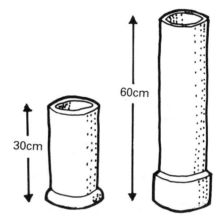

Figure 5.18. Clay pipes suitable for chimney construction. Left – hand-thrown pipe; right – extruded fired-clay drainage pipe.

Chimney sections can also be made by hand in a variety of ways. Thirty centimetre-tall sections can be made one at a time on a wheel, and can be joined together with a collar section. Alternatively, clay sheets can be wrapped around a mould.

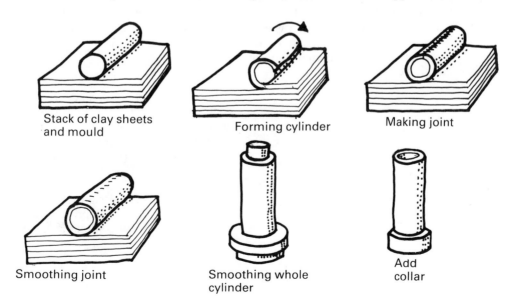

Stack of clay sheets and mould

Forming cylinder

Making joint

Smoothing joint

Smoothing whole cylinder

Add collar

Figure 5.19. Pipe construction in Kasongan, Indonesia.

Corrosion is a problem with metal chimneys and is worst in the 50cm length next to the stove, where the gases are hottest, and just outside the building, where rain strikes the hot chimney.

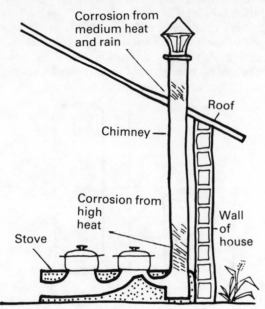

Figure 5.20.   Corrosion in metal chimneys

Chimneys thinner than 20 gauge (1mm) can burn through in less than a year, and usually in less than two. If the cost of thick metal chimneys is prohibitive, it can be reduced by using thicker metal at the high stress areas only.

The joint between the chimney and the roof can leak if it is not watertight. Although a joint may be watertight when first made, any later shrinkage gap should be filled with tar or some other water-proofing substance. Joints should be made so that tar flows down the inside of the chimney and not outside into the kitchen (see Figure 5.21).

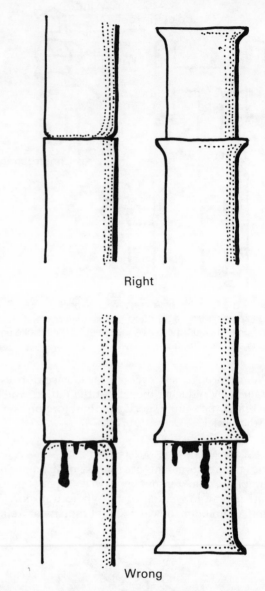

Figure 5.21.   Clay-metal chimney-section joints.

Permanent chimneys, made from fired bricks or cement blocks, can last as long as a house, and will generally have a lower annual cost than cheaper pottery or metal chimneys. In Bhutan, precast cement chimney sections are made in a unique mould producing strong, but not excessively heavy, sections.

The moulds were designed by Bhutanese after discussing the idea with a project engineer (Bachman, 1984, personal communication).

66

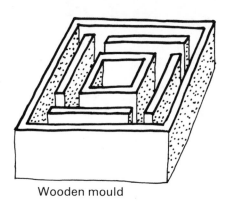

Wooden mould

Concrete sections

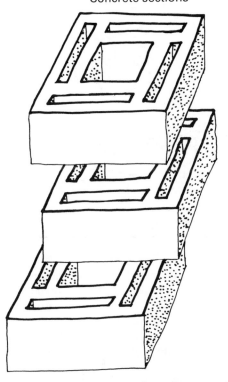

Figure 5.22.   Chimney construction using precast concrete sections. The right-hand drawing shows a stove with cast-iron top and precast chimney sections. (From Bachman, 1984)

Chimneys can be made from mud mix with moulds, but these cannot be transported, are more fragile, have a shorter lifetime, and often require significant input from fieldworkers who consequently spend less time building stoves.

Walls

Thick, heavy walls are often needed in relatively weak mud-mix stoves to provide sufficient strength to support pots and withstand thermal stress. However, theoretical work by Yameogo et al (1982), Prasad et al (1983), and Baldwin (1984), and test work done in numerous countries, show that thick heavy walls reduce the efficiency of stoves and increase both the cooking and warming-up time. Thinner walls, or low-density insulation around strong liners, will improve the performance of most stoves. Thick walls also require more material and labour to construct.

1. MAGAN CHULA (T. KALLUPATTI MODEL, INDIA)

Alternative names
Magan Choolah, Magan Chulah

Description
The stove is made from pottery and is surrounded with mud when installed, the finished stove being approximately 80cm × 45cm × 20cm. The pottery sections can be transported in a 60cm × 35cm × 20cm package. An average-sized stove weighs 8kg and costs US$1.20. The mud surround may weigh up to 60kg. There are two pot-holes on household models. The chimneys are either made of 30 cm long, 10 cm diameter pottery sections (US$0.50/m) or asbestos cement pipe with cap (US$6.50 for 3/m chimney with cap). There is a sheet-metal grate, no door or dampers, and a baffle beneath the second pot-hole.

History and field experience
This stove was developed in the early 1950s at the Gandhiniketan Ashram in T. Kallupatti (Madurai, Tamil Nadu, India 626702) as an improvement on the original mud-mix Magan Chula developed at

Maganwadi in north India. The original design had three pot-holes but by the 1970s all the stoves had only two. The stoves produced at the Ashram are sold through their co-operative outlets, which are all within 60km. By 1987, 17,000 stoves had been produced and sold by the Ashram as a profit-making activity; of these 5,000 had been sold to the Rural Development Office as part of the National Programme. Other potters in the region have copied the design and produce additional stoves. The stoves made at the Ashram can last from four to ten years if treated with reasonable care, but lower quality stoves from other producers often last less than three years.

Limited research carried out in 1983 by ITDG showed that the stove was purchased and accepted where smoke removal and cooking convenience were the main priorities. Where smoke removal was not important, or where there was fear of fire from the chimney, people did not buy the stoves. Broken baffles were often found in installed stoves, and where these stoves were still in use, fuel consumption and cooking time increased to

68

equal or exceed that of traditional stoves. Repair of the baffle improved performance considerably. It is reported that stoves with a properly-built baffle account for fuel savings that are more than a third that of traditional stoves.

The stove is sold for US$1.20 in the co-operatives. A 3m pottery chimney with cap costs US$1.70, and a typical installation charge by a village mason is US$1.50. Until 1983 there were no special promotion or marketing campaigns for the stoves. The Magan Chula is now one of the stove designs approved by the National Fuelwood Conservation Programme, and is eligible for subsidy.

Construction, installation and maintenance

The stove is complex to construct and requires considerable pottery skills; only a few south Indian potters have been successful in making it. The clay mixing and processing has to be carried out meticulously. The raw clay is dug from near-by tanks and allowed to dry in the sun. This is later crushed and mixed with water in purpose-built tanks to form a slurry. The slurry is allowed to settle so that the sand and stones may separate from the clay. The clay is then scooped out of the tank and mixed with a more uniform and finer sand in an adjoining tank. This slurry may then be removed and placed onto hessian cloth to dry out to a plastic-type consistency. Before forming, the clay is extensively wedged, using a traditional technique with the feet.

All the stove components are thrown on potters' wheels with the help of measuring sticks to check the diameters and heights of cylinders. As many as 10 to 20 sets of components may be thrown in one session at the wheel. (Each set consists of 5 cylinders.) It is usually the following day that the component cylinders are joined together using a slip. Where components are prone to slumping they are supported underneath with bricks. The drying process takes about one week during which time shrinking causes many cracks. These are filled with a special paste made up of slip and paper, to form a type of papier maché with clay. After further drying the stoves are fired in an open bonfire using acacia shrub and rice straw as fuel.

The stoves are installed very quickly, and providing the materials are at hand, this may only take an hour. The stove is placed in the required position which may either be at ground level or on a purpose-built platform. Fired bricks are then built up in a rectangle around the stove, using mud and sand as mortar. The gaps around the stove are then filled in with sand. The mud and sand mixture is then used to render over the bricks and across the top of the stove, ensuring the primary air and fuel entrances do not become blocked. The same mixture is also used to build up the baffle inside the second pot position.

The chimney consists of pottery tubes with a cup at one end so that it makes fitting easier. They are joined together and to the stove with a sand and cement mixture. The mud and sand mixture is usually not strong enough for this application. The number of chimney sections required often depends on the position of the roof but it is recommended that a minimum of eight be used, otherwise there may be insufficient draft. The chimney should be taken through the roof of the house and often requires a tile to be removed. The gap between the roof and chimney then needs to be filled properly with sand and cement, otherwise it often leaks water. Finally a cap is fitted to the chimney to reduce the effect from down drafts caused by wind turbulence.

Use of the stove

The stove must always be used with two cooking pots that provide adequate sealing to prevent the escape of smoke. The Magan chula burns a large range of fuels because of its grate, but when using residues such as acacia twigs, rice straw or coconut husks the grate must be checked regularly to prevent clogging. It is best not to overload the stove with fuel as this tends to restrict the air. As with all chimney stoves the chimney must be checked regularly, and in south India it has been found necessary to clean it every six to twelve months. This is done by putting a stick down from the top after removing the chimney cap. The soot can be scraped away from the base of the chimney through its entrance to the second pot. Users have not found it any more convenient to have a special entrance at the base, and this was also found inconvenient to construct.

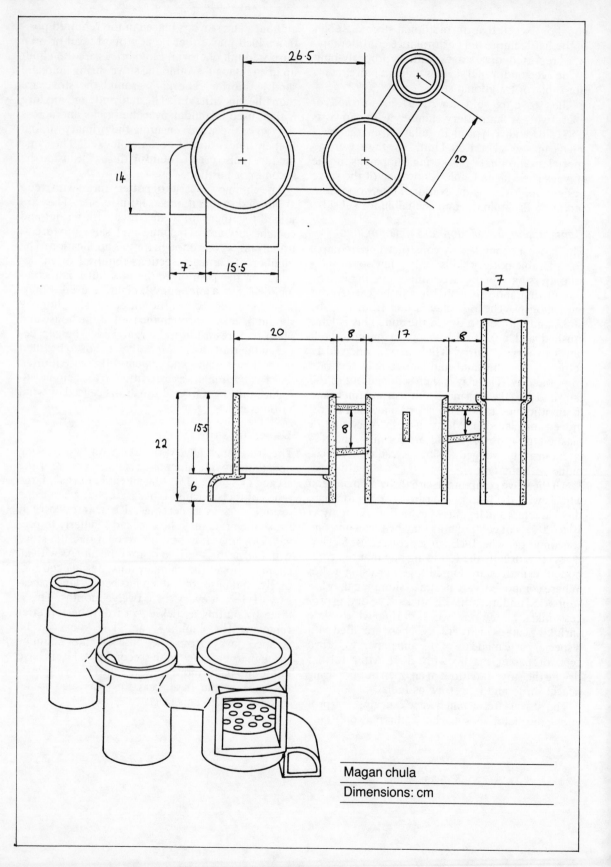

Magan chula

Dimensions: cm

2. NEPALI INSERT STOVE (RECAST/CFDP NEPAL)

Description

This is a two-pot stove consisting of four separate pottery sections – a firebox and first tunnel, the second pot-hole with baffle and rear tunnel, a chimney base, and a sectional pottery chimney. The four weigh about 8kg before being installed surrounded by a mud mix. There are no doors, dampers, or grates. The main pottery section and the chimney base measure 76cm × 24cm × 14cm, and when installed the stove is approximately 80cm × 40cm × 19cm. The four-section chimney is 2.2m in height. The pottery stove costs US$1.20 to produce and US$2.0 to install.

History and field experience

This stove, designed by RECAST working in close collaboration with ITDG, was chosen out of similar designs because of its ease of construction, and its modular nature (which simplifies packing for transport, and also facilitates replacement of individual cracked pieces rather than the whole stove). By 1986 about 12,000 of these stoves had been made and distributed throughout Nepal, with most being made near the capital, Kathmandu. In 1983 two evaluations were carried out on the stoves installed in the Kathmandu valley. It was reported that after nearly one year of use 70% of the families said they used the insert stove for the preparation of all their meals, but most still used another stove for the preparation of livestock feed, liquor and snacks.

A later evaluation of the stove design, and of the social and environmental factors affecting its use, produced the following list showing the importance (in descending order) of these factors:

Stove design	Social and environmental
Cracks and breakage	Fuel availability
Pot-hole spacing	Type of previous stove
Backdraught	Quality of extension
Pot size/fit	Ethnicity
Maintenance and cleanliness	
	User perceptions
Quality control of critical dimensions	
	Family size

At the present time the stoves are given away free, and there is very strong demand. A government-trained artisan helps install the stove and should make one follow-up visit. An extensive monitoring system is being set up to provide information from which the most effective and practical approach can be developed.

The average savings reported from interviews with users, and from laboratory tests, is 35% for cooking meals. Not all the stoves are used solely for all domestic cooking, so the saving per stove distributed averages 20% (Campbell, 1983).

Construction, installation and maintenance

The stove is produced in small pottery units using existing potter's wheels and firing techniques. The type of clay and the amount of sand added are often changed to produce a stronger body. The durability of the stoves is very dependent on the available raw materials, the care taken in their preparation, and in drying and firing of the stove pieces. Dimensional accuracy is obtained using measuring sticks and templates.

One critical aspect of installation is the position of the chimney in areas where high winds are common (see pages 64–5). In the kitchen the area for the stove is levelled and the separate pottery pieces are properly positioned. A mud mix is applied around the pottery pieces to stabilize the stove and to protect the pottery liners from excessive pot weight – a layer of mud is placed on top of the liners so that the pots rest on the mud rather than directly on the liner.

General cleaning of the firebox and tunnels should be carried out daily. Special care must be taken to clean the hidden back tunnel behind the second baffle. When rice straw and other agricultural wastes are burnt the chimney will clog up particularly quickly; easy access to the base of the chimney for cleaning is therefore vital, and thick walls will make this aspect of cleaning more difficult. Chimney blockages will be a major problem after the first six months of stove use unless the chimney is cleaned regularly.

Use of the stove

The stove illustrated is designed for simultaneous use of two pots smaller than 28cm in diameter. A larger model is necessary if larger pots are to be used. Wood or agricultural wastes can be used, but the latter leave a large amount of ash and the oves must be cleaned more often.

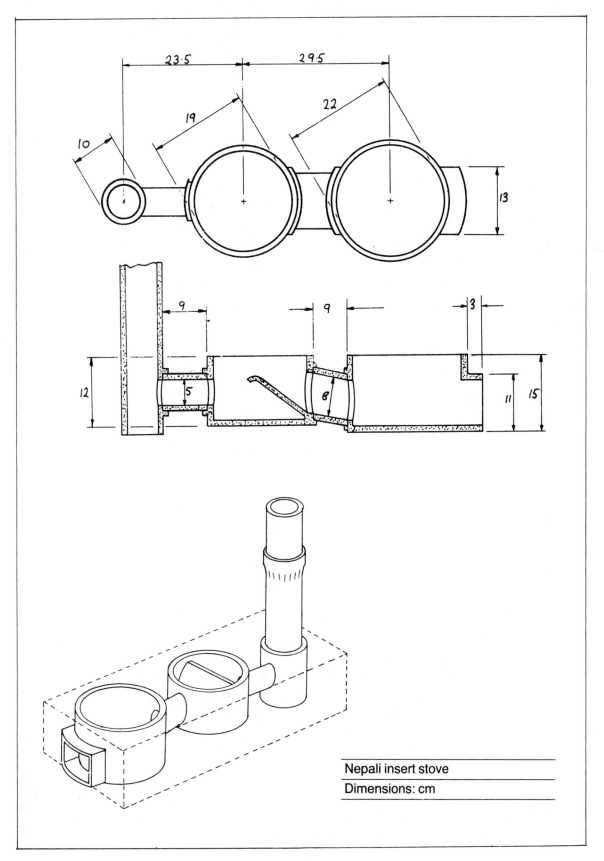

Nepali insert stove

Dimensions: cm

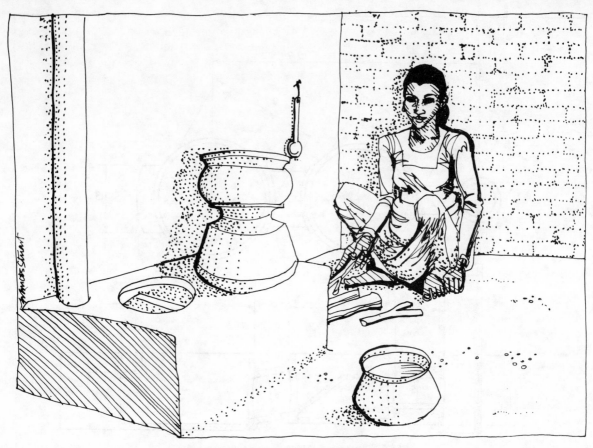

3. NEW NEPALI CHULA (UNICEF, NEPAL)

Alternative name
New Nepali Chulo

Description
This is a two-pot stove consisting of four pottery sections – a door arch, a central two pot-hole with tunnel piece, a rear tunnel and chimney base, and a metal damper connected to a sectional pottery chimney. A cast iron grate is used on some of the stoves. The pottery sections alone measure 70cm × 22cm × 18cm, and weigh about 10kg before being installed in a mud mix; the finished stove is approximately 72cm × 34cm × 29cm. The production costs are US$1.50 for the stove alone, and US$4.60 with the chimney and baffle. The cast-iron grates cost US$1.00–2.00 depending on their size.

History and field experience
This model is the result of years of prototype development and testing by UNICEF, Nepalese potters, and the experience of other people in Nepal and other countries. It was standardized in 1982 and the stoves are presently being produced by potters in a number of towns across Nepal.

The stove is being disseminated through the Small Family Programme, implemented by the Agricultural Development Bank of Nepal with the support of UNICEF. One source (Joseph, pers. comm. 1986) estimates that about 5,000 of these stoves have been distributed all over Nepal, about 1,000 of these deriving from the ADB/N programme. Booklets describing the installation and use of the stove have been produced by UNICEF in English and Nepali. The philosophy behind the introduction of prefabricated stoves is to give the people a properly-designed stove which they can later copy in other locations – it is not intended to be supplied centrally indefinitely.

In May 1983 a small survey was conducted by UNICEF which revealed that this stove was used by more than 90% of the families for cooking food, but was not suitable for the preparation of rice wine or livestock feed, both operations requiring single large pots. While none of the stoves were more than one year old, only 7% had any cracks, implying that they are quite strong and were properly installed. As many as 93% of the users perceived that the stove was saving fuel with an average reported saving of 33%. All those surveyed were pleased with the smoke removal, but 82% felt the stove made cooking slower.

On balance, over 60% of the people thought the stove was more convenient, and 100% were pleased with the smokelessness and would be willing to pay a small sum for the stoves. They felt that the benefits of smokelessness and fuel saving were greater than the costs of longer cooking times and of initial purchase (UNICEF, 1983).

Construction, installation and maintenance

The stoves are made by traditional potters from a combination of wheel-thrown, and slab-shaped pieces. They are installed by covering the liner with mud (adjusting the pot-holes to suit the cooking pots to be used) and fitting the chimney which goes directly through the roof or a wall. Ash must be cleaned out of the stove weekly, and the chimney must be cleaned every six months.

Use of the stove

The stove is designed for two pots to be used at all times. Pots with a diameter of more than 28cm will not fit on the stove shown in the diagram. The 'medium' or normal-sized stove serves a family of five to eight. The models with grates attain higher outputs and can burn bigger logs. The stove is intended for cooking, not heating purposes, and is not designed for charcoal use.

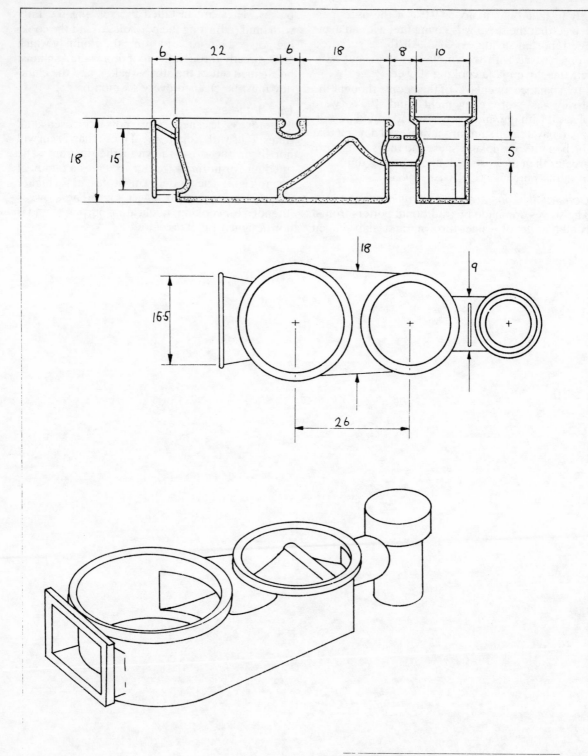

New Nepali chula

Dimensions: cm

4. NADA CHULA (NORTH INDIA)

Alternative name
Nada Chulha

Description
These stoves can be built in different shapes and
sizes in accordance with individual household's
needs, kitchen space available, and the user's aesthetic preferences. The stoves are usually built on
the floor from sun-dried mud slabs, soil and a
special clay-fibre mix. The stoves are fitted with
metal doors and dampers.

The only fixed dimension is the internal height
of the firebox – 17cm. An average-sized two-pot
stove, popular in the plains, measures 70cm ×
40cm × 20cm, and has a 7.5cm diameter asbestos
cement chimney. In mountainous areas, three-
pot, square, T- or L-shaped stoves with two tunnels are more popular, and use 10cm diameter tin
chimneys. The asbestos cement chimneys cost
US$2.50; the metal doors and dampers cost
US$1.00–1.50, and the construction and follow-up
fee is about US$2.00.

History and field experience
This stove emerged as a spontaneous response to
the expressed need for smoke removal, made by
some women of a village that was taking part in an
innovative participatory erosion control and
irrigation project in Haryana, north India. As well
as smoke removal, other benefits of the stove were
protection from excess heat, improved general
cleanliness of the kitchen and house, reduced
cooking time, provision of warm water (and of
room heat if wanted), cleaner pots, and cooking
fuel savings.

Since its introduction the Nada Chulha (named
after the women of Harijan Nada who participated
in its development) has been seen as part of a
technology system, not a technology 'fix'. According to the promoters the system is designed to take
into account 'natural processes such as reconstruc-
tion, relocation, demand for new stoves by newly-
formed families, the proper repair and maintenance of already built ones, and most important,
educating users to use the technology to optimum
advantage' (Sarin, 1983). To accomplish these
goals women builders, who also use the stove,
were trained to build the stoves for others, for a
fee.

Initial attempts at replication of this model in
other areas highlighted the need for proper train-

ing of stove builders, and for devising a suitable organizational structure for dissemination. Dissemination is now only done through collaborating organizations committed to thorough training for builders, and to the provision of the necessary support for effective dissemination. The core of the strategy is to establish a new type of village occupation – for the 'chulha mistri', ideally a local woman who may be self-employed like other village artisans. The chulha mistri's work may provide her with a full-time job, or it may provide supplementary income to a low-income woman. A group of them will have a supervisor or project co-ordinator for a minimum support period of six months.

Initially the full cost of the stove was paid for by the owners. However, to ensure that the poorest households are able to afford the stove, partial or full subsidies have been introduced. Emphasis on the development of local skills, regular monitoring of performance, and helping users understand the technology, combined with a definite desire among women for chimney stoves to reduce the drudgery related to cooking, have all been critical in the success of this project.

A few thousand stoves were built and as a result it has been included among 15 stove models recommended for promotion under the Government of India's 'National Project for Demonstration of Improved Stoves'. This has led to a large number of training courses, and many thousands of the stove have now been built as a result.

Construction, installation, and maintenance

The size of the stove is matched to the pots that will be used, and pot spacing is measured with hand measurements. The stove layout is then drawn on the kitchen floor. Dried mud slabs, 1.8cm thick, are made in moulds, and used to make a skeleton structure for the firebox, tunnel(s) and the outer walls.

The space between the firebox and tunnel walls, and the outside, is either filled with soil or left hollow. The inner walls of the firebox and tunnels are then coated with a 1–2cm thick layer of a clay-fibre mixture that withstand high temperatures. The firebox entrance and the tunnel are roofed with pieces of mud slabs and the stove is finished by applying more of the clay-fibre mix on the top and the outer walls of the stove, leaving the pot-holes moulded to the size of the pots. The chimney is installed with a proper rain sealing at roof level, and a chimney cap. The stove is allowed to dry completely for two to five days before lighting fires of gradually increasing size.

The chimneys and tunnels must be cleaned out regularly because they will clog up in two to three months when wood and agricultural wastes are used as fuel. If there is erosion or cracking of the stove body, repairs should be made by wetting the area and applying more of the clay-fibre, taking care not to change the dimensions significantly. The stove might have to be rebuilt every three or four years by the local trained stove builder.

Use of the stove

The stove can be made for the use of two to three pots and an optional attached oven, depending on the needs of the household. A set of sliding doors is provided on the front of the stove. These are especially useful for retaining heat in the stove body between cooking sessions, and for protecting the cook from excess heat.

For roasting traditional unleavened bread in the firebox mouth, the height of the mouth can be increased by sloping the firebox floor downwards near the opening.

The damper is used to regulate the overall draught, and power output is controlled mainly by manoeuvring the fuel.

When heat sufficent to bring pots to the boil is required in three pot-holes, the firebox is connected to the chimney by two parallel tunnels with one pot-hole above each. When the third cooking hole is desired only for keeping food or water warm, a single tunnel is used. The parallel tunnel stove is extremely popular in mountainous areas and users report substantial fuel and cooking time savings.

5. LORENA STOVE

Description

Lorena stoves are made from a mix of sand and clay and come in a variety of sizes, with three or four pot-holes over one or two tunnels leading to the chimney. The pot-holes are designed so that a variety of pots can be used. There is usually a door in front of the firebox entrance, and a damper in front of the chimney. The cost for an average-sized stove when built by a professional stove builder, and including the chimney, is about US$30 (Caceres, 1983).

History and field experience

The early Lorena stoves were designed at the Estacion Experimental Choqui, in the highlands of Guatemala, after the 1976 earthquake. The basic design came from the smokeless mud chulas of India, designed in the 1940s and 1950s, but was altered to use local materials and construction methods, and to meet a wide range of non-cooking functions, such as acting as a large table, having pot-holes for warming food and water, etc.

Since 1977 a number of organizations have been promoting Lorena stoves and more than 20,000 have been built worldwide. Usage rates of over 90% are reported for the stoves built by some projects, but there is also a significant percentage that are not used properly, reducing potential fuel savings and other performance aspects (Caceres, 1983). There are drastic reductions in reported eye irritation, broncho-pulmonary ailments, and muscular pains for the users of Lorena stoves, compared to users of open fires.

The stoves are made by skilled artisans, by people who have attended training programmes, or by people that copy stoves seen at demonstrations or in others' homes. The estimated lifetime of a well-built stove is four years, after which it must be rebuilt.

Based on interviews with owners of properly built and used Lorena stoves, an estimated 40–45% of the fuel previously used is saved (Caceres, 1983).

Construction, installation and maintenance

The stove is made from sand and clayey soil which are thoroughly mixed and applied in layers or rammed into a large mould. The firebox, tunnel

79

and pot-holes are carved out and the exterior smoothed with hand tools. A chimney is attached and fitted through the roof or wall. Numerous international and locally–produced publications are available (e.g. Evans and Bouttette, 1981) on how to construct a range of designs of Lorena stoves.

The tunnels and chimney must be periodically cleaned for the stove to operate properly. Cracks on the exterior must be patched, and erosion on the inside of the firebox and pot-holes must be patched without significantly changing the dimensions if proper performance is to be maintained.

Use of the stove

Wood and other biomass fuels can be burned in the firebox, and the front door and back damper are used to help control the power output. The first pot-hole is the hottest and is used for most of the cooking. The second pot-hole has considerably less heat output and is good for long simmering. The third and fourth pot-holes are only used for keeping food or water warm. For a slow burning fire the doors and dampers are closed to allow only a low air flow.

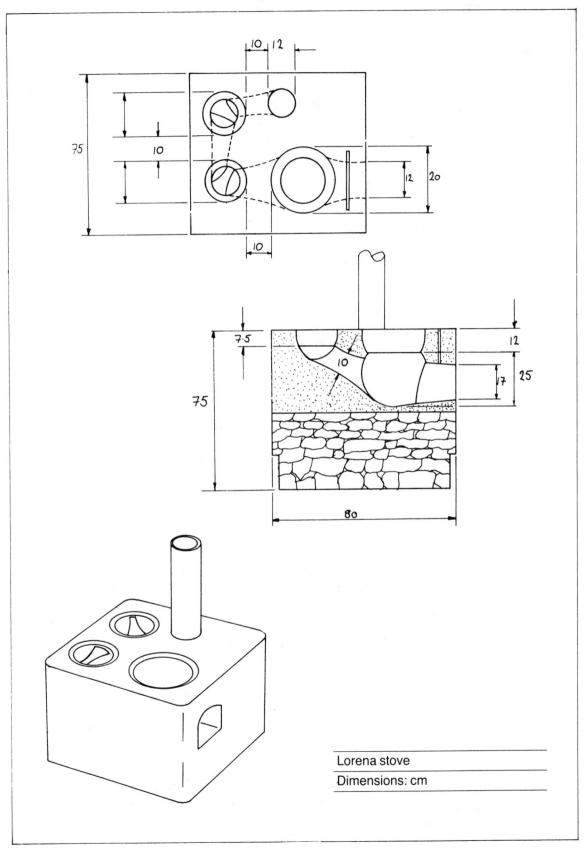

Lorena stove

Dimensions: cm

6. THAI MOULDED STOVE (FOR RICE HUSKS OR WOOD)

Description

The stove is made from a mud mix and is built using internal and external moulds. Extension workers are responsible for ensuring the quality of the construction, and the majority of the work is done by the householders themselves. The finished stoves are 82cm × 32cm × 24cm with a 1.5m (or taller) chimney. There is a feed hopper and a grate to be used when burning rice husks. There are no doors or dampers, but there is a baffle underneath the second pot-hole. Households are charged US$1.00 for the use of the moulds and the skilled instruction combined.

History and field experience

The stove is based on traditional South-east Asian stoves and was designed as part of a project undertaken by the VITA Asia Field Office to provide improved stove options for Khmer refugees in Thailand in 1981. Further modifications of the stove and the construction process were undertaken by VITA-AFO and the Community Based Appropriate Technology and Development Ser-

vices Bureau (CBATDS) of the Population and Community Development Association of Thailand, in 1981 and 1982. Dissemination outside of the refugee camps is being undertaken by CBATDS in north-east Thailand, where the stoves are part of their integrated programme. Problems of high cost and cracking were experienced with cement versions of this stove, but the properly-made mud-mix stoves have proved to be cheap, long-lasting, and to have a good performance. When rice husks are not available, the grate is removed so that maize cobs and wood can be burned.

Construction, installation and maintenance

A mud mix is rammed between internal and external wooden moulds, which are taken out when the mix has dried slightly; the stove is finished with a spoon or trowel. The grate is made by fitting the hooked end of each of approximately twenty 5.5mm steel rods onto a horizontal bar placed across the entrance, just inside the doorway. These rods are supported at the other end by a

82

second bar across the firebox chamber. The chimney is attached and tied to a supporting wooden or bamboo pole.

Ash must be cleaned out of the tunnels regularly and repairs should be made to cracks on the stove.

Use of the stove

To start the stove a small pile of kindling is placed at the bottom of the grate. Rice husks are poured onto the grate until they are level with the hopper rim (see diagram). The kindling is then lit. Every two to five minutes the ash is pulled out of the base, and/or rice husks are pushed down the hopper to get fresh fuel onto the grate. Air is pulled through the bars into the charred and burning rice husks and the flames are forced up to the pots by baffles. The power output is decreased by slowing the feed rate. For maize cobs and wood, the steel bars are removed, and it is used as a typical wood stove.

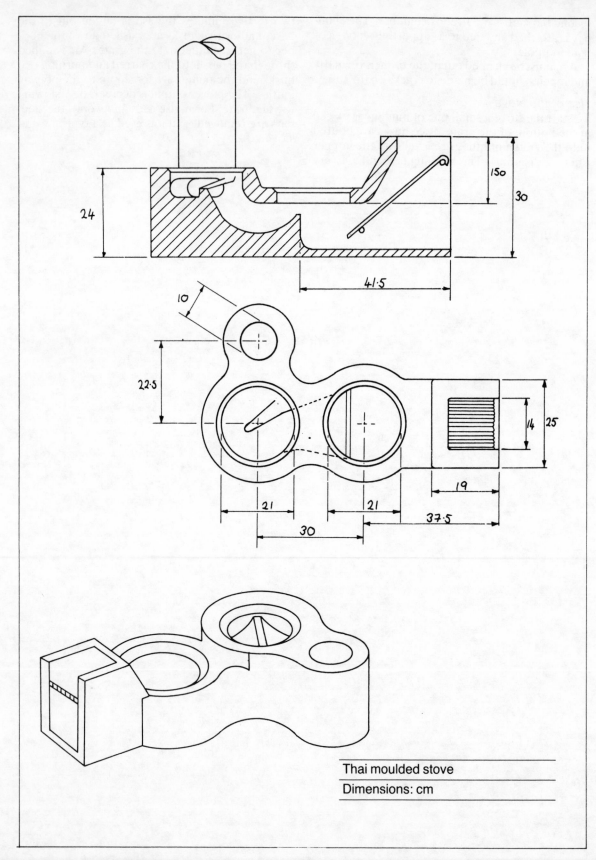

Thai moulded stove

Dimensions: cm

7. POGBI STOVE

Decription

The two-pot stove has a massive mud-mix straw base, and a thick steel or cast-iron top plate. There is a grate in the firebox and a single small door for the firebox entrance and the primary air. The stove is designed to use two specially-designed pots that are sunken nearly all the way into the stove. The metal top plate of this design would cost at least US$20 in Sri Lanka or South India, the stove will require two or three man-days to construct, a chimney must be purchased and installed with the stove, and special pots must be purchased as the stove operates inefficiently with most traditional designs.

History and field experience

The stove was designed in Upper Volta (now Burkina Faso) by Waclaw Micuta of the Bellerive Foundation of Switzerland in the late 1970s as a proposed improvement on the Nouna stove – a similar design, but with a thick cement top plate. A few hundred stoves have been built in Burkina Faso, Kenya, and Pakistan, as part of stove promotion programmes of the Bellerive Foundation. The cast-iron top plates should last many years, but many of the steel ones will warp with heat. The straw in the stove body within 5cm of the firebox will burn out and repairs will need to be made to the firebox walls.

Construction, installation and maintenance

The stove body is made from a mix of clayey soil and straw formed into 3 to 5cm-thick by 30cm-long pieces; these are rammed into a sturdy mould so that no air pockets are left. When sufficiently dry the mould can be removed and the stove is left for a longer period of time to dry. If the stove has been made in a central place it must be transported to the kitchen, and as it weighs over 150kg a very strong cart or a motor vehicle is required. After placing the stove in the kitchen the metal top plate (made elsewhere, from 3mm or more thick steel, or from cast iron) is placed on top of the stove, making sure there are no air gaps around the top. The chimney is then installed.

Maintenance required is periodic cleaning of the chimney and tunnels, patching of eroded parts of the mud walls, repair of the grate (which rusts rapidly if made from mild steel rods), and the repair of any external cracks.

Use of the stove

Wood must be chopped small enough to fit through the small door, and long pieces must be supported so that they lie flat on the grate. Special pots which sink well into the stove body must be used; if unsuitable pots are used the flames will travel through the stove with little pot contact and there will be a significant decrease in performance. The heat input ratio between the two pots cannot be altered, but the second pot gets a greater percentage of the total heat at high power outputs. Power output is controlled by manoeuvring the wood and closing the entrance with a brick-shaped door.

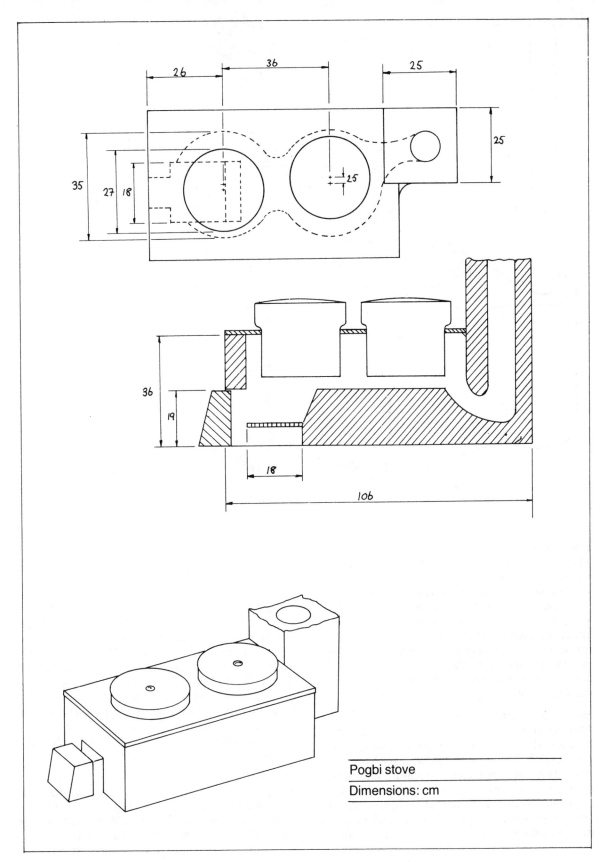

Pogbi stove

Dimensions: cm

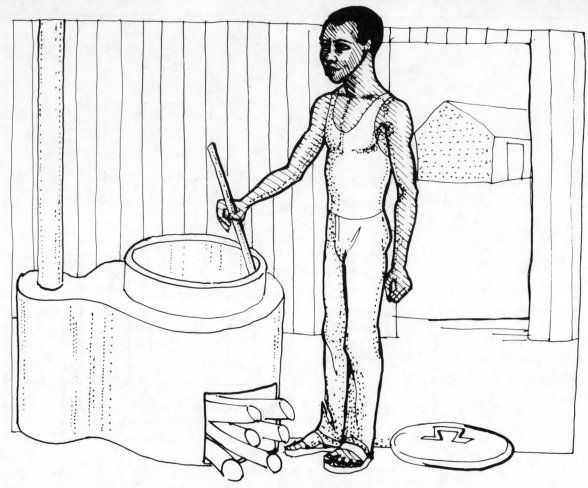

8. COMMUNITY STOVE (designed by Waclaw Micuta)

Description

The stove is an adaptation of large traditional European cast-iron stoves, made instead with bricks and mud mix. The body of the stove is built with a mud mix and the firebox is lined with bricks. The pot sits inside the stove resting on a ledge, just above the firebox. The pot is also supported by its rim which rests on a metal top plate. Most of the pot wall is exposed to the hot gases. The grate is made of steel bars and there is one door for both the firebox and the primary air entrance.

History and field experience

This design was also developed and promoted by Waclaw Micuta. A small number of these stoves has been built for large kitchens in Africa and Asia. They are reported to save more than three-quarters of the wood previously used for food requiring long cooking periods. There is insufficient experience to predict their lifetime, but periodic maintenance of the mud-mix walls is probably essential. A widespread dissemination programme for schools and other institutions in Kenya was planned for 1987.

Construction, installation and maintenance

The stove must be built on a solid foundation. Mud mix is packed around moulds and frames. The bricks are positioned in the firebox and then the walls are built up. Allowance must be made for shrinkage of the mud mix. After the stove is dry the metal top plate is attached to the walls. Periodic repairs to the walls are probably necessary, and the chimney must be cleaned to prevent blockage. Thin steel-bar grates will burn out every few years and must be replaced.

Use of the stove

The pot is brought to a boil in the usual manner, and once the stove walls are hot, and the food is boiling, very little additional fuel is needed to keep the food cooking. The door can be closed to reduce the draught and conserve the heat in the stove.

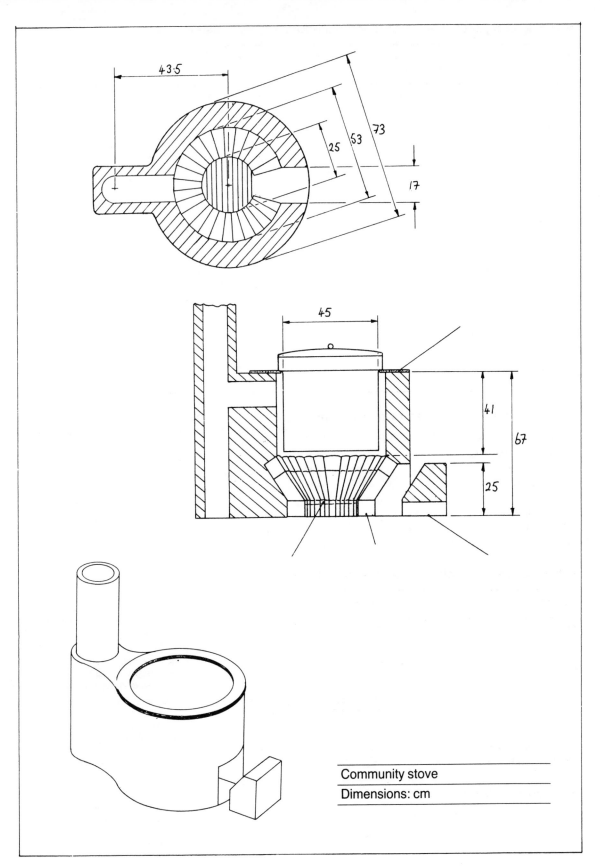

43·5

73

53

25

17

45

41

67

25

Community stove

Dimensions: cm

Table 5.1: Comparative test results for multi-pot chimney stoves

Stove	Efficiency (PHU)	Power output kW	Heat input ratio	Source and comments
1. Magan Chula	19–21	3–6	—	ITDG (1984). Good for burning wet fuel, and fuel with short flames
2. Nepali insert	20–24	approx 4	3:1	RECAST, Nepal (1983)
3. New Nepali Chulo	22–24	4	3:1	RECAST, Nepal (1983). Low power output is major user complaint. Field experience with cast-iron grates suggest that they increase power output, ease the burning of big fuel, and increase the proportion of heat going to the second pot
4. Nada Chulha	—	—	—	
5. Lorena	13.6	—	—	VITA (1983)
	13–18	—	—	Bennett (1980). Efficiency increases as the stove gets hot.
6. Thai	13.3	7	—	VITA (1981). Original prototype
moulded	21	7	—	VITA (1982). Improved version
rice-husk burner	5–10	—		VITA (1983). Stoves built by extension workers with noticeable defects
	11–18	—	—	VITA (1983). Stoves build properly by extension workers
7. Pogbi	35–40 and 20–25	—	3:1	For more details see *Modern Stoves for All*
8. Community	25.8	—	—	See *Modern Stoves for All*

Stove problems – causes and solutions

REPAIR GUIDELINES FOR MULTI-POT CHIMNEY STOVES IN THE FIELD

The first step is to check that the stove to be repaired has been constructed according to the original plan(s). If the stove does not follow the original plan this will most probably be the reason for unsatisfactory performance, given the same operating conditions (pots, fuel, chimney height, etc.) for the original stove and the stove being repaired. Determine whether any modifications have been made and the reason why

The next step is to discover, by interview, what problems the user may have with the stove, and to observe a fire burning if possible.

The common problems which will be encounteed, their causes, and the various solutions available to remedy them, are tabled below.

Table 5.2: Stove problems – causes and solutions

Problem	Cause	Solutions
Always slow to cook	Firebox too deep and flames not touching first pot	– Reduce firebox height by raising the floor
	Low draught and very little flames	– Increase tunnel size* – Increase baffle gap† – Increase chimney height
	High draught and flames flaring straight out without good pot contact	– Reduce baffle gap – Decrease back tunnel size – Decrease front tunnel size – Decrease chimney height
Slow cooking problem developed after a few hours use	Clogged chimney, chimney cap or tunnel	– Clean out chimney, chimney cap and tunnel
Burning too much fuel and burning it quickly	High draught	– Reduce baffle gap – Decrease back tunnel size* – Decrease front tunnel* – Decrease front door area* – Decrease chimney height

Problem	Cause	Solutions
Smoke always coming out of front door of stove	Low draught	– Increase tunnel size* – Increase baffle gap – Increase chimney height
Smoke coming out of front door of stove when windy	Poor chimney placement as wind is forced down chimney	– Change chimney position
Not enough heat to second pot	Baffle gap is too great and flames do not have good pot contact	– Decrease baffle gap
	First tunnel is too small and total power output is low	– Enlarge first tunnel
	Baffle gap is too small and total power output is low	– Increase baffle gap slightly
	Baffle angle is wrong	– Change angle*
Too much of total heat going to the second pot	High draught	– Reduce baffle gap – Decrease back tunnel – Decrease front tunnel size – Decrease chimney height
High fuel consumption	Draught too large, or too small	– Increase or decrease the height or position of baffles – Check diameter/height of chimney – Increase or decrease fuel entrance or air entrance*
	Pots wrong design or size	– Check pot with stove design recommendations
	Combustion chamber too large, or too small	– Check combustion chamber shape and size in design recommendations
Cooking performance poor ie. slow to cook	Power output low	– Check moisture content of fuel – Increase fuel load – Increase draught, reduce baffle height, increase chimney height
	Poor heat transfer	– Check draught
Difficult to ignite	Cold or wet stove	– Light fire with as much paper and kindling as possible
	Blocked chimney of flue	– Clean stove
	Wet wood	– Use drier wood to start, adding wet wood only when stove is well alight
Difficult to burn wet wood	Insufficient draught	– Increase chimney height – Decrease baffles – Clean stove
Stove very smoky	Insufficient draught	– Increase chimney height – Decrease baffles
	Fuel load too large	– Reduce fuel load
Excessive soot deposits	See 'Stove very smoky'	– Clean stove and chimney
Insufficient heat to second pot	Insufficient draught	– Increase chimney height – Decrease baffles
	Baffle wrongly positioned or wrong size	– Check position and size of baffle
Excessive heat to pots	Too much draught	– Increase baffles – Decrease chimney height
Smoke exits from the fuel entrance or fire burns back out from the entrance	Wrongly positioned chimney – wind blows down it	– Re-locate chimney or cover with cowling
	Insufficient draught	– Increase chimney height – Decrease baffles

NOTE: * These solutions not applicable for all pottery stoves   † These solutions not applicable for pottery stoves not surrounded by mud

CHAPTER 6

Multi-pot chimneyless stoves

Introduction

Multi-pot chimneyless stoves are traditional throughout much of Asia, and most of the following designs are similar to the traditional stoves in their area of origin. The improvement in perform-ance over that of traditional stoves is largely due to a more enclosed firebox, a tight-fitting front pot, and a baffle underneath the second pot which is often partially shielded. They are easier and cheaper to build than chimney stoves, and the field

Figure 6.1.   Typical multi-pot chimneyless stove.

1. Firebox entrance
2. Secondary air holes
3. Firebox
4. Pot-holes
5. Tunnel and baffle
6. Exit gaps

Figure 6.3.   Size of secondary air holes. If these are too large cracking will occur.

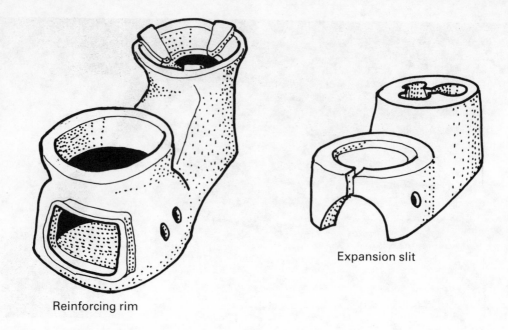

Reinforcing rim

Expansion slit

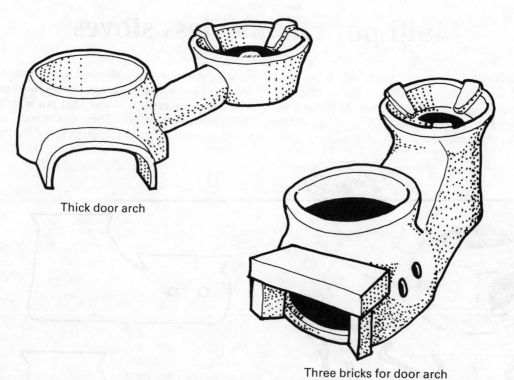

Thick door arch

Three bricks for door arch

Figure 6.4   Methods of reinforcing and protecting the fuel entrance

performance is less likely to be significantly worse than the laboratory performance as these stoves do not have the inherent problems associated with the correct installation and maintenance of a chimney. Neither are there doors, dampers or grates that could be used incorrectly.

All of the stoves described are for 20–24cm pots and the designs must be scaled up for satisfactory performance with larger pots.

Fuel entrance

The fuel entrance into the firebox should be wide enough to insert and manoeuvre the fuel, although smoke will escape through a high doorway or an open front (a problem that is most noticeable with poor quality fuels). A 5–10cm long entrance arch reduces the chance of smoke coming back out. An arch can be an integral part of the stove, or made afterwards from bricks or mud mixes. The arch above the firebox entrance receives a great deal of heat stress and allowance should be made for this in the construction, e.g. by having a reinforcing rim around the doorway, a thick entrance arch, or an expansion slit in a mud-mix stove. Doors are not useful on these designs.

Secondary air holes

'Dead' spots at the back or sides of the firebox, where there is not enough air, are a common problem and secondary air holes are used to get air into these areas. Small holes are better than large holes on pottery stoves, for structural reasons. They should be positioned on the stove so that they can be cleaned easily (e.g. away from the kitchen wall).

Firebox

The firebox is slightly spherical in a number of the designs, to allow the flames to develop fully in the combustion chamber. The firebox height should be approximately half the pot-hole diameter plus the fuel bed thickness. Grates have not been found to improve the performance of these types of stove. To preserve charcoal and insulate the fire, many people leave a thick ash layer on the firebox floor, and allowance should be made for this in the design by increasing the height of the firebox slightly.

Pot-holes

The first pot-hole should be as large as possible to maximize the heat transfer area. The second pot-hole does not need to be as large because the hot gases will naturally rise around the pot and a conical shape will fit both small and large pots.

Tunnel and baffle

A large tunnel that angles steeply upwards to the second pot promotes a good draught and more even heat distribution between the two pots. The baffle is the base of the tunnel and should end part-way underneath the pot. The tunnel should be large to allow for a build-up of ash; if tunnels are too small the total power output will be low, combustion will be poor, and the second pot will heat up very slowly.

Exit gaps

Raising the second pot and increasing the size of the exit gaps increases the draught and improves the combustion and power output, especially with wet or poor-quality fuels. A small pot shield can improve the performance, particularly where there is some wind around the stove. For 17–25cm pots the exit gap area should be at least to 60 sq cm, which would require a 1cm gap around a 20cm diameter pot. Larger gaps will increase the flow and power output, but will decrease the efficiency somewhat. Most users will feel that increased power output offsets a slight drop in efficiency.

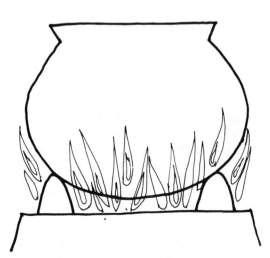
Exposed second pot

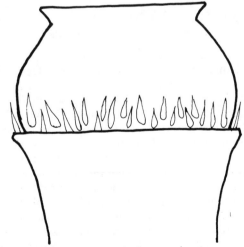
Semi-shielded second pot

Figure 6.4. Exit gap around second pot.

9. TUNGKU SAE (DIAN DESA, INDONESIA)

Description

This pottery stove is made from wheel-turned sections and slabs. The doorway leads to the fire-box directly underneath the first pot-hole. A tunnel formed by slabs is inclined steeply upwards to the second pot, which is raised on three supports. The stove is 58cm × 25cm × 25cm, weighs 6kg, and costs about US$0.40 to produce. It can be used with or without mud-mix insulation.

History and experience

The Tungku Sae was developed by Dian Desa (an Indonesian appropriate technology organization) in 1980 in conjunction with ITDG. It was modified further following field trials and is now being produced by potteries near Yogyakarta, Indonesia. Early in 1983 Dian Desa transferred the production of stoves by individual artisans to small groups of potters organized to make the stoves in assembly line fashion. This reduced the problems of variable quality, and, for example, enabled raw materials to be obtained in bulk, provided more work space, etc. More management was needed but at a reduced level per stove as production increased. Over 1,000 stoves per month were being produced in 1984.

In 1983 the major supply was to village development programmes of the Indonesian government, but a few thousand stoves were sold through village shops. By the end of 1983 about 6,000 stoves had been produced. Evaluations carried out in 1983 by Dian Desa showed that the stoves were very well received where the pot sizes and types of food cooked suited the design. Where very large pots, or single pots, were used for cooking, the stove was not accepted. The reported fuel savings vary from 25–50%.

In 1984 Dian Desa embarked on a major programme to identify the potential market for the stoves, and ways to increase production without the requirement for large management inputs. Currently, only one factory is producing. A major evaluation is under way, and a study of marketing methods is being carried out. Around 20,000 stoves in total have been marketed throughout the lifetime of the project.

Construction, installation and maintenance

The construction process is described in detail on pages 204 to 208. Briefly, the two cylinders are thrown on a wheel, and when slightly hard placed on a work table; the rest of the stove is constructed around them from clay slabs. The openings are cut with a knife. In one production unit the average production rate is 100 stoves per month per full-time worker. Proper materials, uniform construction and firing are necessary if this fairly complex stove is to be made.

The 6kg stove is strong enough to use without extra support from a mud covering, but a clay/rice husk mix (2:1 by volume) can be used to make a 3–5cm thick insulation which will weigh only 15kg. A 10cm thick sand clay mix insulation will weigh about 40 kg, and absorb considerably more heat. The pottery liner without insulation is portable, but it is more prone to breakage. An insulation layer protects the pottery from impact and reduces the heat stress on the pottery.

The tunnel and smoke vents should be cleaned to allow for proper gas flows. Up to 5cm of ash in the firebox helps to prevent the embers from going out, but the build-up of too much ash will block the tunnel. The ventilation holes should be kept clean and cracks in the insulation should be repaired with more mix.

Use of the stove
The stove performs best when both pot-holes are used simultaneously. When only one pot is used this can be lifted up with pot sherds or pebbles to form a shielded fire.

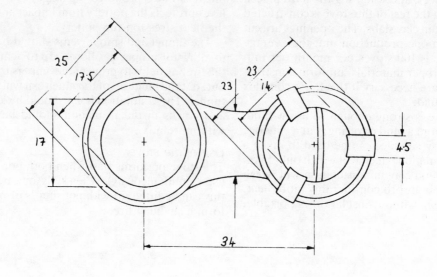

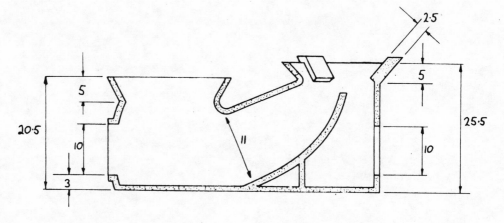

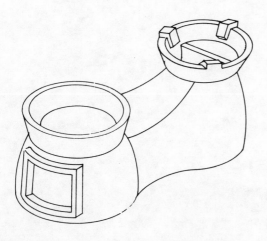

Tungku sae

Dimensions: cm

10. SRI LANKAN POTTERY LINER

Description

This pottery stove has the same internal dimensions as the successful mud stove design that was used in Sri Lanka by the Sarvodaya Shramadana Movement. The stove is made from two components, these can remain separate or be joined during their 'green' states to form a one-piece two-pot stove. The first component is made from a large cylinder slightly bigger towards the bottom; there is an arched doorway in the front and an oval tunnel leading off at a right angle to the door. On the left-hand side there is a small lid in the cylinder to provide secondary air for the combustion chamber. The second component, a small cylinder flared at the top has a section cut away such that it meets with the end of the oval tunnel on the first component. Inside the flared section are three equally-spaced buttresses to support the second pot. When the stove is installed inside a kitchen it is covered with a mud layer for increased durability and protection against knocks, and may measure 56cm × 36cm × 23cm.

History and experience

The stove was designed in 1981 by the Sarvodaya stove project, in collaboration with ITDG, when problems associated with inaccurate construction and the use of poor materials were being experienced in the mud-stove dissemination programme.

By 1986 about 20,000 stoves had been sold in Sri Lanka through two programmes, the community-based Sarvodaya programme, and the Ceylon Electricity Board's National Stoves Programme. The cost of the stove is about US$1.00, divided equally between the cost of the component pieces and installation by an artisan.

The stove was promoted only in rural areas and has been most popular where people either purchased wood, or where the women were major income earners.

More recently further development amongst some potters has shown that the two-piece stove can in fact be made as one piece, and this has definite advantages because less installation work is required, and marketing is much easier. Although current production of the one-piece stove is limited, by 1987 production will have increased to 100,000 per year.

Construction, installation and maintenance

The firebox can be made by coiling techniques, or can be thrown on a potter's wheel. The second pot-hole is turned on a wheel. The stoves are fired in simply updraft kilns. The design requires that the two pieces be properly orientated and then surrounded with a mud mix. Ash must be cleaned from the tunnel, and the deposits of soot must be periodically scraped from the exit gaps so that smoke is allowed to escape.

Use of the stove

The fuel is fed in at a right angle to the pots so that both can be easily reached by the cook. Both pot-holes should be used for quick cooking and the greatest fuel savings, but a single pot or kettle can be used by lifting it with pot sherds, or by suspending it from a wire.

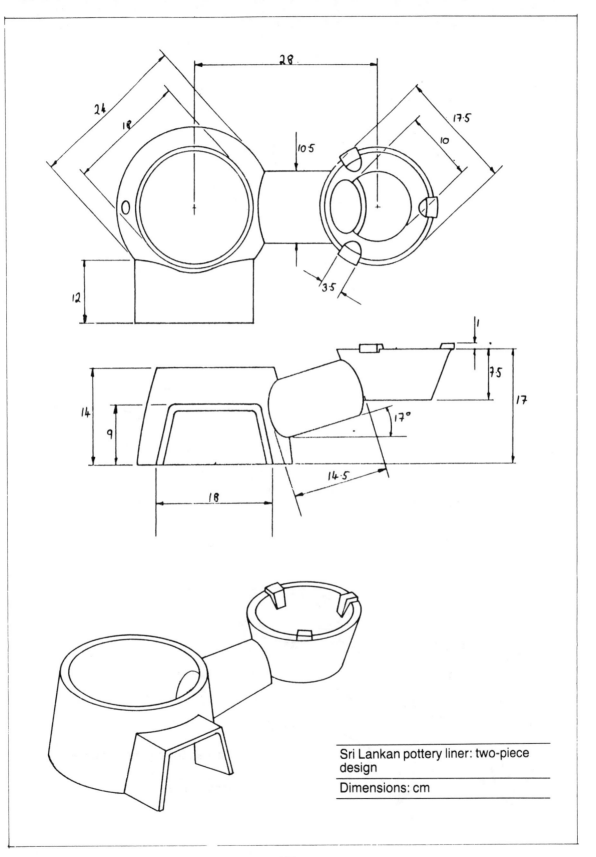

Sri Lankan pottery liner: two-piece design

Dimensions: cm

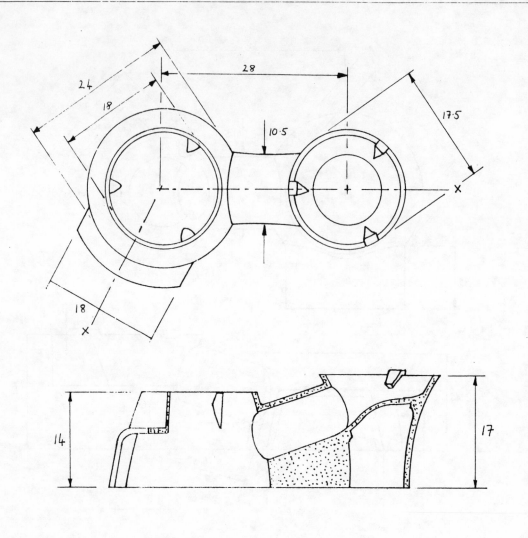

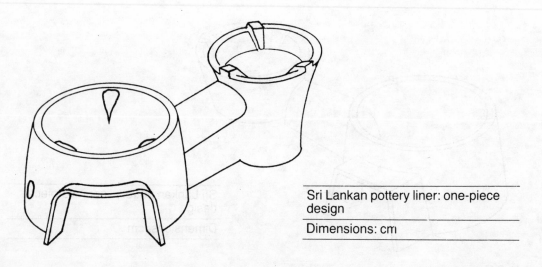

Sri Lankan pottery liner: one-piece design

Dimensions: cm

11. TUNGKU LOWON (DIAN DESA, INDONESIA)

Description

This stove is constructed by carving out a block made from a mud mix. The walls are about 10cm thick. The stove has one pot over the firebox with a 12cm tunnel leading to the raised second pot-hole. The steeply inclined tunnel is important for good draught and heat transfer to the second pot. Smoke escapes through four to six openings with a total cross sectional area of 80 sq cm. The doorway is large enough so that wood can be manoeuvred easily in the firebox. Two ventilation holes lead into the firebox, and poor draught is corrected by enlarging the smoke vents and/or the tunnel. The raised second pot-hole improves the draught, especially with wet or low quality fuels. The walls are about 10cm thick. A typical model weighs 70kg and measure 80cm × 38cm × 25cm.

History and field experience

The stove was designed by the staff of Dian Desa in Indonesia as a hybrid of a small Lorena stove and the traditional device. The chimney of the Lorena was removed to reduce the cost and allow the smoke to be used for crop drying. When built properly the stove cooks faster and is more fuel-efficient than either traditional stoves or the chimney stoves. The Tungku Lowon requires less skill in construction and maintenance than a chimney stove and can be made in a shorter period of time.

Dian Desa promoted this stove primarily by training field workers of other organizations. While properly-constructed Tungku Lowons are still in constant use after more than two years, field evaluations revealed that many stoves became disused after only a few months because of inaccurate construction, and also because of breakages resulting from the use of poor materials. Dian Desa decided that the benefits of the mud stoves were insufficient to justify the cost and logistical difficulties of providing proper training for all stove builders, of ensuring careful choice of materials and of accurate construction. Instead they concentrated on developing the pottery Tungku Sae (stove No. 9).

A version of the Tungku Lowon design has also been promoted across Africa in numerous projects with only mixed results, sometimes due to poor construction.

Construction, installation and maintenance

Sand/clay mixes are the most popular construction material. Additives such as ash, cow dung, fibres, starch, brick dust and natural glues are added by various builders to improve the thermal strength of the stove. The mix is either laid down in one large slab, or packed around two empty cans which are later removed to form the pot-holes. The carving of the stove is usually done one day after the mix has been laid.

Any cracks that form in the stove should be wetted and filled. Ash as clay or cow dung as clay slips are often applied to the firebox if there is a problem with flaking or crumbling.

Use of the stove

As with other multi-pot chimneyless stoves, the stove is most efficient when both pot-holes are used. Care must be taken not to push fuel into the tunnel, which will reduce the air available for efficient combustion. Large pots can be supported on pottery sherds, and small pots or a kettle can be supported just inside the firebox in some way.

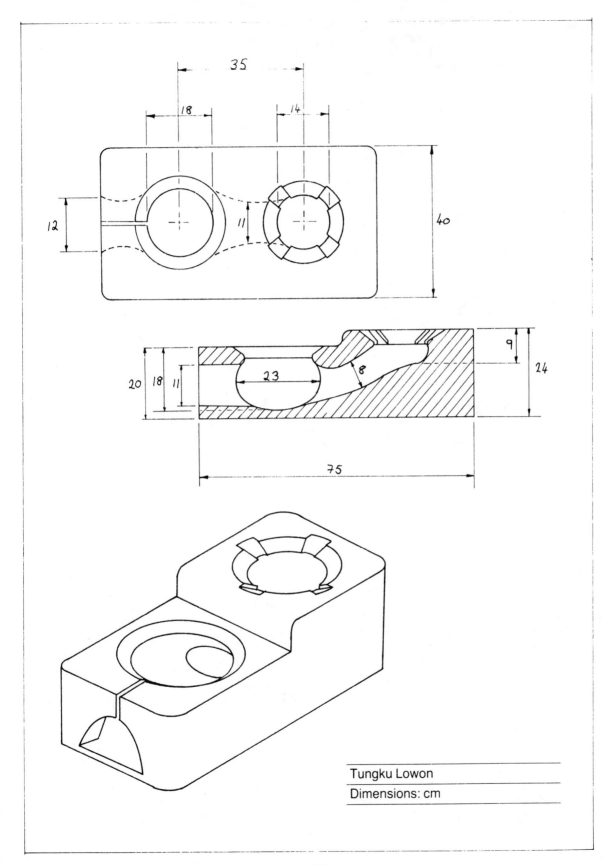

Tungku Lowon

Dimensions: cm

12. TERI IMPROVED CHIMNEYLESS FUELWOOD COOKSTOVE (INDIA)

Description

This is a one-piece hand-moulded pottery stove made from a low-fired mix of clay and grain husks (2:1 or 3:1 by volume). The pottery stove is 50cm × 23cm × 18cm and is usually insulated with a mud mix. The stove weighs approximately 5kg and costs US$0.40. It has two pot-holes with the first pot sitting tightly over the firebox and the second raised on pot supports. There are no doors, dampers, or baffles.

History and field experience

The stove was designed by the Tata Energy Research Institute, Pondicherry, India, in 1980. The significant design constraints were that the cost of the improved stove should not greatly exceed that of the traditional stove and that local potters could veto any complicated design changes.

Over 100 stoves were distributed in a field trial in 1982 and 'fuel savings of 28%, 38% and 30% are reported from groups using agricultural wastes, mixed fuels, and fuelwood, respectively' (Gupta, 1983). The users had some complaints, but over

75% reported satisfactory performance in terms of fuel saving and cooking time. While this stove has not achieved widespread dissemination (because in India, without a chimney, it does not justify for Government subsides) it is included here because many of its features have been successfully incorporated in other designs.

Construction, installation and maintenance

The stove is made from a mix of clay and rice husks (between 2:1 and 3:1 by volume), forming the shell of the stove by coiling and then smoothing out the coils. After drying in the sun for one day the top half of the stove is added. The stove is fully dried, then fired in a bonfire kiln. The pottery stove is installed in mud in the same manner as the traditional stove.

The stoves last from six months to more than two years. The ash must be cleaned out at least weekly, and more often if agricultural wastes are burnt.

Use of the stove

As for the Sri Lankan Pottery liner, stove No. 10

106

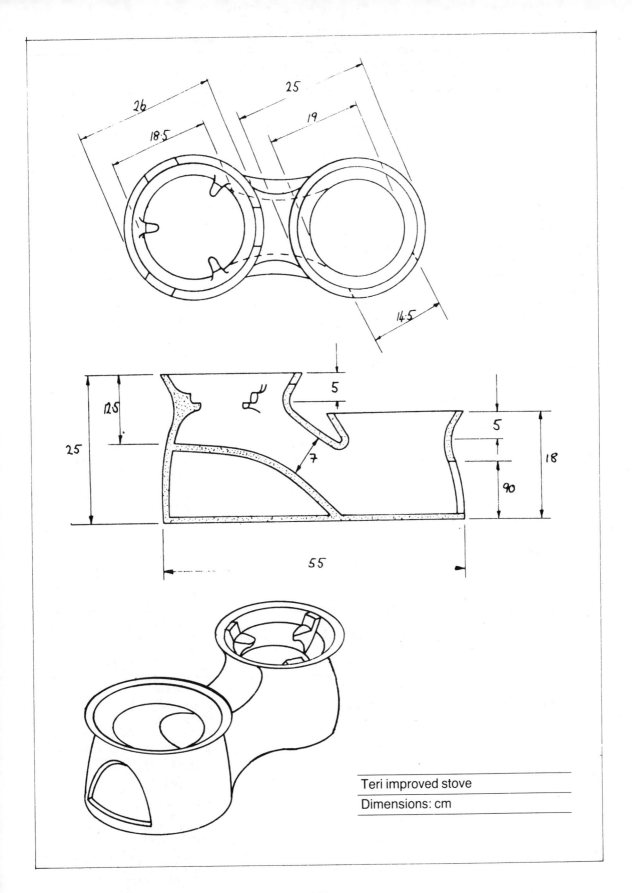

Teri improved stove

Dimensions: cm

Table 6.1: Comparative test results for multi-pot chimneyless stoves

Stove	Efficiency (PHU)	Power output kW	Heat input ratio	Source – and comments
9. Tungku Sae	23–27 18	3–5		ITDG (1984) Recent tests in Nepal using local fuel and pots
10. Sri Lankan pottery liner	20–23	3–5	1.8:1 to 1.1:1	ITDG (1984). Slightly slower than other pottery stoves
11. Tungku Lowon	20–23	3–5	1.3:1 to 1.5:1	ITDG (1984) This stove can produce high carbon monoxide levels if improperly constructed, or when used at high power (Joseph and Loose, 1982)
12. Teri improved fuelwood cookstove	22–29 17–22	1.6–1.9 2.3–2.5	2:1 1.3:1	Gupta (1983). Aluminium pots Gupta (1983). Clay pots

Table 6.2: Stove problems – causes and solutions

Problem	Cause	Solutions
Always slow to cook	Firebox too deep and flames not touching first pot	– Reduce firebox height
	Poor combustion (which may be caused by low draught, or insufficient air through doorway or secondary air holes)	– Increase size of exit gaps – Increase tunnel size
Slow cooking problem developed after a few months of use	Clogged tunnel or exit gaps	– Clean out tunnel and exit gaps
Smoke coming out of front	Low draught, or effect of wind	– Increase size of exit gaps – Protect from wind, or move stove
Not enough heat to second pot	Flames not hitting second pot	– Direct flames to strike the second pot by positioning of the baffle and exit gaps – Decrease distance between first and second pot
Insufficient heat to the back pot	Insufficient draught	– Increase fuel entrance, decrease baffle height, open exit gaps
Stove very smoky	Wet fuels	– Use drier fuel, or smaller sticks
	Insufficient air	– Increase draught, open fuel entrance, decrease baffle height – Introduce more secondary air
High fuel consumption	Draught too large, or too small	– Increase or decrease chimney height – Increase or decrease baffle height
	Pots unsuitable design or size	– Check that the pot over the firebox – sits firmly on stove, without air leaks
	Combustion chamber too large, or too small	– Re-train potters/improve quality control
Cooking performance slow	Power output low	– Increase fuel load – Increase draught
	Wet fuels	– Use drier fuels or smaller sticks
	Poor heat transfer to pot	– Clean carbon deposits from bottom of pots
Stove life span less than 6 months	Improper construction materials	– Ceramic components should be fired to at least 700–750°C – Increase the amount of silica sand in the material, or add rice-husk ash – Complain to stove maker
	Mishandling	– Handle with care
	Rapid cooling of stove surface from spilled liquids and water	– Decrease surface porosity by coating with a layer of low firing clay – Decrease porosity of basic construction material

CHAPTER 7

One-pot chimneyless stoves

Introduction

One-pot chimneyless stoves (also known as shielded fires) are the simplest and smallest of the stove types and seem to be the most direct progression from the three-stone fireplace. The highest constant field performance figures have been obtained from them. Some of these stoves have been used in Asia and Africa for many years. They are usually portable, are relatively low cost, and can often operate over a wider variety of power outputs and at higher efficiencies than the other types.

Much of the recent work on this type of stove has centred on improving existing designs, by adding a shield around the pot and by altering the shape and size of the firebox.

Firebox entrance

Specific design guidelines are related to the way in which the cook expects, or is expected, to operate the stove. On the Thai wood-burning and the Alor Island stoves the doorway is fairly large to allow the cook to manoeuvre the wood in order to control the power output. On the first three stoves

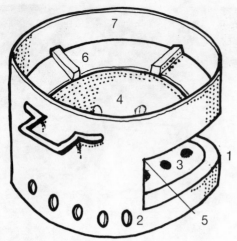

Figure 7.1. Components of a one-pot chimneyless stove.

1. Firebox entrance
2. Primary air entrance
3. Grate
4. Secondary air holes
5. Firebox
6. Pot seat
7. Pot shield

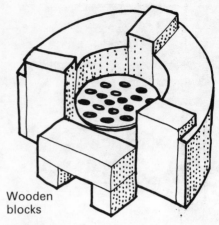

Wooden blocks

Figure 7.2. Simple shielded fire.

described here (the Gambian Noflie, the West African metal cylindrical, and the Louga-type stoves) the doorway is relatively small to prevent the cook from putting too much fuel in the firebox. In practice, the doorway must be related to the type of fuel used and to the accepted method for operating the stove, even if this entails a drop in efficiency. Closed-door designs will give the highest efficiency if sufficient primary and secondary air enters the firebox, but these may be unacceptable to users.

Primary air entrance

On the basis of the dimensions of successful Thai and ITDG stoves with grates, it is apparent that there should be primary air entrances with a minimum size of 30 sq cm.

Grates

Grates significantly improve the performance of every stove to which they have been added, with the exception of the Louga-type stove. The addition of a grate to a simple shielded fire is one of the simplest effective improvements that can be made. Tests carried out on the simple stove shown below gave efficiencies of 22–25% at 3–4kW in Sri Lanka and Nepal (Stewart, 1981, 1983).

Grates bring in air directly underneath the wood and charcoal, and promote better mixing of fuel and air. The optimum percentage of grate opening depends on the amount of secondary air holes and

the size of the doorway. Grates with openings forming 10–20% of the total area are common for the metal stoves, but the Thai stoves have 25–50% openings on pottery grates. The grate area can be calculated using the formula given in the previous chapter (page 60) for one-pot chimney stoves.

The use of grates promotes the combustion of the charcoal and is therefore not desirable for stoves required for long unattended simmering, or if the user wishes to leave hot embers in the ashes to facilitate easy relighting of the stove.

Secondary air holes

Specific design guidelines for secondary air holes cannot be made beforehand without detailed information on the stove design, fuel, user practices and earlier test results. The proper placement and size of secondary air holes has been found to be critical for the all-metal Gambian stoves (Joseph and Loose, 1983; Bennett, 1984), and their presence significantly reduces the performance of some prototype pottery, wood-burning stoves in Nepal (Sulpya, 1983). Secondary air holes introduce structural problems in non-metal stoves. A higher grate opening area or more secondary air holes are necessary for wet or poor quality fuels; the optimum relationship can only be developed from systematic testing.

Firebox

Cylindrical or cone-shaped fireboxes are used for stoves with a grate. The cone shape design helps keep the grate covered with charcoal.

When the firebox height is too small for the fire, combustion will be suppressed and there will be considerable smoke, and charcoal build-up. When

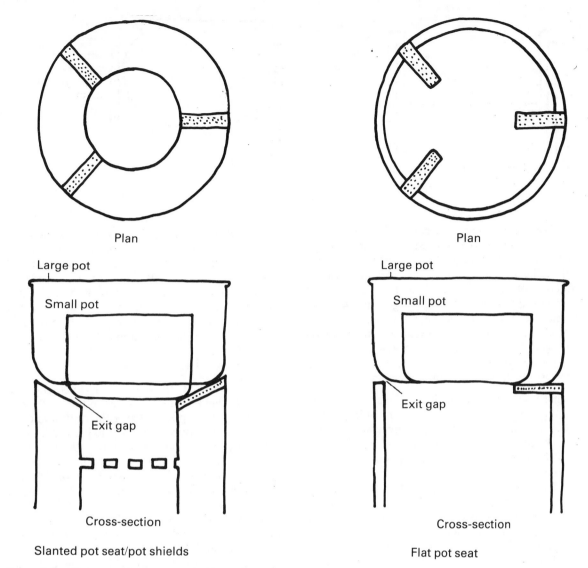

Plan   **Plan**

Large pot

Small pot

Exit gap

Cross-section

Slanted pot seat/pot shields

Large pot

Small pot

Exit gap

Cross-section

Flat pot seat

Figure 7.3. Pot supports on one-pot chinmeyless stove.

the firebox height is too large, combustion will be more complete but heat transfer will be less effective. Smoky fires and large charcoal build up are two reasons why many traditional open fires are taller than the experimental optimum, and it may be prudent to avoid these problems in small fireboxes by increasing the height somewhat – despite the resulting decreased efficiency.

Based on surveys of traditional one-pot chimneyless stoves in West Africa. Baldwin (VITA, 1984) suggests that the height of the firebox should be approximately half the diameter of the pot. For bulky fuels the height can be calculated from the middle of the fuel bed.

Pot seat

Pots are supported on top of these stoves by small lugs 1 – 2cm wide, or are held 1 – 2 cm away from the shield of the stove.

Pot shield

The pot shield can be a tapered continuation of the pot seat so that a wide variety of pots can be used (see left-hand diagram of Figure 7.3.) as in the Thai and Alor Island stoves. Alternatively the pot shield can be a vertical cylinder but this is only suitable if one size of pot is used. Ideally a straight-walled pot would maximize heat transfer.

111

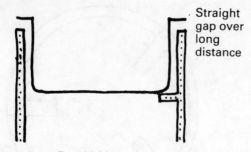 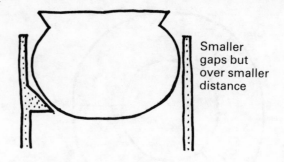

Straight gap over long distance

Smaller gaps but over smaller distance

Figure 7.4.   Pot shields.

A pot shield reduces the convective losses from the pot to the surroundings, and increases the convective and radiative heat transfer to the pot walls. The size and shape of the gap significantly affects both the increased heat transfer and the power output of the fire. Gaps larger than 4cm will have little effect on the heat transfer or power output, but the following explanation and graph by Baldwin (1984) (Figure 7.5) explains a theoretical relationship between the gap size and length, the total power output, and the efficiency.

'Increasing convective heat transfer from the hot gases to the pot is the single most important way to improve a stove's performance . . . it is necessary to expose the entire surface of the pot to the hot gases, forcing the gases against the sides of the pot . . .'

In the graph below we see that the efficiency of convective heat transfer increases very rapidly with the pot to wall gap (G) and only slowly with the channel length (L). It is also imporant to note that one may often have a trade-off between the efficiency and the heating rate. Long narrow gaps can have very high efficien-cies but low heating rates compared to wider gaps. This means that a compromise must some-times be made between fuel consumption and the patience of the user in bringing a pot to a boil. In addition, the sensitivity of the efficiency on the pot to wall gap requires precise control of dimensions – possible only through mass pro-duction – and the careful matching of stoves to pots.'
(Baldwin, 1984)

Based on experiments and calculations, Baldwin concludes that a 4–8mm gap, depending on the size and shape of the pot, will give the optimum com-bination of high power output and high efficiency. Other designers, such as Sulilatu (1983), recom-mend larger gaps (10mm) to allow for soot build-up. For round pots in cylindrical pot shields, the gap can be considerably smaller than for straight-walled pots.

When designing stoves with pot shields it is important to consider the range of pot sizes that will be used and the overall performance for cook-ing, i.e. not just how to achieve the optimum performance for a single pot/stove combination.

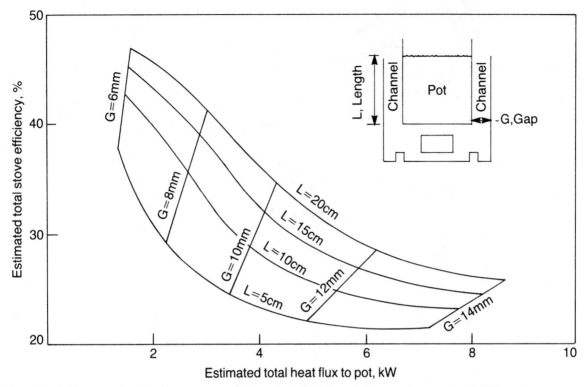

Figure 7.5.   Heat transfer from hot gases to pot. (Pot diameter 0.3m, starting gas temperature 600°C, wall well-insulated, from Baldwin, 1986, based on De Lepeleire, 1983).

Mark 1

13. NOFLIE STOVE (THE GAMBIA)

Description

These metal stoves are made in three sizes (to suit three pot sizes) and according to two different designs – the newer design is cheaper to make. They are made from oil barrel metal and the medium size is 33cm wide × 27cm high and weighs 3.7kg. There is a firebox, grate and pot support welded onto an outer shell. The firebox entrance has a door and there are two handles. The medium-size stoves cost $6 for the straight-walled design and $7.50 for the slanted-wall type.

History and field experience

Initial design and test work was carried out in The Gambia by the Department of Community Development and ITDG (Joseph and Loose, 1983). It was then tested and optimized in the UK. The stove designs were taken to The Gambia where they were further modified by ITDG and the local

stoves technical team, so that they could burn a mix of briquettes and wood in one device and be more easily made by the local craftsmen. In the field tests that followed thorough laboratory testing the new users were initially sceptical about the ability of such a small stove to cook quickly, but were quickly impressed by the speed, fuel efficiency and relative smokelessness. The stove was given its name – the 'Fourno Noflie' – which literally means 'a stove where you can be at ease' or 'a stove that is easy and simple to operate'. After a positive response to the first 50 stoves in use, 400 more were built for use in an expanded field test early in 1984. Some 2,000–3,000 stoves were built in extended field trails in Banjul, Greater Banjul and smaller towns.

114

Mark 2

Construction, installation and maintenance

The steel pieces for the stove are cut out of old oil barrels using templates, and then tack-welded together. The stoves are portable, but when used on sand it is important to check that the primary air holes and grate do not become clogged. Repairs to sections that rust away can be made by local metal workers.

Use of the stove

The stove can burn briquettes, briquettes and wood, or wood alone. The door is made to allow just three pieces of chopped wood to fit inside. The power output is controlled by the amount of fuel in the firebox. The door can be shut to improve the burning of the briquettes or small pieces of wood.

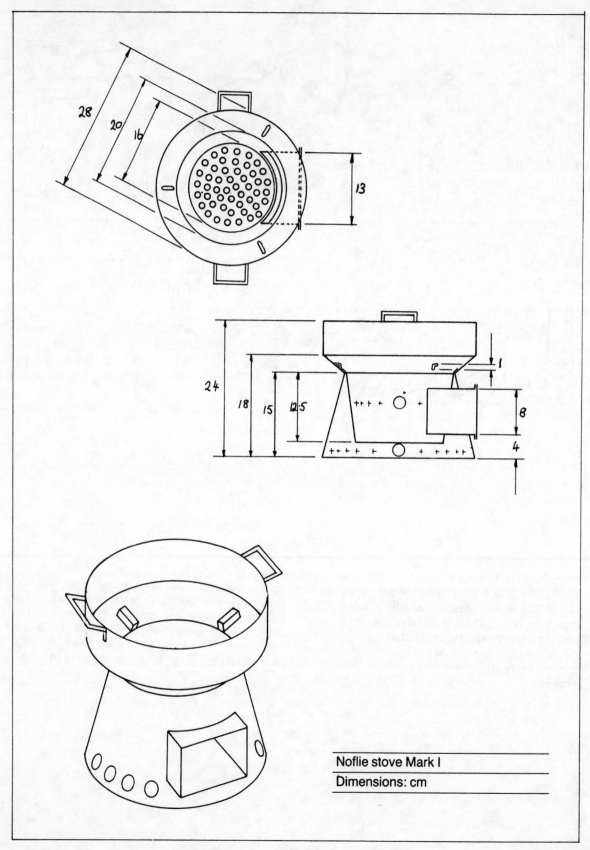

Noflie stove Mark I

Dimensions: cm

116

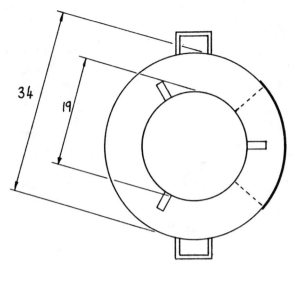

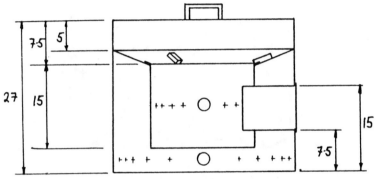

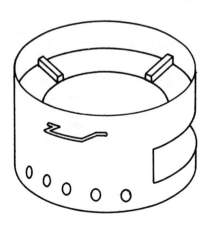

Noflie stove Mark II

Dimensions: cm

14. WEST AFRICAN CYLINDRICAL STOVE WITH GRATE (BURKINA FASO)

Description

This stove design is made to fit only one pot size correctly. Smaller pots can be used, but the gap is then too large and fuel consumption is reduced considerably. The stove is simply a metal cylinder with support tabs cut out from the base to allow primary air in and to support the grate, attached (riveted welded) pot supports, and a rectangular fuel entrance. The diameter of the stove is the diameter of the pot, plus 0.8–1.2cm (i.e. a 0.4–0.6cm gap). The height of the pot from the grate is 0.4 × diameter of the pot. Holes are punched in the grate to give an open area of 10–20%.

History and field experience

The stove was designed by VITA staff and other personnel working principally in Upper Volta (now Burkina Faso). They have been made and were being trial-tested in Burkino Faso and Mali in early 1984. The stove has proven particularly suc-cessful in Senegal, where over 10,000 have been produced. Substantial numbers have also been produced in Mali and Burkina Faso and it is one of the recommended designs for dissemination in West African Sahelian countries.

Construction, installation and maintenance

Most of the stoves are made in small metal workships using templates. The stoves can be made using welds, rivets or seams. They are portable and require no installation. Repairs and replacement parts can be made by local metal workers.

Use of the stove

A pot of a specific size must be used with the stove if the potential savings are to be realised. The fuel must be small enough to fit in the small door. When used on sandy soil the stove or grate must be slightly elevated so that it does not rest in the sand.

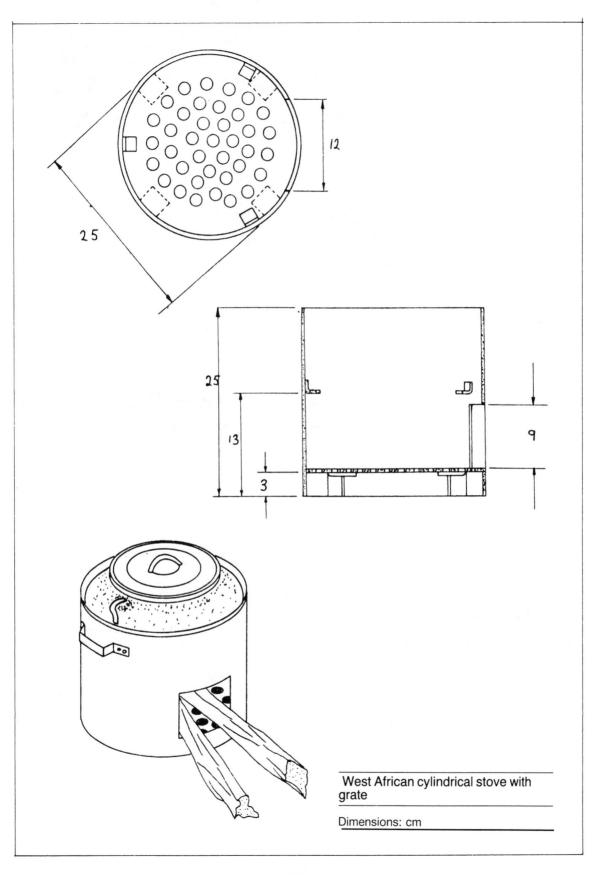

25

12

25

13

3

9

West African cylindrical stove with grate

Dimensions: cm

15. LOUGA OR COUMBA GAYA (SENEGAL)

Description
The stove consists of a thick circular wall surrounding and shielding a pot with one entrance to the firebox situated directly beneath the pot. The internal diameter is the diameter of the pot plus a 1–4cm gap all the way around the pot. The stoves are made from mud mixes and can weigh up to 80kg.

History and field experience
The stove was first designed in 1980 by a team from the Aprovecho Institute working in Senegal. The stove had been widely promoted throughout West Africa and more than 100,000 have probably been built. In Burkina Faso alone, 80,000 had been built by the end of 1986. There is a great deal of variability in the performance and lifetime of the stoves due to the original design, the materials, and degradation due to use, rain and thermal stress; the average lifetime is often less than two years.

Construction, installation and maintenance
The stoves are constructed from mud mixes using the pot as the guide. The pot is often supported on three rocks or bricks, or a metal stand. The stove requires considerable labour, but relatively low skill. The stove should be protected from the rain if it is built and used outdoors. Cracks should be repaired with more mud mix.

Use of the stove
The stove is made for one pot's diameter. Smaller pots will fit if the pot supports are large enough, but larger pots cannot be used. The fire is started with kindling, and wood is fed in through one door. An air hole at the back of the stove may be necessary to improve combustion. The power output is controlled by the quantity of fuel in the firebox.

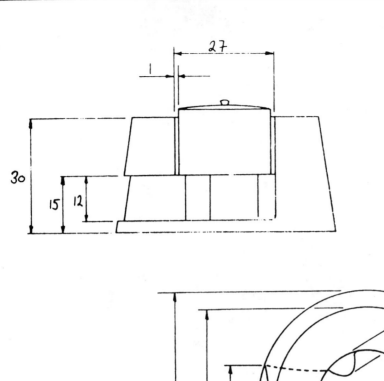

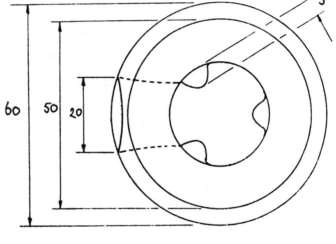

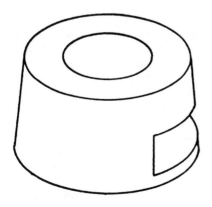

Louga or Coumba Gaya

Dimensions: cm

16. ROYAL THAI FORESTRY DEPARTMENT CHIMNEYLESS WOOD-BURNING STOVE

Description

The stove is made from a mix of river clay and rice-husk ash that is moulded, finished and fired like the Thai charcoal stove (see page 143 and page 216 onwards). The grate is also made from pottery. For greater strength and portability the stove body can be placed in a galvanized sheet metal bucket and insulated with a rice-husk ash/clay mixture (12:1 by volume). In this case the top, firebox entrance and primary air entrance edges must be sealed with cement mortar. Diameters from 18–40cm can be used on the slanting pot seat with an exhaust gap of 0.8–1.0 cm. The whole stove is 25cm high and 28cm wide. The firebox is lined with a refractory material consisting of a rice-husk ash/clay mixture (5:1 by volume). The stove weighs 8–10kg, and has an estimated lifetime of five years; early production costs were $4.50, but could be less for larger scale production.

History and field experience

The stove was designed after testing all the available one-pot chimneyless stoves in Thailand and trying to combine the best features at a reasonable cost. Further modifications were made to simplify the construction and lower the cost by using refractory clay without any outside insulation, and a galvanized sheet metal bucket. The use of the stove is not different, and is often more versatile, than the existing commercial wood-burning stoves; nor does it require any change in use by people who traditionally use home-made stoves. The RTFD began demonstrating and field testing the stove early in 1984 and now some six village groups are manufacturing them for local sale. Several thousand have been produced and sold. Its widespread dissemination is likely to remain doubtful, however, because of the very high price.

Construction, installation and maintenance

The stove body and grate are made in the same

manner as the Thai charcoal stoves (page 141–145). The stove is portable and new grates can be purchased in shops.

Use of the stove

Firewood is fed through the feeding port and laid horizontally on the grate which is 12cm from the bottom. The fuel is lit with kindling and the heat output is controlled by careful positioning of the fuel in the combustion chamber, and by adding or removing it as appropriate. Firewood burns well in the stove and charcoal formation is low. Wet wood can be warmed when the stove is alight by insertion through the ash-removal port (under the grate). A wood support in front of the door is useful if long pieces of wood are burnt. Burning firewood pieces can be extinguished by immersing the burning ends in a sand pile. The ash should be periodically removed from below the grate.

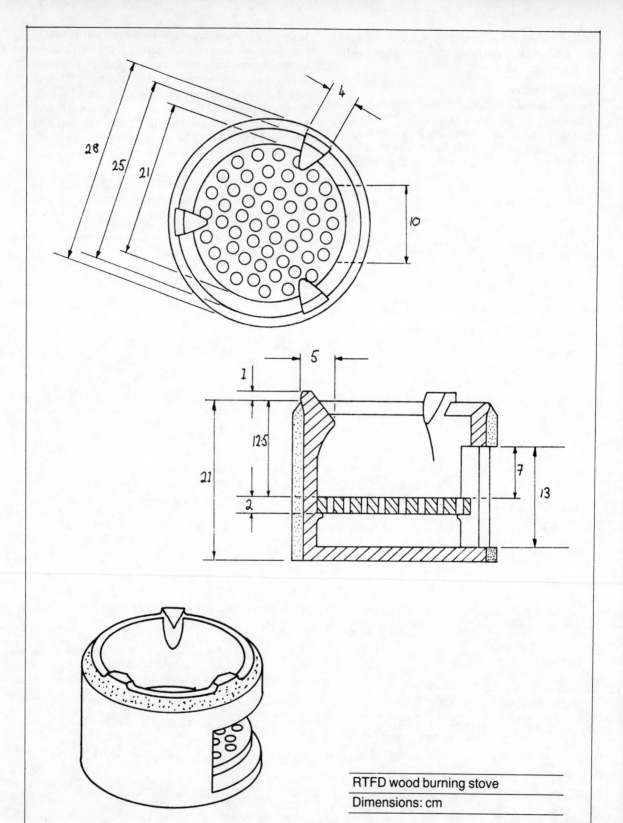

RTFD wood burning stove

Dimensions: cm

17. ALOR ISLAND[1] STOVE

Description

This pottery stove is shaped like a cooking pot, with an extra large lip with pot supports and a large oval door cut in one side. It is 30 cm wide and 22cm high and weighs approximately 1.5kg. The stove costs US$0.35 to produce and deliver to the market, and has a probable lifetime of one to three years when insulated. The stove is used in dry savannah areas where the fuel used is nearly always dry.

History and field experience

The stove is designed for cooking patterns requiring one pot and long simmering periods. It was designed in 1982 as an adaptation of a traditional Javanese stove to meet local cooking practices and construction skills. The main producers were seasonal female rural potters who trade their wares (now including stoves) in the regional cities around Flores. The stove is sold in small shops for US$0.50. Marketing to promote the product in the urban market is the principal type of dissemination assistance that is being provided.

Construction, installation and maintenance

The stove is constructed in the same manner as a coiled pot. A plate-like base is made, coils are attached in a circular fashion, and then the pot is scraped to the proper thickness and shape. Templates are used to ensure that the pot-hole and door are the correct size. The stoves are fired, with other pottery wares, in a bonfire. This fired pottery liner is insulated before use with a 5–7cm layer of mud mix. No maintenance is necessary except for periodic ash removal.

Use of the stove

The depression at the base of the stove is left filled with ash to give a level bottom. The fire is lit in the stove and controlled like an open fire. Low power outputs are much easier to maintain compared to an open fire.

1. Alor is a small island off the coast of Flores, Eastern Indonesia.

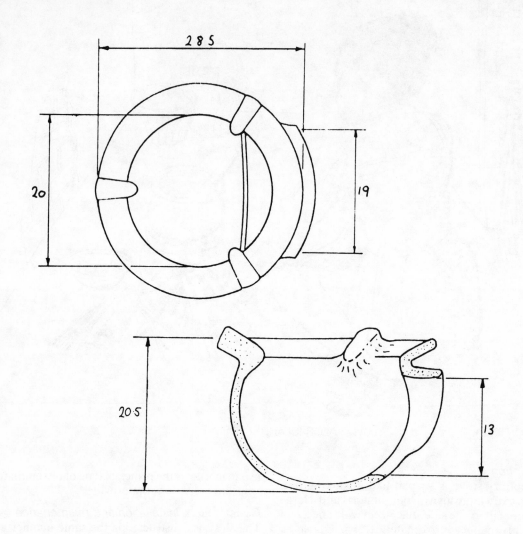

285

20

19

20·5

13

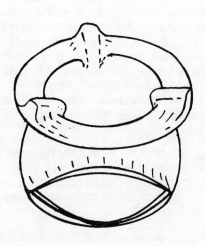

Alor island stove

Dimensions: cm

18. ROYAL THAI FORESTRY DEPARTMENT RICE-
HUSK CHIMNEYLESS STOVE ('MEECHAI' STOVE)

Description

This portable stove is a perforated metal cone with
a cylinder sitting on three projections inside the
top half of the cone. The pot is placed on top of the
cylinder. The cone rests in a steel ring which has
three wooden or metal legs. The rice husks are fed
between the cone and the cylinder – the flames go
up the inside of the cylinder. The stove is made of
sheet steel and lined with a rice-husk ash/clay
mixture for insulation. The stove costs US$7.60 to
produce and the expected lifetime is two to three
years.

History and field experience

The stove was developed in Kampuchea and was
'discovered' by Thai extension workers of the
Population and Community Development Association who saw them, made from scrap metal,
being used by refugees in the Kao-I-Dang refugee
camp. The PCDA was the first to promote the
stove in Thailand. The RTFD made improvements
to the design and changed the material used to
make it more efficient and more durable – the
principal improvement being addition of the inner

insulation. Thousands of the stoves have been
made in Thailand, but the popularity of the
Meechai remains strictly limited.

Construction, installation and maintenance

The stove consists of two parts, the receptacle cone
being made of sheet steel 0.7mm thick with top and
bottom diameters of 45cm and 10cm respectively.
277 holes of 9mm diameter are drilled around the
lower part of the cone. The inner side of the whole
of the cone is lined with 1cm-thick rice-husk ash/
clay mixture (5:1 by volume) as insulator, the holes
being made through it when the mixture is still wet.
The cylindrical body is made of sheet steel of the
same thickness as that for the cone, and is similarly
lined, or it can be made from pottery. The stove is
then fitted into its stand. The gap through which
the rice husks flow between the cone and cylinder
is 2–2.5cm. The insulation may crack off, but it can
be repaired by the user with the same type of
rice-husk ash/clay mixture.

Use of the stove

Rice husks (half hull, not pulverized) are poured

127

into the stove between the cylinder and top part of the outer cone until there are sufficient husks lining the inner walls of the lower section to stop the downward flow. These husks are ignited using dry leaves, straw or waste paper placed inside the lower section of the cone through the cylindrical section of the stove. When the fire is well alight (usually within one minute) the pot is placed on the stove cylinder. The burnt rice-husk ash must be removed from the bottom part to allow more husks to flow into the combustion chamber. Regular attention, approximately every one to three minutes is required to keep the rice husks flowing.

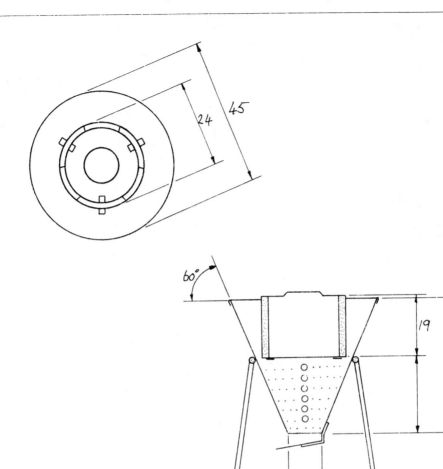

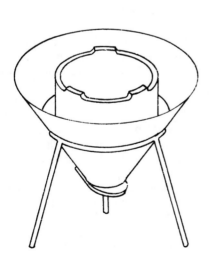

RTFD rice-husk stove ('Meechai' stove)
Dimensions: cm

19. GAMBIAN CERAMIC WOODSTOVE

Description

This one-piece, one-pot stove is made entirely from pottery and is cylindrical in shape, with the top slightly flared to accept the spherical bottom pots typically used in The Gambia. The stove is approximately 32cm in diameter at the top and stands 22cm high. The fuel entrance (without a door) is off to the side and is positioned so that long pieces of wood can be inserted into the firebox while resting on the ground. The stove does not have a grate nor secondary air inlets, and all air for the combustion process enters through the doorway.

The pot is supported directly above the firebox by three equally-spaced pot rests on the inside of the flared section of the stove at the top. These pot rests maintain a 1cm gap between pot and stove wall to maximize heat transfer while allowing the exhaust gases to escape around the base of the pot. Under each pot rest is a buttress to give extra strength to the stove walls.

History and field experience

The Department of Community Development began work on an all-ceramic stove for The Gambia in 1984. The massive mud stoves being promoted at that time showed few signs of ever achieving widespread acceptability, and a simple portable one-pot stove made from a cheap material was seen as one way of achieving greater dissemination in the rural areas that have neither access to metal in order to make Noflie stoves, nor the cash to buy them.

Test work through laboratory and field trials showed that the design had the potential to save 30–50% fuel compared to the open fire. Achieving significant savings has not been difficult, but proving the stove's durability and ease of manufacture has. Further development work in this area is currently being pursued by the Department of Community Development with the assistance of UNSO. Although the one-pot ceramic portable stove has not achieved widespread acceptance in The Gambia, primarily because the project is in its early stages of development, experiences of a similar stove in Burkina Faso have been very encouraging regarding performance, acceptability and cost. Providing more durable clay bodies as well as easier construction methods are evolved, the all-ceramic stove perhaps offers amongst all other materials the greatest potential for achieving low cost combined with high performance.

Construction, installation and maintenance
The stoves are made by potters using soil and slab techniques.

Use of the Stove
Fuel is fed in through the firebox door and a limited range of pots can be used on the same stove.

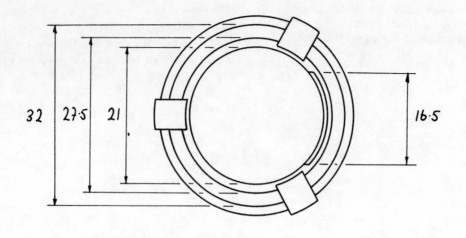

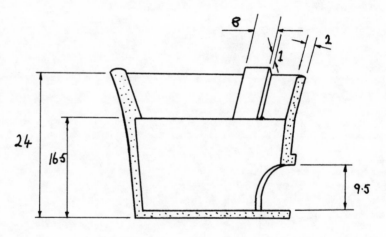

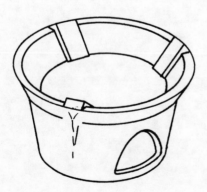

Gambian ceramic wood stove

Dimensions: cm

20. KUNI MBILI, KENYA

Description

This cylindrical, portable, wood-burning stove (the name means 'two sticks' in Kiswahili) weighs 9kg and is made from both metal and ceramic components. Current models are 32cm in diameter by 25cm in height. The stove is designed for flat-bottom aluminium pots, ranging in diameter from 20cm to 35cm, and these are supported directly over the firebox by three metal-hinged rings, a standard fitting used on all portable stoves in East Africa. The stove is also fitted with a grate and an ash pan which prevents ash falling directly onto the floor. Three feet can also be fitted which raise the stove slightly and provide greater stability on uneven surfaces.

History and field experience

Work began on this stove in 1983 by KENGO in Kenya as a result of many field experiences showing the need for innovative ideas to be developed. This was because conventional features such as pot shields for enhancing the stoves' performance were not acceptable, cooks requiring a high level of pot-size flexibility.

The use of a ceramic combustion chamber within a metal cladding evolved as a way of achieving fuel savings without reducing the stove's ability to accept a wide range of pots, and making the stove portable at a price people could afford.

The early laboratory work in 1983 did indeed show that performance could be improved by insulating combustion chambers while maintaining a relatively simple stove configuration. Additional laboratory work in 1984 provided further guidance on achieving more efficient ceramic configurations. By the end of 1985 a range of stoves had been tested in Kenya, with mixed results concerning their acceptability within the home as replacements for the open fire. Further trials are currently being carried out on modified stoves that should improve acceptability. Regarding performance, in April 1986 tests indicated that the Kuni Mbili had been fully optimized and that the percentage heat utilized was in the region of 28% at 2.5kW to 10kW for a 30cm diameter pot.

Although as many as 4,000 of the stoves may have been built and sold in Kenya, their future as a replacement for the open fire is not yet assured, despite measured savings in the order of 50–60%. The price and low acceptability rates still remain problems that need to be overcome if this promis-

133

ing concept of using metal and ceramic components is to be realised.

Construction, installation and maintenance
The ceramic liners are produced by women's groups using simple external moulds. These are purchased by metal-working artisans who make the metal cladding and insert the liner, fixing it with a cement vermiculite mix.

Use of the stove
The stove may be used with either agricultural residues such as maize stalks, or long pieces of wood with cross-sections no greater than 3cm × 3cm. The fuel is fed into the firebox through a side entrance situated close to the base so that the very long pieces will rest upon the ground. The exhaust heat and gases leave the stove around the base of the pot in such a way that heat transfer is enhanced.

Power regulation can be achieved by removing excess fuel and closing the fuel entrance door.

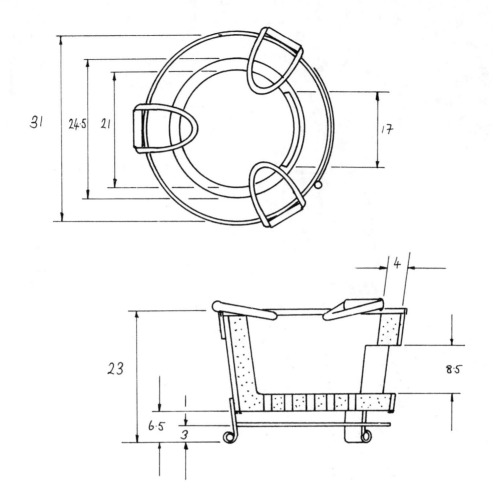

Kuni Mbili

Dimensions: cm

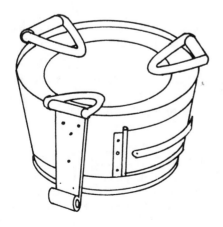

21. WASTE-BURNING STOVE, (SAWDUST AND RICE-HUSKS), KENYA

Description

This is a very simple metal cylinder with an integral base and detachable top. The top has a hole in the centre that concentrates the fire onto the centre of the pot. Three supports attached to the lid maintain a 1.5cm gap to allow gases to escape around the base of the pot. Air enters the stove at the base of the cylinder through a short tunnel that also helps to prevent the waste particles collapsing, blocking off the supply of air. Similar stoves are made in Asia, of both clay and metal.

History and field experience

Very little development work has been carried out on these traditional waste-burning stoves, although the concept of burning compacted residues can be found in most developing countries. It is most commonly used by communities that have access to abundant supplies of waste residues (such as sawdust or rice-husks) at no cost. The Royal Thai Forestry Department have tested similar types of stoves to the Kenyan model and achieved efficiencies in the region of 13–16%. Although this performance is relatively high for traditional stoves, power control and regulation is extremely difficult, and the stoves generally have low specific fuel consumption levels. The widespread application of these types of stoves has not been promoted because of the limited amount of access people have to cheap, abundant supplies of residues. However, where the opportunity does exist these stoves are an excellent alternative either to conventional wood- or charcoal-burning stoves.

Construction, installation and maintenance

The stoves are made from scrap metal by informal sector artisans. In Asia, they are made by potters as thrown items.

Use of the stove

A circular form, either a bottle or cylinder, is placed inside the stove and the residues are packed firmly around it. The form is carefully withdrawn leaving the centre hollow. Some residues such as rice-husks are difficult to control and may need mixing with more fibrous residues. The air inlet is also kept clear of particles. The fire is lit from the base, usually by lighting small sticks and feeding them through the entrance. It may also be lit with paper or kerosene, but with this method it is generally considered to be more difficult to sustain the fire. The fire will quickly ignite the residues, producing a smokeless flame at the top which is ideal for cooking upon. The fire will continue to burn until the residues have been consumed. Controlling the heat output can be achieved by closing off the air inlet. Re-establishing the fire is more difficult, and having some sticks alight in the stove helps this process.

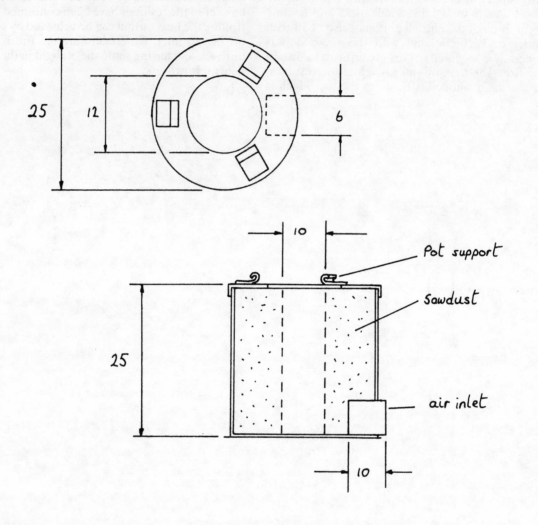

Pot support

sawdust

air inlet

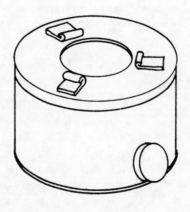

Waste-burning stove

Dimensions: cm

Table 7.1: Comparative test results for one-pot chimneyless stoves

Stove	Efficiency	Power output	Source – and comments
13. Noflie			
slanted wall	31	3.0	
	27	4.5	Joseph & Loose (1982) Stoves made in UK, hardwood fuel
	33	6.0	
	31	5.6	Stewart (1984) Gambian stove with larger pot to pot seat gap, tested in UK, softwood fuel
	27	—	Bennett (1984) Tests in Gambia, with hardwood
	26	—	Bennett (1984) Tests in Gambia, with groundnut shell briquettes
straight wall	35	5.6	Stewart (1984) Gambian stove, tested in UK, with softwood
14. West African cylindrical with grate	29	2.5–4	VITA (1983) 4mm gap
	25	2.5–4	VITA (1983) 10mm gap
15. Louga	15–20		Various reports from West Africa
	34		Test conducted by the WSG in Eindhoven, Netherlands
16. Royal Thai Forestry Dept. chimneyless wood-burning	27	5.7	RFTD (1983) Test carried out on design being promoted
	14	5.0	RFTD (1983) Lowest efficiency for commercially available stove
	20	5.0	RFTD (1983) Average efficiency for commercially available stove
	26	6.0	RFTD (1983) Highest efficiency for commercially available stove (three times as expensive as RTFD model)
17. Alor Island	—	—	Flickinger (1983) In an open shed with a slight breeze, the stove saved 50% of the fuel compared to an open fire when the boiling time was the same, and 30% when the boiling time for the stove was 30% less than for the open fire
18. Royal Thai Forestry Dept. rice-husk chimneyless or Meechai	16–19	9	RTFD (1983) Boils 3.7kg of water in 12 minutes in 24cm diameter pot, with very little smoke
19. Gambian ceramic	19–25	6–4	ITDG, *Laboratory evaluation of the Kenya wood-burning stove*, April 1986
			ITC, *Gambia National Stove Project, end of mission report*, Feb. 1984
20. Kuni mbili	25–27	6–7	ITDG, *Laboratory evaluation of the Kenya wood-burning stove*, April 1986
21. Waste-burning	13–16	—	Chagoria Hospital, Kenya, Nov. 1982
			RTFD, *An evaluation of Thai cooking stoves*, 1981

Table 7.2: Stove problems – causes and solutions

Problem	Cause	Solutions
High fuel consumption	Combustion chamber wrong size	– Check dimensions
	Wrong pot size	– Check pots
	Wet fuel	– Dry fuel before use
Slow to ignite	Wet fuel	– Use plenty of small sticks and paper to light fire
	Insufficient air	– Ignite with pot off the stove
	Wind	– Ignite sheltered from wind
Stove slow to cook	Power output low	
	– damp or wet fuel	– Dry fuel
	– grate blocked	– Clean stove
	Poor combustion	– Check primary and secondary air openings are not blocked
	Insufficient fuel	– Increase fuel load and use smaller sticks
Stove very smoky	Too much fuel	– Reduce fuel load
	Primary or secondary air vents blocked	– Clean stove
	Pot size too big	– Reduce pot size to ensure there is sufficient gap for exhaust gases to escape
Stove life-span short	Cracking of ceramic components	– Mishandling – Ceramic mixture, or firing, wrong
	Metal components burnt out	– Replace with thicker metal
	Ceramic insert falls out of cladding	– Re-insert and fix with cement/sand mix 1:2 (by volume)

CHAPTER 8

Charcoal stoves

Introduction

Stoves that burn charcoal are the predominant type used in the cities and towns of Africa, and the use of charcoal is increasing at a rapid rate as the urban population grows. Charcoal stoves are less widely used in most of Asia, and, where they are found, it is in urban areas. A major exception is Thailand, where charcoal is a major fuel in both urban and rural areas.

From an energy point of view, charcoal is not a positive conversion of wood. Even though traditional charcoal stoves are usually more efficient than traditional wood stoves, 60% to 80% of the energy is lost in the process of converting wood to charcoal (based on typical kiln yields of 10% to 20% on a weight basis), thus negating any savings even from the more efficient stoves. Economically, however, charcoal has many advantages over wood because of lower transport, handling and storage costs per unit of energy. It is also more convenient to use, giving a smokeless fire that requires considerably less tending to keep a constant heat output. Most current charcoal users purchase both fuel and stoves, and they are therefore usually interested in purchasing improved charcoal stoves.

The design guidelines for charcoal stoves are different from those for wood- or waste-burning stoves for a number of reasons. The fuel contains more energy per unit of volume and can be packed tightly. Most of the heat transfer is by radiation from the stationary charcoal bed rather than radiation from moving flames. Work by Samootsakorn (1981) showed that major heat losses in charcoal stoves result from the heat energy stored in, and radiated from, the walls of the stove. The fuel only needs to be tended every half hour, or longer, rather than every three to ten minutes as with many wood- and waste-burning stoves. Once alight there is usually no smoke from a charcoal fire, so chimneys are not necessary.

Charcoal stoves are lightweight, portable, have one fire per pot, and have no chimney. Design improvements to increase cooking performance centre around changes to the stove body surrounding the firebox. Work in Thailand and Kenya indicates that the most important variables that affect performance are wall material (insulated pottery is best), the density of the ceramic material (which should be light and porous), the area of the grate hole (which should be about 76 sq cm for a grate of 14cm diameter), and the area of the exhaust gap.

Primary air entrance

Having a door to the primary air entrance allows some adjustment of the power output, but in some designs a door is not included because it is not considered necessary or practical. The power output can be increased by fanning air through the primary air entrance.

Grate

The grate should have sufficient open area to allow good mixing of air underneath the charcoal. The openings should be less than 2cm wide to reduce the amount of small charcoal pieces that will fall through, but greater than 0.5cm so that they will not get blocked. The percentage of open area varies from 16% on the Kenyan Ceramic Jiko, to 50% on the Royal Thai Forestry Department's charcoal stove. If the open area is too small not enough air will enter the combustion chamber, but if it is too great an excess of air will decrease the flame temperature. The optimum percentage depends on the type and size of charcoal used.

The replacement of sheet-metal grates with ceramic grates increased the charcoal bed temperature, the power output, and the efficiency of test stoves at ITDG. For metal grates, the efficiency was higher for a grate with 15% open area, 12% lower for a grate with 30% open area, and 40% lower for a grate with a 90% open area.

Combustion chamber

Slightly conical combustion chambers are used on nearly all improved charcoal stove designs. This helps keep the charcoal packed as it burns down to a small amount and promotes more even combustion at a higher efficiency. The combustion chambers are 9 to 10cm high for use with 20 to 30cm pots, with the top diameter 25-45% larger than the grate diameter.

Pot seat

The pot usually sits with a 1 to 1.5cm gap for the exhaust gases; larger gaps allow more heat to escape. The pot seats are always made to accommodate a range of pot sizes. Many designs have the pot supported on metal supports if the combustion chamber is made of a weaker material.

Pot shields

Pot shields do not increase the efficiency as much as they do in wood stoves, as most of the heat is transferred onto the bottom of the pot. They do add marginally to the efficiency, but the reduced versatility and added weight and cost of large pot shields can rarely be justified. The Thai stove integrates a partial pot shield into the pot seat.

Stove body

In hundreds of tests at the Royal Thai Forestry Department, on commercially available charcoal stoves weighing 4-12kg, the most significant correlation was that heavier stoves have lower efficiencies. However, very light stoves which have low heat capacity walls (e.g. thin steel) do not attain high power outputs, high efficiencies, or steady burning, without full combustion chambers. Insulating the combustion chamber with fired pottery, low-density pottery, a clay/rice-husk ash mix, pumice stone, cement/vermiculite mixtures, or other heat resistant insulators, has usually increased the efficiency significantly. Insulating the outside of a cast-iron combustion chamber also increases the efficiency significantly.

The outside shell of a charcoal stove should be robust if the stove is to be moved around frequently.

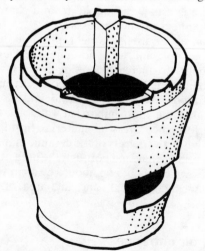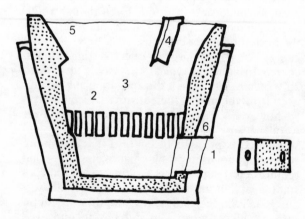

Figure 8.1. Components of a typical bucket stove (Thai Bucket). The cross-section shows the essential parts of a charcoal stove.

1. Primary air entrance
2. Grate
3. Combustion chamber
4. Pot seat
5. Pot shields
6. Stove body

22. ROYAL THAI FORESTRY DEPARTMENT IMPROVED CHARCOAL BUCKET STOVE

Description

The stove is made of high quality fired clay with 1cm thick refractory lining (rice-husk ash/clay mixture, 5:1 by volume) on the inside. The outside insulation between the stove body and the metal bucket is made with rice-husk ash/clay mixture (12:1 by volume). The top outside diameter is 30.5cm and the height is 25cm. The complete stove weighs approximately 10kg. The special design features include a conical rim, and slanted pot rests that can accommodate various sizes of pots, from 16–32cm in diameter, and also many sizes of woks (with a constant 1cm air exhaust gap). The grate is also unique; it is 4cm thick and has 61, 1.2cm diameter, equally-distributed holes (the percentage hole area totalling about 30%). The stove costs approximately US$5.0 to produce and will last two to three years in domestic use. The production cost will be lower when it is produced in greater numbers.

History and field experience

The design is the result of what is believed to be the most exhaustive charcoal-testing project ever undertaken. All designs of charcoal stoves available in Thailand were tested, and the data was analysed to develop optimum design criteria for a single stove that could use a variety of pots and pans. The design was simplified to ease construction and lower the cost. A demonstration and promotion campaign was started early in 1984, and the users of the first 400 stoves were impressed with the new stoves.

By 1986, the stove was being manufactured by one capital-intensive factory, several traditional stove manufacturers and a number of village groups, and some 10,000 were in use. The stove is now subject to a nationwide marketing campaign which aims to have over one million in use within five years.

Construction, installation and maintenance

The stove body and grate are made from a clay/rice-husk ash mixture in moulds. After the preliminary moulding they are finished by hand, dried and fired. They are then put in a metal bucket with a protective insulation between the stove body and bucket. The construction process is described in detail on pages 216 to 221. The stove is portable, and new grates can easily be purchased and installed.

Use of the stove

The charcoal is lit with kindling and after two to three minutes the charcoal bed is burning and the pot can be put in place. The insulating layer reduces heat loss and keeps the charcoal bed very hot. The chamber only needs to be partially refilled to maintain maximum output. Closing the air inlet door will reduce the burning rate considerably. Left-over charcoal can be retrieved at the end of cooking by putting it into a covered jar or a sand pit to extinguish it.

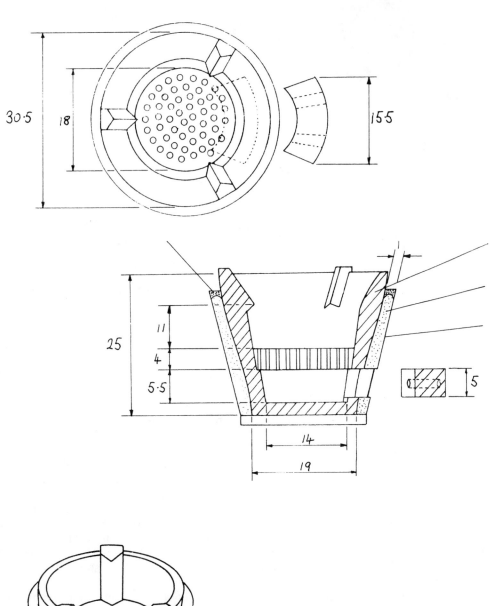

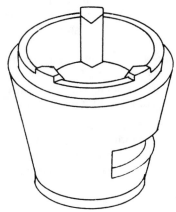

RTFD improved charcoal bucket stove

Dimensions: cm

23. TIMCO CHARCOAL STOVE (SRI LANKA)

Description
The stove is comprised of three pottery pieces – the stove body, the grate, and a tray underneath to collect the ash. The stove is 17cm high and 24cm wide, and weighs 3kg. It can hold up to 400g of charcoal and burns about 250g per hour. The power output cannot be controlled. The stove will last six to twelve months in heavy use but the grate will only last three to six months before it must be replaced. The production cost is US$0.60.

History and field experience
Before 1980 charcoal was not used as a domestic fuel in Sri Lanka. In that year the government requested the Ceylon Institute of Scientific and Industrial Research (CISIR) to design a simple charcoal stove in order to utilize charcoal made available from a land clearance scheme and to replace the use of stoves requiring imported kerosene. Since 1980 over 30,000 stoves have been sold in private shops in major towns with the State Timber Corporation as wholesaler (hence the name 'Timco'). Cooking with charcoal is more expensive than wood but cheaper than all other options. Most of the charcoal stoves are used for only part of cooking needs, and have not totally replaced other types of stoves.

Construction, installation and maintenance
The stove is made and fired by traditional potters using traditional techniques. The stove is portable when it is cold and any piece can be replaced.

Use of the stove
Kerosene or kindling is used to light the charcoal. Once lit there is no power output control. The stove has no handles, gets very hot during use, and is difficult to move.

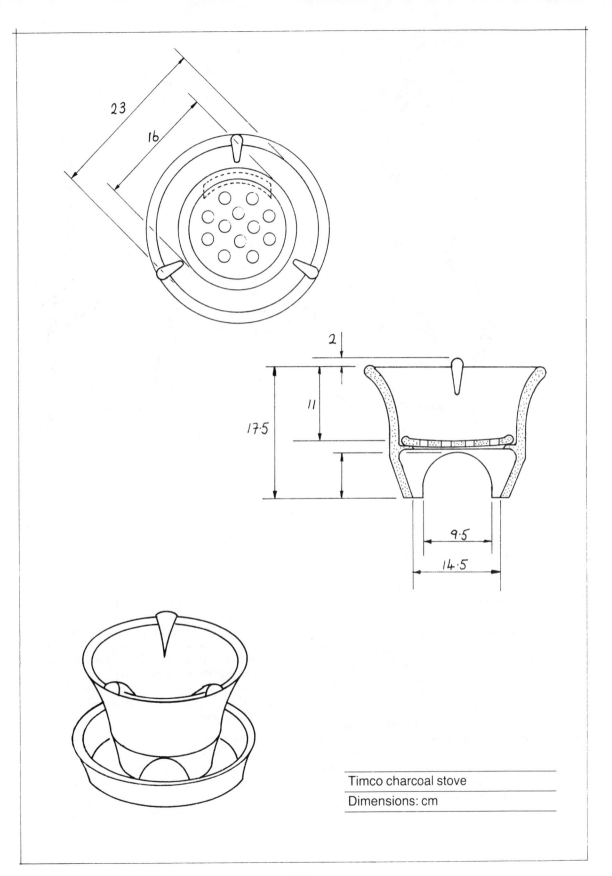

2

23

16

17·5

11

9·5

14·5

Timco charcoal stove

Dimensions: cm

24. KENYAN CERAMIC JIKO (KCJ)

Description

A pottery liner and a pottery or metal grate are held in a metal cladding with a wide top and a wide base (for stability) by a thin mix of cement and vermiculite. Metal pot supports are attached to the metal cladding and a door controls air intake through the primary air entrance. The standard model weighs about 6kg.

History and field experience

This stove is the result of the adaptation of the traditional ceramic charcoal stoves of Thailand to Kenyan conditions. In 1982 three Kenyans went to Thailand to study the stove industry. Upon their return they began to work in the informal and formal manufacturing sectors to produce similar stoves. The bell-bottom design was developed by Maxwell Kinyanjui to simplify construction, improve stability when pots were stirred vigorously, and to increase consumer appeal.

By the end of 1985, the KCJ was the subject of a dissemination programme funded by ATI, who estimated that by that time, some 150,000 stoves had been sold, the vast majority in Nairobi, where KCJs now account for probably 50% of stove production.

Construction, installation and maintenance

The pottery liner is made from a clay/rice-husk ash mix which is formed in a mould. The grates can be made from metal or pottery. The metal claddings are made by traditional metal workers mainly using oil barrel steel. The fired liners are placed in the metal claddings with a thin layer of cement/vermiculite to hold the liner in position. The stoves are portable and the grate can be replaced. When the liner cracks it must usually be replaced.

Use of the stove

The charcoal is lit with kindling or kerosene. When the stove is hot it can be run at full power with the door open, or half power with the door shut. The retained heat in the pottery liner allows long simmering with relatively small recharges of charcoal.

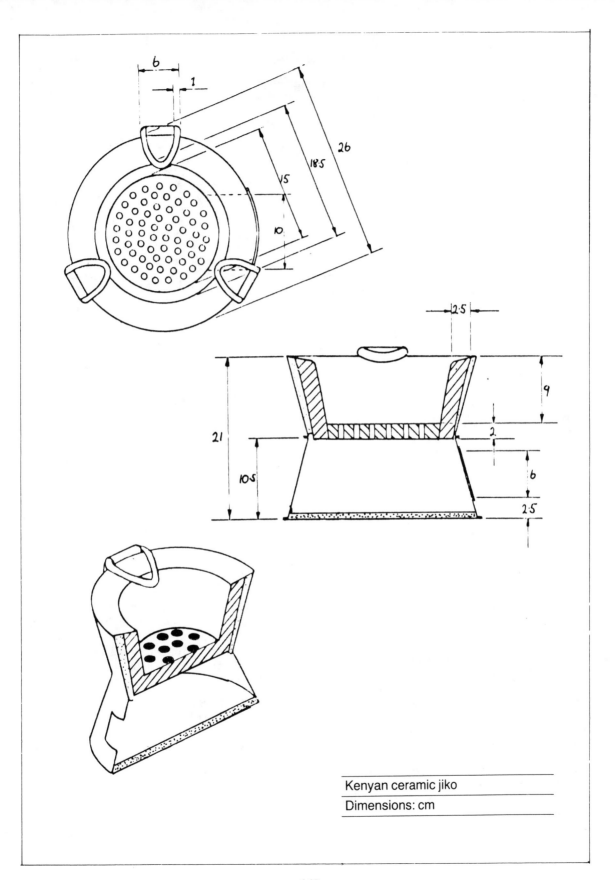

Kenyan ceramic jiko

Dimensions: cm

25. CEMENT/VERMICULITE-LINED STOVE (KENYA)

Description

A mixture of cement and vermiculite (1:3 by volume) and water is used to line a traditional metal stove with a maximum thickness of 4cm throughout, or on the top half only. A door on the primary air entrance allows the power output to be controlled.

History and field experience

The stove was designed and made in Kenya in 1982, based on an original idea from Papua New Guinea. A few thousand stoves were produced, principally by metal workers who put the lining into the stoves they already made, but by 1984 it was reported that production had dropped dramatically because the lifetime of the lining was only a few months.

Construction, installation and maintenance

A mould, usually a plastic bucket, which is the desired shape of the firebox, is placed inside a traditional metal stove. The prepared cement/vermiculite mix is packed into the space between the mould and the outer metal shell. The lining is kept moist for three days to develop strength. The grate is placed in the stove, and it is then ready for use.

The intense heat weakens the cement, and cracking starts in the lining. Rough handling rapidly increases the deterioration. The replacement of half the cement by refractory plaster significantly increases the thermal strength, but the weight and cost also rise.

Use of the stove

The stove is lit with kindling or kerosene. It heats up quickly, can operate at high and medium power outputs with a full charge, or be used for long simmering with small amounts of charcoal because of the insulated firebox.

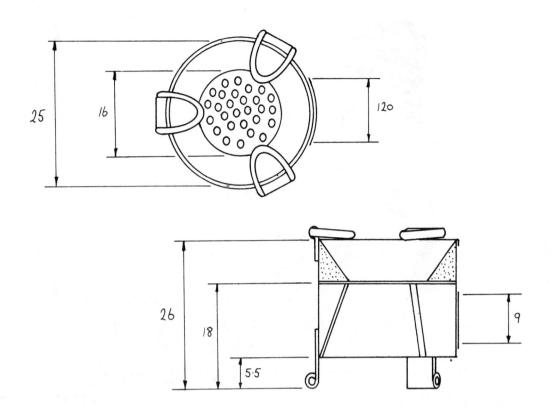

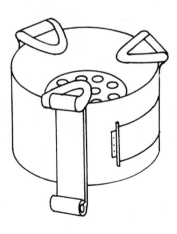

Cement/vermiculite-lined stove

Dimensions: cm

26. RAJAMUNDRY CAST-IRON CHARCOAL STOVE (INDIA)

Description
This small cast-iron stove is made at the Rajamundry Iron Works in Andhra Pradesh and is sold throughout India. The stove is made of 5mm-thick cast iron with a removable grate, weighing 2.8kg and costing US$3.50 (1983).

History and field experience
Charcoal is a relatively minor domestic fuel in India and is used primarily by tea-shops, restaurants and commercial users. Charcoal stoves are mainly used for preparing hot water and grilling. They are made from a wide variety of materials including steel, pottery and cement, but cast-iron is the longest lasting material. The stoves are now available in markets throughout much of India.

Construction, installation and maintenance
The stoves are made in a large cast-iron foundry, but the moulds used are relatively simple. The stoves are used without an insulation layer (see drawing), but as can be seen from the table of results (page 154) insulation significantly improved the performance. The ash is cleaned out of the pit below the firebox. Replacement grates can be purchased.

Use of the stove
The charcoal is lit with kerosene or kindling. The charcoal burns slowly until the cast-iron walls heat up, and then burns much more rapidly. Only 150–200g of charcoal can be placed in the firebox. There is no door to control the air flow and power output.

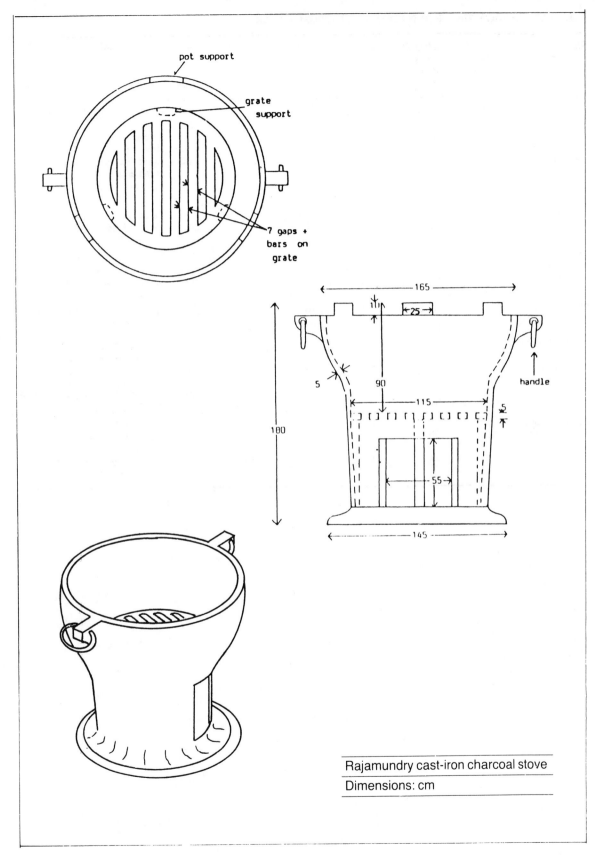

pot support

grate
support

7 gaps +
bars on
grate

165

25

90

115

5

5

180

55

145

handle

Rajamundry cast-iron charcoal stove

Dimensions: cm

Table 8.1: Comparative test results for charcoal stoves

Stove	No. of tests	Efficiency (PHU)	Power output (kW)	Time to boil 2l water (mins)	Charcoal used (g)	Evaporation rate (g/min)	Source – and comments
22. Royal Thai Forestry Dept. charcoal stove	N/A	32–34	3.2				RTFD prototype. 400g original charge. Very high power output
	4	23					Low efficiency for commercial stoves
	>100	27					Average efficiency for commercial stoves
	4	30					Highest efficiency for commercial stoves
23. Timco charcoal stove	10	30					De Silva (1980) in Sri Lanka
	2	35.0		15		20	Stewart (1984) in UK
24. Kenya ceramic Jiko	4	32	2.5	16	234	22	Stewart (1983). Primary air door OPEN during simmer
	4	28	1.8	16	176	12	Stewart (1983). Primary air door CLOSED during simmer
25. Cement/ vermiculite-lined stove: (half-lined)	4	34.3	2.3	16	219	23	Stewart (1983). Primary air door OPEN during simmer
	4	28.3	1.6	16	156	9	Stewart (1983). Primary air door CLOSED during simmer
(fully-lined)	4	30.5	2.3	15	556	19	Stewart (1983). Primary air door OPEN during simmer
	4	28.5	1.9	15	383	13	Stewart (1983). Primary air door CLOSED during simmer
26. Rajamundry cast-iron stove	2	32.0	1.3	31	161	11	Stewart (1984) as purchased
	2	39.7	1.5	23	167	18	Stewart (1984) with 1.5cm ceramic blanket insulation
	2	44.4	1.6	21	166	21	Stewart (1984) with 5cm glass wool insulation

PART III

GREAT TREES FROM LITTLE SEEDLINGS . . .

Once a design has been tested and tried out in a number of homes, maybe 50, maybe 500, a picture will have emerged as to whether the stove is really popular *and* does genuinely save fuelwood. If it isn't or if it doesn't then you should proceed no further, but go back to the beginning and redesign the stove.

If, however, the stove does appear to be successful, then the pressure will be on to get it more widely used in the area of operation. It is at this stage that many stove projects flounder because the practitioner lacks the skills to expand the project, and the resources are not usually made available to assist until the programme has successfully achieved a higher profile.

Training is probably the most important consideration when trying to expand a project beyond its own workshops, or outside the special relationship a practitioner might have built up with one or two artisans or a group of villagers. As projects expand so practitioners will need to train groups of artisans and villagers on a less intensive basis, and as the programme develops still further, the need for training of trainers will grow.

As projects emerge from the protected environment of subsidized workshops and free materials and transport into the real world of people allocating their scarce resources of time and money to a range of activities and products, so there will be a need to check that the stove being promoted is really affordable (in time or money) by the people it is aimed at. In the case of manufactured stoves, it must be clear that the device is attractive enough to artisans in terms of the income it could generate.

Getting people to buy or build the stove can still be a major problem even if the economics look right, and marketing is an area often overlooked in stoves projects. Most successful stove projects have had an active marketing element in terms of getting the product to the people, as well as getting the people to want the product.

Finally, we examine different production methods that have been tried around the world, both in ceramics and metal and, more briefly, in other materials. Chapter 12 aims to provide useful hints and pointers for practitioners seeking to adapt and improve existing production skills.

This part does not seek to make the stove practitioner into an expert trainer, economist, marketing specialist or production engineer. The aim rather is to provide practitioners with sufficient knowledge and confidence to carry out these tasks when, as is so often the case, specialists are not available.

CHAPTER 9
Training

As a stove practitioner you will, almost certainly, find yourself training others in various aspects of stoves work. Training is a skill in itself. This chapter does not attempt to make you an 'expert' in training but it does attempt, within the context of stove programmes, to identify the various target groups, types of training and training methodologies that have proved successful in stove programmes, and potential pitfalls. It is hoped that the contents of this chapter will help to enable stove practitioners to acquire enough knowledge and confidence to plan and implement a training programme within their own stove projects.

What is training?

– Training is the transfer of skills from one person, the trainer, to another, the trainee.

– Training is usually a significant proportion of any stove programme.

– Training can be an important vehicle for the expansion of a stove programme.

– Training can be a simple effective process if well planned and implemented.

Planning a training programme should be a continuous process, involving:

– identifying training needs
– planning of the overall project training programme
– planning training courses/sessions
– implementing training courses/sessions
– evaluating the effectiveness of the course/ programme
– modifying objectives, replanning programme/ courses based on results of evaluation.

Identifying training needs

From the overall objectives and programmed activities of a stove project it should be possible to identify training needs; that is, to identify where and when additional skills will be needed in order to achieve those objectives.

For example

If the stove project objectives state that a certain number of stoves are to be disseminated and monitored in a certain region within a two-year period, clearly these stoves must be built by people skilled in this activity, who may need training. If stove production is to be effectively monitored, a number of fieldworkers/extension workers will be needed. If there is a change in cooking habits or stove operation, perhaps the stove users will require training. It should be possible to identify how many people need training and whether the project has the capacity to do this, or whether more skilled trainers are needed.

In this process you will also need to identify the target groups, i.e. the type of people to train. Possible target groups include:

- Home builders/users
  Training in building, using and maintaining the stoves
- Artisan potters/trainee potters
  Training in building stoves and how and why the stove works
- Artisan metal workers/trainee metal workers
  Training in building stoves and how and why the stove works
- Stove users
  Training in using and maintaining stoves
- Extension workers/trainee trainers
  Training techniques, building stoves.

Training would usually take one of the following forms:

- one-to-one/counterpart – long term
- one-to-one on the job – short term
- informal group training – one or more sessions held in villages etc.
- formal courses – one or more sessions held at training centres.

Many of the techniques and pitfalls are common to all forms of training. However, this chapter aims to cover primarily informal group training which is often the most appropriate for stoves programmes.

Choosing trainees

The criteria for choosing trainees differ for different target groups. However, it it important to identify trainees who are enthusiastic, capable of undertaking the training, capable of fulfilling the role envisaged for them on completion of the training course, and who are likely to remain with the project for a reaonable period.

For example
User builders – usually if potential users are sufficiently enthusiastic to undertake training they will be able to fulfil their role, returning home to build and use a stove.

When identifying the target group, be aware of any local taboos against certain groups building with mud etc.

Commercial builders – when identifying artisans for training, it is useful to understand their existing businesses, who does which tasks within a group of

artisans, what the profit margins on existing work are, how and where raw materials are obtained, what is the existing marketing structure for products, what are the existing products, do they involve similar raw materials/skills etc. This information should have been gathered during the initial situation assessment (see Chapter 1).
It should be noted that many artisans have seasonal work in their trade, and that training will have to fit in with these seasons. Artisans cannot be trained either when they are working flat out or when they are away working in the fields at harvest time.

If the project plans to train artisans (potters, metal workers, masons) to build stoves, it is advisable when possible to work with artisans who already have relevant skills that can be built on. If the stove design replaces an existing stove already being built by those artisans, these are fairly easily identified. However, if the 'improved' stoves do not replace an existing artisan-built stove, it will be necessary to work with artisans who have the time and resources to start a new product line. If existing skilled artisans are to do this, the stove will be competing with their current products, and unless the profit margin is sufficiently large, they may not be prepared to take the risks. Training in small business management may be helpful, or it may be necessary to consider recruiting trainee artisans and instructing them in the basic skills of the trade before training them to build the stoves. If this approach is adopted there may be more need for initial project support for the manufacturing process, for example by supplying materials, tooling, quality control and marketing.
For example
In a small river-side town in West Africa several metal workers had been trained to build an improved wood-burning stove design, and yet just one metal worker had produced a few stoves to sell. The problem was that the most profitable product for these artisans were nails for boat repair, and the potential earnings for a hard-working metal worker was of the order of $10 per day – and the stoves work would not pay this amount. Therefore the time, effort and resources put into training these people were effectively wasted because the objective had been to get stoves into the local market place for sale, but the wrong people had been selected.

TRAINEE TRAINERS
Group size: ideally 2–6. These are the most difficult trainees to identify. Here you will be looking for people with the qualities that enable them to teach others. It often helps to identify potential trainers within a group that you are teaching, for example, to build stoves. Some of the qualities that

trainers will need (this goes for you too) are:
- a desire to be an instructor
- the necessary technical skills
- patience, not 'bossiness'
- enthusiasm, hard work
- possibly some literacy
- a willingness to learn
- likeability, an easy-going nature
- acceptability to the future target groups, i.e. sex, language, age, reputation etc.
- pride in their skill.

These people will also need the time, resources, and motivation to be trainers. This usually means that this should be their job (or part thereof) and they should therefore be or become employed by the project, or other interested parties, in this capacity.

TRAINEE GROUPS

Groups sizes: ideally 4–6, not more than 8. When artisans are busy working, training may have to be carried out on a one-to-one basis at their place of work.

The planning and implementation of training sessions is simplified if the groups are chosen such that trainees have similar levels of:
- existing skills
- experience (although some variation in experience can be useful)
- literacy/education
- motivation
- social status.

Mixed sex groups can sometimes be disadvantageous for women.

For example

If you are planning to teach a group of village women to build their own stoves, and several local teachers from a nearby school ask to join the training, you might well find that one group completely dominates the sessions to the detriment of the other; it is usually more productive to run two separate courses for such groups.

THE TRAINING PROCESS

There are special techniques for training of manual or technical skills such as those needed in stove making. Such training should have three main components:

Words   – spoken or written
Seeing   – demonstration, films or samples
Doing   – exercise or practice.

All three forms are needed for complete training, but in about the following proportions of training time:

Lectures   10%
Demonstration   20%
Exercise and practice   70%

Remember, practical skills such as stove-building are best learnt by doing not by watching and listening – this includes the training of trainers, who obviously need to possess the skills they are to teach as well as needing practical training in how to transfer those skills.

An ideal instructor/trainer needs the following qualities. He or she must be:
- a complete master of the work to be taught
- confident with no doubts about how to do the job
- polite, but firm about discipline
- patient and sympathetic with trainees' problems
- impartial with trainees
- enthusiastic and keen on the job.

THE LEARNING PROCESS

There are four basic points to keep in mind:
- Try to think in terms of the learning process and the trainee, not the training process and the instructor, e.g. the easiest method of giving out information is by lectures, but the most effective way of learning is by practice.
- Training is not the same as education and does not use the same methodology – the role of education is to transmit knowledge and to develop the capacity to think – training's job is to transmit the ability to do a job well.
- The result of a training course should be that the trainees go back and do their work better than they did before, or do work they could not do before – not just that they have learnt something, or know how to do the job, or enjoyed the course. Otherwise you have failed, wasted your time (and theirs) and the organization's money.
- Remember that, although you are training people in particular skills, they will 'pick up' many other things from the course – tidiness, respect for tools, pride in skills, politeness and respect for people with different backgrounds, honesty in admitting mistakes, enthusiasm, time-keeping and discipline, etc.

From the trainee to the trainer:
If you tell me, I'll forget
If you show me, I'll remember
If I do it, I'll learn.

Course planning

It is important to identify what you want the course to achieve, that is, to set the course objectives. The course can then be divided into one or more sessions, and each of these should:
- have a specific objective
- be programmed to take place at a time convenient to all the trainees
- be planned to take place at a location conve-

nient for all the trainees, but with a minimum of distractions
- have a basic written timetable (the '10% lecture, 20% demonstration, 70% practical work' format given above is often suitable)
- incorporate a very simple task for the first hands-on practical work. This builds confidence
- make use of teaching techniques familiar to the group when possible
- incorporate a method of session evaluation, i.e. have session objectives been achieved?
- incorporate the planning of any future follow-up activities with the participation of the trainees.

At the start of the course, discuss with the trainees what you propose to do on the course, ask about their skills and experience if necessary and modify the programme to suit their needs. After the first practical session, re-evaluate their skill levels to see if you are expecting too much.

For example:

In a course for training metal workers to produce metal stoves, one of the sessions planned was to teach the use of templates in order to produce accurate stove components. The session plan was designed as follows:

Session III: Use of templates

Objectives: that the trainees should demonstrate
        – an understanding of the need for accuracy
        – the ability to use the templates properly
        – the ability to produce accurate stove components

Date:
Location:
Duration: 3 hours
Trainer:
Trainees:

Subject	Activity	Time	Tools and materials
Importance of accuracy in stove production	talk demonstration practical	5 min. 10 min. 40 min.	examples
Use of templates to produce components	talk demonstration practical	10 min. 20 min. 60 min.	templates chisels anvil scribers rulers hammers
Question	trainees' questions	10 min.	
Evaluation	comments	10 min.	
Plan follow up visits		10 min.	
Clear up		5 min.	broom water

Figure 9.1.

TRAINING MATERIALS AND TOOLS

All the technical activities should be tried and tested before the session. Training materials and tools should be prepared well in advance. Training materials should be clear and concise, preferably in a format familiar to the trainees. For example, cartoons are only a suitable form of training material if used in an area where people are used to them. Technical drawings are only applicable when working with technicians trained to understand such material. Training materials should, when possible, be tested in advance; written instructions should be worked through step-by-step to check that they are correct and easy to follow; diagrams or cartoons should be presented to people (within the target group) who should then be asked what they understand them to represent. Do not try out new materials or techniques on a course, without adequate practice beforehand. Make sure that enough tools and materials are ready for the practical work – with a course of 6–8 this may mean working in pairs on two different exercises at the same time.

All tools and equipment to be used during training should be readily available to the trainees after the training. Either the trainees should use their own tools and equipment, or the items used on the course should be given or sold to trainees afterwards. For example, when teaching mud-stove construction to village women, do not use an unfamiliar, unavailable ruler to measure, but use hand measurements – or find a household article that will serve as a measure. For example, a plastic ballpoint pen is often used in Mali to measure the firebox height and the gap around the pot for the 'Trois pierres ameliorés' stove (a version of the Louga).

EVALUATION AND FOLLOW-UP

Evaluation should be a continuous process throughout the project. Evaluation of training can be done at several levels:

Training session/course evaluation
- did the session achieve its objectives, i.e. were all the trainees able to demonstrate that they had learnt the skill being taught?

Training programme evaluation
- is the programme achieving its objectives, i.e. on return to work do the trained personnel perform better than before, or do work they were unable to undertake before, and is the work advancing the project?

The session/course evaluation can be done at the

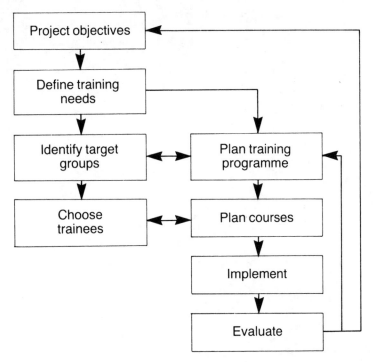

Figure 9.2

end of each session of the course either from the results of the practical work or by setting an informal test. At this stage, it is often valuable to ask the trainees to comment on the course's content and implementation (which sessions or activities they found most useful or enjoyable, which sessions they found least useful, whether they have any suggestions for future courses, etc.)

In order to evaluate the training programme, it is essential to carry out a follow-up exercise, that is, to visit the trained personnel in the field after a suitable period of time and assess the effect of the training course on their work. Follow-up can also be a useful method of re-motivating people and assessing if any further training could be useful. Be ready to spend several hours with each trainee in their workshop to see their problems, to complete their training and to improve future courses.

It is important that the evaluations and follow-up are providing continuous feedback into the planning of future training sessions and courses to enable continuous improvement to the training process (Figure 9.2).

CHAPTER 10

Will the stove pay?

Some simple tools for finding out

For all stoves it is important to work out whether the stove will 'pay'; that is, will the benefits people get out of the stove more than compensate for the costs in money, time or effort spent in acquiring it. Any stove that is *perceived* not to be 'worth it' will not catch on, and as soon as subsidies are removed it will disappear without trace.

Perceptions are all-important here. While we may be able to show in a laboratory that a stove can save fuel or time or reduce smoke in the kitchen, it is people's perceptions of these savings that will determine their willingness to purchase or install one and to recommend it to their friends. For example, a saving of 20% of fuelwood might be perceived as no saving at all, while in some programmes savings of 30% have been perceived as substantial.

SELF-BUILT STOVES

If stoves are entirely self-built and require no spending of money at all, the main consideration for people will be whether they can spare the time to build their own stoves. Wealthier people will tend to pay other people to construct for them, so it is important to assess the time availability of poorer people both to build their own and to build stoves for others who are wealthier.

It is likely that people will only be able to carry out the work at slack times of the year when there is no planting, weeding or harvesting to be carried out. 'Slack time' is a misnomer; even at the slackest times, women – who are likely to be the principal stove builders – have many tasks to carry out: firewood collection, carrying water, preparing and cooking food, caring for the family, off-farm income-generating activities, etc.

For people to allocate their precious time to learn how to build and use an improved stove, to fetch the right materials and to actually build it, let alone use it in practice, they must be convinced that the stove yields genuine benefits. These benefits are likely to be of a non-monetary nature. The most likely perceived benefit will be in time-saving, collecting firewood and, possibly, in reduced cooking times. Health and safety aspects may also be considered important.

There is no way you can measure and quantify the perceived costs and benefits of self-built stoves effectively. Some attempts have been made to calculate the time spent carrying wood before and after the introduction of an improved stove, but fuel collection is often so complex as to defy measurement. Different people collect wood at different times; families share wood resources; children's bundles vary widely in weight and quality.

What is important is to talk to people – and to ask those not directly connected with the project to talk to people – about their perceptions of the stove. Enthusiasm will be reflected by the appearance of the stove: is it used often, is it well-maintained? The more popular the stove is, the more likely it is to succeed in spreading.

If people do not attend your training sessions despite the above, do not immediately assume that the stove is unpopular. Examine other possibilities first: is the training at the wrong time of the year – are people too busy; is your advertising of the course wrong – are people aware the training was to take place; are people aware of the improved stove; is the training itself wrong – are men running the course, putting women off; or is the training in a place where women cannot get to easily?

COMMERCIAL STOVES

By commercial stoves, we mean any stoves where people have to spend some money; where something has to be manufactured and someone has to buy it. This includes self-built stoves where the stove is built around a ceramic liner to standardize internal dimensions.

With any commercial stove there is an automatic conflict of interest between the consumer – who wants the stove as cheaply as possible – and the producer – who wants to make as much money as possible. It is essential that any stove can satisfy the interest of both these groups; otherwise it will never take off in large numbers, without at least some form of subsidy.

COMMERCIAL STOVES FROM THE CONSUMER'S PERSPECTIVE

Any stove project will have amassed a wealth of information about consumers' perceptions of the stove during the pilot phase. What may not have become so clear is whether a stove is affordable, by whom, and more importantly how much consumers are prepared to pay.

This information can be unclear for a number of

reasons. Many projects hand out stoves initially for free or at very subsidized prices. Hidden subsidies can continue for much longer: producers are often helped with free transport for raw materials and the finished stoves; early stoves are often produced in project workshops where producers do not face any overhead costs.

Subsidies can be very dangerous. If a stove is well designed (and by that we mean from the consumer's point of view) subsidies should not be necessary, because the stove should have been designed to be affordable by, usable by and relevant to the needs of the consumers.

In normal market activities new products start expensive and become cheaper as they take off. Higher prices help to establish a product's credentials ('it must be good – look at the price!') and help to recompense those producers who took the initial risks. Furthermore, it is better that wealthy consumers take the risks first in trying out a new stove as they can afford to do so. Special offers and other marketing ploys can help with the promotion of the stove, but not subsidies.

With subsidies, the stove appears cheap and is adopted – still, most likely, by wealthier people. Then, as always happens, subsidies will be withdrawn because the project cannot afford them any more. The price rockets up, removing the stove from the reach of poorer people and killing the market stone dead as the wealthier already have the improved stove at the subsidized price.

It is important, therefore, that before moving to a broader programme of stove dissemination you have a clear idea of what the stove costs to produce (see the next section) and what consumers are prepared to pay. There are two useful tools you can use to see whether it is likely that consumers will pay for the stove.

a) Payback period

This tool is only really useful when people are paying for their fuel. This is normally in urban areas but increasingly now people are paying for their fuel in rural areas too. Various economists have tried to put a price on fuel which was collected free, but never with any real success. What is important when wood is free is the people's own perceptions of the stove's benefits, not those of an economist. It is unlikely, when wood is free, that poor people already with very stretched resources will pay more than a very little for their stove.

When woodfuel (wood or charcoal) is purchased on a widespread basis, it is fairly easy to calculate a payback period. Firstly you need the market price of the fuel in question. Never rely on government official prices – they are seldom adhered to. Do not ask people yourself if you are visibly 'an official' or someone not from the area: sellers will tell you less

than they really get if you are perceived as an official, or more than the market price if you look like a stranger who does not know the prices; buyers will either way tend to exaggerate the price they paid. You must rely on local contacts to find out the local prices – and not local prices per bag but per unit in which people usually buy the fuel, which may be a bag or margarine tin or such like. These fuel costs tend to be much higher than bag prices.

Secondly, you need to estimate what the minimum price of the stove will be, that is, the minimum price that producers would be prepared to accept to produce the stove (see the next section).

Thirdly, you need to know how much fuel the improved stove will actually save. These are not laboratory savings but genuine savings identified during your field tests – savings you can be confident will be made in practice. These savings should be measured in terms of fuel used per time-period (day, week, month) for a traditional stove less fuel used for an improved stove over the same length of time.

There are then two payback periods you can calculate: for a new investment and for a replacement. The payback period for a new investment is:

$$\frac{C_i}{S_f}$$ where C_i = cost of the improved stove
S_f = fuel savings over a given time period.

The answer will be in units of time the same as the time-period of the fuel savings.

The payback period for a replacement investment (that is when a new stove is purchased when the old stove has worn out and needs replacing anyway) is:

$$\frac{C_i - C_T}{S_f}$$ where C_T =– cost of traditional stove

What use is the payback period? In many countries, especially in urban areas, people receive their income on a monthly basis – even the unemployed will receive money from employed relatives on a similar basis. Especially amongst poorer people, there is likely to be little saving and thus it becomes vital that a stove should have a payback period of a month – or certainly little more than that. Wealthier people may have savings and short payback periods may be less important. If people are paid on a weekly or fortnightly basis, payback periods may have to be even shorter. A long payback period indicates that the stove will not be purchased by the mass of poorer people.

Even in rural areas, payback periods can be useful if people are buying their fuel. Incomes in rural areas tend to vary with seasons rather than months and there may be surplus cash only once or twice a year after harvest. If people can see that the new stove will pay for itself within that period of relative affluence, people will be more enthusiastic about purchasing the stove. In Thailand, for example, some 90% of all household purchases are made from December to May when the harvest is in.

One thing to beware of – poorer people often buy fuel in very small quantities which can be very much more expensive than buying larger amounts. This can have the effect of making payback periods much shorter, and therefore the stove financially very attractive. You must remember, however, that if people cannot afford larger quantities of fuel it is unlikely they can afford the capital cost of an improved stove except at very specific times of the year.

b) Kitchen investment levels

When carrying out your field trials, it is worth gathering together information about the sort of domestic items people have in their houses, how much they cost, and how often they are replaced. This will give you some idea of the amount of money people have to invest in their kitchens, and the priority the kitchen is given in household budgets. The sort of items include existing stoves, pots and pans, washing bowls, water jars and kerosene lamps.

Try and work out these kitchen investment levels for people of different incomes. Sometimes, there are national statistics which can guide you in this. If not, try and grade people by subjective criteria and by using local contacts.

You can then work out – very roughly – how much different groups of people can or do spend on their kitchens over a year.

For poorer groups, especially, it will be hard to increase investment in the kitchen substantially or to save money to buy a stove. Thus a stove needs to be of a similar price to, or below that of, the most expensive utensil currently purchased regularly (i.e. at least once a year), and must cost less than annual expenditure on kitchen items.

Wealthier groups, with access to savings, may not be worried about this. However, in most countries, wealthier groups are only a small minority and catering for their market only will not significantly affect fuelwood use. Example 1 shows how payback period and kitchen investment levels can be worked out in practice.

COMMERCIAL STOVES FROM THE PRODUCER'S PERSPECTIVE

Production of stoves can be carried out in a variety of different ways. Many projects start off by making stoves in their own small workshop. This is fine at the very early stages, but once you have a design which appears to have potential for adoption, you should think very carefully about becoming directly involved in more serious production.

Existing producers will always be in a better position to exploit the potential market. The stove project should be there to stimulate those producers and the markets and to bear the risks during the initial start-up phase. Stove projects, therefore, need to provide:

– training
– marketing
– production advice and quality control
– finance, if banks are unwilling to invest.

Who are these 'existing producers'? Where a new stove is replacing an existing one (especially true for charcoal stoves), the answer is obvious: the producers of the existing item.

Where no stove is currently being manufactured, you should examine producers of similar items and involve them in the production of improved stoves. Thus, potters making water jars may be persuaded to make ceramic stove liners, while metal-working artisans making cooking pots might be best placed to make metal stoves.

Producers come in all shapes and sizes, but for the purposes of this exercise, we shall divide them into two groups: informal and formal producers. The difference between the two is hard to define precisely but an attempt is made in Table 10.1. Basically, informal-sector businesses operate outside the legal framework of a particular country: they do not pay taxes and they do not recognize minimum wage, health and safety or employment laws. They are not registered and seldom have legal title to the land on which they operate. Their potential for expansion is severely limited: they have little access to credit, capital accumulation is very difficult because they have no security and informal entrepreneurs have a fear of growing anyway, because they might become too visible to the authorities. They do have their advantages, however: their setting-up costs are minimal, their flexibility of production is great as long as risks are minimized, and their productivity can be remarkably high. Furthermore, they often make use of resources not available so readily to formal sector businesses – such as scrap metal – and can make products much more cheaply in certain cases than can their formal-sector counterparts. The informal sector is thriving in many countries; while individual businesses have little potential for expansion, there is great potential for new people to enter this sector and expand employment opportunities much more rapidly than in the formal sector.

All these businesses, whether formal or informal, are effectively commercial concerns and share certain similarities.

a) Any product must earn enough to cover all

Table 10.1: Differences between formal and informal businesses

	Informal	Formal
Title to land	No	Yes
Registered business	No	Yes
Adheres to business laws	No	Probably
Access to credit	No	Yes
Formal employment contracts	No	Probably
Ability to take risks	Nil	Varies with size
Capital accumulation	Very low	Varies with size
Size	Small	Varies

expenses and to pay back any loans used to finance the assets necessary to make it.

b) Any new product will only be taken on if it does not conflict with existing more (or equally) profitable activities.

c) Commercial businesses are unlikely to take risks until a market has been established. This is especially true in the informal sector where capital funds are in very short supply.

The tools needed to assess whether production will be attractive to these different businesses will vary considerably. Obviously, a formal-sector business in the urban areas will have many more options for investment and the investor will thus be interested in having an accurate rate-of-return estimate to compare with other options. An informal-sector artisan may be interested simply in being paid the right amount for the time taken, and be more concerned with receiving firm orders than with longer term profitability. Rural women's groups will most likely want a level of income to enable them to purchase certain commodities (school fees, clothes, etc.) which are currently beyond their means.

TOOLS FOR APPRAISING PRODUCTION OPTIONS

The following tools will have application for particular forms of business, although they will need some adaptation to individual circumstances.

a) Production economics

For a formal-sector business most costs of production and distribution are measurable: raw materials, wages, rents, service charges and transport costs are all fixed or have market rates. Thus a fairly accurate estimate of profitability can be made at different prices and levels of output. This is not possible in the informal sector where costs tend to be fluid, uncontrolled and very adaptable to individual circumstances.

An example of formal-sector production economics is given in example 2. This is taken from a stove manufacturing unit in Sri Lanka. Costs are in Sri Lankan Rupees.

All costs can be divided into three types:

(a) Variable Costs: Costs which vary directly with production. Such costs include raw materials, direct processing costs, direct transport costs and labour paid on a piecework basis.

(b) Semi-variable Costs: Costs which are fixed over a limited range of output but are variable over a large range or over a long period of time. Such costs include wage labour, salaries, some transport costs and repairs and maintenance.

(c) Fixed Costs or Overheads: Costs which have to be met by the business whatever the level of output. Such costs include rent, lighting, sewerage, depreciation, non-direct transport costs, and bank interest.

In the example, all semi-variable costs have been treated as fixed costs (overheads) since the output range is not varied too much. It should be noted that the longer the time frame, the more variable all costs become. In the very long term, all costs are variable.

Variable costs are effectively equivalent to the extra money you will have to spend to produce one extra unit. Fixed costs will have to be paid come what may.

The 'contribution' of a stove, then, is how much money selling that extra stove will contribute towards overheads or fixed costs. The contribution of one unit, therefore, is the selling price less variable costs.

In this example, two production options are compared using a wheel or a mould for producing the ceramic liners. Annual sales are calculated by estimating how many stoves will be sold and multiplying by the selling price. Annual contributions are worked out by multiplying the number of stoves sold by the unit contribution.

Here you can see that the factory loses money whichever production method is chosen. The analysis tells you more, however. For the factory to break even using moulds, for example, it will need to earn contributions of R115,560 to pay for overheads. This will require the production and sale of 51,360 stoves (115,560 ÷ 2.25). This is called the breakeven point. Any production over 51,360 stoves will make a profit. The higher the overheads are as a proportion of costs, the higher the breakeven production level will be. On the whole, as well, the higher the overheads the riskier the business since if sales fail to reach targets, these costs still have to be met. The more capital-intensive the business the higher the overheads will tend to be.

b) Monthly Cash Flow Statement

An example taken from Kenya of a Monthly Cash Flow Statement is given in example 3. A Cash Flow Statement is quite simply that: it shows flows of cash in and out of the business on a monthly basis. Payments and receipts should be shown in the month when the money actually leaves or arrives at the business, not when the cost is incurred or the sale made. Costs like depreciation, which are only book entries, should be excluded totally.

Each month, then, will have an opening and closing balance. The balance will tend to get worse in the early months until the business is making a profit, when it will start to improve. The worst negative balance is equivalent to the minimum finance necessary for the business to survive this critical starting period. Thus in this example Sh224,236 are needed as an absolute minimum of finance to get the business going. In practice, the business should be looking to total credit in the region of Sh250,000 to be safe.

This Monthly Cash Flow Statement is essential to secure adequate financing for a formal-sector business.

c) Discounted Cash Flow (see example 4)

Discounted Cash Flow Statements use Annual Cash Flow Statements, which are exactly the same as Monthly Cash Flow Statements. For each year of the project cash outflows and inflows are recorded. Depreciation costs – and also bank loan interest and principal repayments – *must not* be included. Where machinery is replaced (as in Year 3 in the example) it should be shown at full cost. It should be noted that the setting up of the unit – before production begins – is shown in Year 0.

Each year then has either a net inflow or outflow of cash. Each year's cash flows are then discounted to the present using a discount rate which ideally should be the rate of return of the best alternative project available to the business or the rate of return currently being achieved by other projects of the business. In practice, the easiest discount rate to use is that currently being charged commercially by banks for term loans.

If the Net Present Value (NPV) is greater than zero (i.e. the sum of all future cash inflows discounted to the present is greater than the sum of all cash outflows similarly discounted) then we know at least that the project can pay back any loans required to set the business up, and leave a profit for the owner of the business. The IRR (Internal Rate of Return) is simply that discount rate which yields an NPV of zero. Therefore, if the IRR is greater than the discount rate, the project is worth going ahead with.

You can then vary the selling price to see what is the minimum selling price that still yields a positive NPV or an IRR equal to the bank's interest rate. If you have access to a computer these calculations are very simple. Spreadsheet packages like Lotus 123 provide you with NPV and IRR formulae to do the work for you.

If you have to do the calculations manually, the formula to use is:

$$NPV = NCF_0 + \frac{NCF_1}{1+i} + \frac{NCF_2}{(1+i)^2} + \frac{NCF_3}{(1+i)^3} \ldots \frac{NCF_n}{(1+i)^n}$$

Where NCF = Net Cash Flow in year $0, 1, 2, 3 \ldots n$
i = Interest rate (15% is written 0.15)

There is no formula for Internal Rates of Return. You simply change the interest rate in the above formula until $NPV = 0$. As a short cut, take an interest rate which yields a positive NPV and another which yields a negative NPV. The IRR can then be estimated as:

$$IRR = i_+ + \frac{NPV_+ \times (i_- - i_+)}{NPV_+ + NPV_-}$$

where i_+ = interest rate yielding position NPV
i_- = interest rate yielding negative NPV
NPV_+ = NPV value at interest rate i_+
NPV_- = absolute NPV value at interest rate i_-
That interest rate is then the approximate IRR.

d) Informal economics

All the above tools are fine for formal-sector businesses, but in the informal sector the ground rules are constantly changing. The circumstance in one village – the prices of raw materials, say, or the opportunities for paid employment – may be totally different from the one next door.

All we can do in this circumstance is to set parameters in terms of minima and maxima for costs and prices and indicate the sorts of incomes that people can expect to earn from working in this area, and whether it is likely to prove attractive, by considering other possibilities for production or employment.

The best thing to do is to look at what other products the business makes and how much it costs to make these in terms of labour time and material costs. You can then carry out the same exercise with an improved stove, and calculate a selling price that makes it attractive to the producer. Initially, this price will have to be more than equal to that of other products, to make it worthwhile to make the change and the investment in time and lost sales to learn how to make the new product.

From this you can then predict short-term and long-term prices for the improved stoves. Prices will tend to fall over time, to match the prices for other products as more producers start making the improved stoves and competition forces prices down.

You can also set parameters so that you can quickly assess whether a particular artisan or informal business is in a position to take on the new product, by setting a range of maximum costs for raw materials and labour and minimum prices for the finished product. Examples of such informal economics are given in examples 5 and 6.

Example 1. The consumer's perspective

RURAL STOVES IN SRI LANKA

ECONOMICS OF IMPROVED STOVES TO THE CONSUMER

1. Payback period

In many parts of rural Sri Lanka fuel is a free commodity. The most common fuel is wood from jungle areas, but around the coast substantial amounts of coconut husk and branch are burnt. In both cases, the household (usually women and children) collect sufficient fuel from their own land or from nearby jungle. The poorest tend to use lower-grade fuels (smaller branches, palm fronds, rice husks).

Where fuel is free it is difficult to cost and hence to calculate a payback period for a stove. The opportunity cost of labour used to collect fuel will be low for much of the year, except when there are labour shortages at times of planting and harvesting. There is, however, a growing market for fuel in the towns, and in Hambantota District we found women selling wood to passing trucks for R5 for a 10kg bundle. In Manikine in Kandy District, itinerant sellers sell wood for R20 a hundredweight or approximately R4 for a 10kg bundle. It can be said, then, that the opportunity cost of burning 10kg of wood is the loss of the sale of 10kg of wood – in other words R4–5. While this is not totally realistic (since households tend to use lower grade fuels for themselves and sell the higher quality wood) these figures can give a rough guide.

Current fuel usage for a family of 5–6 members is 30–60kg per week. At a cost of R5 per 10kg, weekly fuel expenditure amounts to R15–20 per week.

Just how much wood does the Sarvodaya stove save? There have been widely varying reports. Herath (1984) reported 9.3% savings in controlled cooking tests. Stewart (1983) reported that in field tests, savings of 25–33% were achieved. Abeyratne (pers. comm., 1985) suggests savings in the region of 50–60%, and our own conversations with stove owners suggest savings of up to 50%. For our calculations here, we shall assume savings of 30%.

At this level of fuel saving, weekly fuel expenditure drops to R10.50–21 per week, a saving of R4.50–9 per week. If the stove costs R30, then the payback period is 3–7 weeks.

2. Kitchen investment levels

In poor houses, the family may own 3–5 pots while a rich house would have cooking pots for each day plus others for special occasions and dishes, totalling ten or more. There are six standard pot sizes, ranging in price from R2.50 to R8 with an average price of R5. Each year every household buys at least one new pot to celebrate New Year.

Households also possess water jars costing approximately R10 each, at least one and sometimes as many as five. Other items include curd pots and aluminium washing bowls.

The total value of kitchen items, then, can vary from R25 to R150. Assuming a two-year life for most items this suggests an annual expenditure of R12 to R75 or R1 to R7 per month. Poorer groups may be able to spend less than R1 and wealthy groups may spend considerably more than R7. This appears to be confirmed by the findings of the Labour Force and Socio-Economic survey 1980/81, although kitchen items are not listed separately and we must assume that they form a proportion of

Table 10.2: Number of households and average expenditure on major items by expenditure groups, Sri Lankan, rural sector, 1980/81

Expenditure group (R/month)	No. households	Total expenditure	Monthly expenditure (R) Semi-durable goods	Consumer durables	Total
All groups	2,266,677	1,155.39	3.86	18.12	21.98
Less than 300	55,498	225.75	0.15	0.44	0.59
300– 500	185,666	413.86	0.56	0.24	0.80
500– 600	147,404	550.09	1.06	2.71	3.77
600– 800	401,488	699.62	1.23	2.40	3.63
800–1,000	375,522	896.79	2.12	4.78	6.90
1,000–1,500	626,736	1,221.03	3.38	11.64	15.02
1,500–2,000	261,905	1,705.98	6.65	23.64	30.29
2,000–3,000	157,458	2,360.99	12.10	52.55	64.65
More than 3,000	55,000	4,490.21	25.81	292.40	318.21

Source: Department of Census and Statistics, 1983

total semi-durable and durable household goods. Monthly expenditure by expenditure group is given in the table below.

What is clear is that expenditure of R30 per month on durables and semi-durables is only achieved by the very wealthiest (only 20.9% of all households). A R30 stove may therefore be beyond the reach of a large proportion of households. Where wood is currently not monetized, the stove would have to have major non-monetary attractions to justify the expense for the poorer half of the population.

The 'lumpiness' of rural incomes, however, means that an annual investment of R30 is likely to be accessible to over 80% of the rural population.

Example 2. Production economics

Rural stoves in Sri Lanka

Centralized stove factory (1)

	Wheel	Mould
Variable costs		
Clay (2)	.74	.74
Labour (3)	7.00	6.00
Firing (4)	3.40	3.40
Rejects (5)	.78	.71
Delivery (6)	1.90	1.90
TOTAL VARIABLE COST	13.82	12.75
SELLING PRICE	15.00	15.00
Contribution to overheads	1.18	2.25
Annual overheads		
Quality controller (7)	10,400	10,400
Supervisor (8)	19,500	19,500
Labour (9)	8,320	8,320
Management charge (10)	10,000	10,000
Factory overhead (11)	10,000	10,000
Depreciation (12)	21,500	29,500
Interest (13)	27,200	27,840
	106,920	115,560
Annual Sales (14)	300,000	300,000
Annual contribution	23,600	45,000
Net Profit (Loss)	(83,320)	(70,560)
Net Profit Percentage	Negative	Negative
Return on Capital	Negative	Negative

Notes

(1) All the costs are based on the Sumagi Tile Factory, Dankotua.

(2) Clay costs R120 per cube (100 cubic feet) at the mine site. Transport costs another R25 per cube to bring it to the factory gate.

The Sumagi pugmill – an ancient machine powered by a Massey Ferguson tractor – can process 3.66 cubes of clay per 8 hour shift. Operating costs per shift are:

10 gallons diesel at R36.96/gallon	369.60
2 pints oil at R90/gallon	22.50
Machine minder at R50/day	50.00
5 × labourers at R32/day	160.00
Total operating costs	602.10
Operating costs per cube	164.51
Plus: Cost of raw clay and transport	145.00
Marginal cost of processed clay per cube	309.51

No charge for depreciation or maintenance has been made, since it is assumed that these marginal costs are zero.

The Sarvodaya two-pot liner weighs 9.45kg wet. One cube of clay weighs 3983.61kg, which is enough for 421 stoves. The marginal cost of clay per stove is, therefore, R0.74.

(3) It is assumed here that all labour involved in stove-making will be paid piece rate. In practice, it is likely that they will be paid a basic wage plus bonus – ie. not a truly variable cost.

Wheel-working potters can currently earn up to R1,000 for a six-day week. In timing tests, it took an experienced rural potter 20 minutes to make a stove. At speed, this could be reduced to 15 minutes. Thus a potter working 48 hours on stoves alone could manufacture 140 stoves, allowing for down-time, etc. A potter would thus expect payment of approximately R7 per stove to compete with existing earnings.

Moulding requires less skill and could be carried out by Sumagi employees currently earning R32 per day, or R192 per six-day week.

According to Laurie Childers (19—) these costs could be reduced somewhat (say, to R5 per stove) for thrown work. This is not enough, however, to make such a centralized unit profitable.

One worker could mould six stoves per day or 36 per week. At R6.00 per stove this gives earnings of R216 per week, which should prove attractive to these workers.

(4) The small kiln at Sumagi uses 16 cubic yards of firewood to fire 5,500 tiles to 850°C. The total weight of these tiles is 33,000 lbs fired. 200 stoves weigh 3,080 lbs fired, which, pro rata, should use 1.5 cubic yards of firewood. The different nature of stoves, and the extra space they occupy, suggest that 4 cubic yards would be needed per firing of 200 stoves.

Fuelwood costs R130/cu yd from the rubber plantations and a further R40/cu yd for transport. Total fuel cost per firing is, therefore, R680 or R3.40 per stove. No loading/ unloading charge is made since there is excess labour available for this at no marginal cost.

(5) Reject rate is estimated conservatively at 7% and is calculated at 7% of clay, labour and firing costs.

(6) Assumes average distance of delivery is 100 miles round-trip. A 5-tonne lorry carrying 500 stoves is used.

Ceylon Ceramics Corporation (CCC) charges R9.50 per running mile, which is comparable to urban commercial rates. This works out at R1.90 per stove.

(7) Quality controller would be a newly-qualified graduate with credits in chemistry and physics, hence the low pay.

(8) One supervisor is charged for. This may be more than is necessary and this cost would be reduced, or used to employ a more highly qualified person part-time.

(9) The labourer is employed in wedging, assisting with kiln loading and unloading and general tasks.

(10) Estimate. CCC charges at 21% on-cost, which would be over R50,000 but this is very high.

(11) Estimate. CCC charges at 19–20% of variable costs, which would be R30,000. This is very high for a private factory.

(12) Depreciation is charged as follows:

Item	Value	Depr. rate	Annual depr.
Building	85,000	10%	8,500
Kiln	60,000	20%	12,000
Sundries	5,000	20%	1,000
Moulds	8,000	100%	8,000
			29,500

Throwing stoves removes the need for moulds, and thus reduces depreciation to R21,500.

(13) Interest rates in Sri Lanka currently vary between 12 and 16% in the commercial sector. 16% is used here for conservatism, and interest is charged on:

	Wheel	Mould
Capital Costs	150,000	158,000
Working Capital	20,000	16,000
	170,000	174,000

(14) 20,000 stoves at R15 per stove.

Example 3: Monthly cash flow statement

Monthly cash flow statement for a centralized KCJ manufacturing unit – Kenya (Ksh)

Month	1	2	3	4	5	6	7	8	9	10	11	12
Capital Costs (1)	198000											
Overheads (2)	9880	9880	9880	9800	9800	9800	9800	9800	9800	9800	9800	9800
Variable Costs (3)		2684	5367	8051	10734	13418	16101	18785	21468	24152	26835	26835
Total Cash Outflows	207880	12564	15247	17931	20614	23298	25981	28665	31348	34032	36715	36715
Sales (4)		5000	10000	15000	20000	25000	30000	35000	40000	45000	50000	50000
Net Inflow/Outflow	(207880)	(7564)	(5247)	(2931)	(614)	1702	4019	6335	8652	10968	13285	13285
Opening Balance	0											
Closing Balance	(207880)	(215444)	(220691)	(223622)	(224236)	(222534)	(218515)	(212180)	(203528)	(192560)	(179275)	(165990)

(1) As for Riruta.
(2) As for Riruta, excluding Depreciation and Interest (85,239/– p.a.) and including Manager's salary and rent (34,000/– p.a.)
(3) Taken as 53.67% of sales.
(4) Assumes the same sales mix as for Riruta.

Example 4: Discounted cash flow

Urban stoves factory, Sri Lanka (R'000)

Year	0	1	2	3	4	5	6	7	8	9	10
Capital Costs	158	8	8	8	8	73	8	8	8	8	73
Variable Costs	—	75	150	150	150	150	150	150	150	150	150
Overheads		58	58	58	58	58	58	58	58	58	58
Total Cash Outflows	158	141	216	216	216	281	216	216	216	216	281
Sales		150	300	300	300	300	300	300	300	300	300
Net Inflow/Outflow	(158)	9	84	84	84	19	84	84	84	84	19

NPV: 137,654 (discounting at 16%)
IRR: 34.29%

Example 5. Informal economics

RURAL STOVES MANUFACTURE, SRI LANKA

These figures are based on the pottery businesses of Cyril Amitepale in Maniking village in Kandy District, Mr. V. P. Wijeysiri of Kirimagedere village in Hambantota District and of other potters in the same village.

1. Current income

The main alternative products which a rural potter could produce are cooking pots and flower pots.

Product	Price	Potential daily production per skilled worker	Potential daily income
Curd pots	1	40	40
Rice pots			
– small	2.5	20	50
– large	6*	15	90
Flower pots	4	20	80
Stoves	15	7	105

* R10 during New Year.

The former is a declining market while the latter is static or falling due to substitution of cement pots for ceramic. Thus any income comparison may not be realistic since the long-term choice facing rural potters may be stove production or unemployment.

Stove production is, therefore, attractive. However, it is likely that, during the New Year when rice pot prices rise, production of stoves will tail off and the potters will concentrate on these.

2. Operating costs

– In Hambantota, clay is free from the base of dried-out tanks. Transport costs vary depending on the distance from the tank. A tractor costs R150 for a large load of 110 balls of clay (one ball of clay being enough for three stoves). Clay, therefore, costs approximately R0.50 per stove.

– In Kandy, there are no tanks and Cyril Amitepale has to pay for his clay. A tractor load currently costs him R100 which is enough for 250 stoves. The tractor hire costs him a further R80. Clay, therefore, costs R0.72 per stove, although Cyril has to keep on changing sources and costs may vary.

– Labour is all family labour. Other potters sometimes help out but not on a formalized basis.

– Kiln loading and unloading is by the potters themselves. There is no opportunity cost since these activities are skilled and without them the pottery work would be worthless.

– Firing uses whatever local materials are available. Thus in hilly areas like Kandy, wood and sawdust tend to be used. On the coast, coconut husks and some coconut wood is used.

Cyril Amitepale uses R500 of firewood per month and R40 (transport only) of sawdust. This works out at R1.80 per stove at his current production level of 300 stoves per month. V. P. Wijeysiri uses 1,000 coconut husks per firing, costing R40 plus R40 transport. He also uses 10–12 pieces of coconut wood costing R10–12. (A coconut palm costs R40–50 and is enough for four firings.) Thus firing costs are R0.92 per stove at a kiln capacity of 100 stoves per firing.

– No other financial costs are incurred, since the property is rent-free and there are no power costs.

– An imputed cost needs to be calculated to cover the costs of replacement of capital items (namely the kiln and shed) and an interest charge for setting-up and working capital made even if no interest is being paid. This charge should be at the opportunity cost of capital facing the potter (i.e. that interest which could be earned by the potter if (s)he invested his/her money elsewhere). Thus, an existing potter's opportunity cost of capital nears zero, since the selling price of his or her assets would be very low (if anything) and thus the potter could not re-invest that capital. If a new potter sets up, then the opportunity cost of capital is calculated based on the full capital cost of the equipment and buildings.

3. Capital costs

A 100-stove kiln uses 1,000 bricks which cost approximately R500 in rural areas. However, many potters fire their own bricks, although Cyril Amitepale said that the level of orders for stoves means that were he to build another kiln, he would buy the bricks and hire a mason. A 100-stove kiln would cost, therefore:

Bricks × 1000	500
Mason × 5 days	325
	825

The building housing the kiln would use:

100 linear feet of timber @ R5/ft	500
12 sheets corrugated iron 32 ga. 8' x 2' @R80/sheet	960
	R1460

A carpenter would build this in five days, or the potter could build it. Many potters use coconut fronds rather than corrugated iron for roofing. It should be noted that the cost of timber in rural areas is very variable (as is the quality) and R5/ft is taken as an average.

The total costs of the kiln and housing, therefore, will range from near zero (i.e. self-made bricks, self-built, coconut frond roof, cheap timber) to more than R2,500 (purchased bricks, built by mason and carpenter, corrugated iron roof, quality timber.)

The pottery shed is likewise very variable in cost and quality. Some potters work in 'lean-to's' attached to their house, self-built with very low quality materials. Others have built more spacious sheds with corrugated iron roofs and sturdier timber poles. Shelving for drying pottery does not appear to be used much: pots are laid out on the ground to dry. It is not known how many pots are damaged this way by children, dogs, chickens etc.

A shed could, thus, vary from the R8,000+ of the urban pottery shed to little more than zero.

Total capital costs, therefore, can vary from R10,000+ to as little as a few hundred rupees (the opportunity cost of the potter's labour for constructing the assets). The life of the asset would vary accordingly, but even the cheapest kiln and shed would last several years.

4. Working capital

Working capital requirements are very small. Only the costs of clay and fuel will be paid for before cash is received for finished goods.

Since it will take approximately one month from clay collection through preparation, potting, drying and firing to final cash sale, a month's working capital should be allowed for:

Fuel	368–540
Clay	200–288
	R568 – 828

5. Total capital requirements

Total capital requirements for a new operation, then, are:

Kiln	200– 2,500
Shed	200– 8,000
Working Capital	500– 900
	R900 – 11,400

6. Returns to the potter

Costs per stove completed should be in the following region:

Clay	0.5–0.8
Fuel	0.9–2.0
	1.4 – 2.8

$$+ \text{Reject Rate @ 10\%} \quad \frac{0.14 - 0.28}{R1.54 - 3.08}$$

Selling at R15 per stove, this yields a gross profit of R13.46 to R11.92. If we assume a capacity of 400 stoves per month (or 5,200 stoves per year), this yields a gross profit of R69,992 to R61,984.

From this needs to be deducted depreciation and interest. On assets worth R500 – R10,000, if we assume a life of 2–10 years, depreciation is R250–R1,000. Interest at 15% of total capital requirements of R900–R11,400 is R135–R1,710.

Thus net annual profit – or rather net earnings distributable to family members – is:

Gross Profit	69,992 – 61,984
Less: Depreciation	250 – 1,000
Interest	135 – 1,710

Net Income to potter's family R69,607 – 59,274

At a production level of 25 stoves per week per potter, capacity of 100 stoves per week would require four potters.

7. Labour creation

To manufacture 20,000 stoves per year, 16 potters would be employed full-time.

Capital cost per workplace: R225 – 2,850
Average income per potter: R14,818 – 17,401

8. Price sensitivity

It is likely that as competition builds up prices will fall. Even if the price of a liner fell to R10, it would still prove attractive, especially when sales of other items were slack. Furthermore, as demand for other items is falling anyway, this could put further downward pressure on stove prices.

At R10 per stove, annual gross profits would be in the range of R43,992 to R35,984 or a net income per potter of R10,902 to R8,318.

Example 6. Informal economics

DECENTRALIZED KCJ PRODUCTION, KENYA

Introduction

By its nature, the informal sector is not conducive to formal economic analysis. One can discuss production methods, costs of raw materials and labour or distribution channels; one can conduct detailed analysis and recommend a specific option; and the informal sector will go ahead and do the exact opposite (or, more likely, it will do a number of different things). This is not because the analysis is wrong, but because there are so many non-economic factors at work and because the economic factors themselves can fluctuate so wildly; an economic analysis in the formal sense is too narrow.

Production of claddings
Setting-up costs

Below are set out costs given to us by Vitelus Okoth at Shauri Moyo, and also costs given by Opole (1983). As can be seen, there are significant variations. It is likely that in the less-integrated informal sectors, the costs will be higher as more tools would have to be bought from the formal sector. Opole also reports a 1,000/- training fee for new fundis (artisans) at Shauri Moyo. It is suspected that this was a charge for trainees introduced by KENGO or others. It is unlikely that fundis would have to pay this fee normally, especially if they are related to an existing fundi. This cost is, therefore, left out of our calculations. The likely setting-up cost is given on the right.

Item	Okoth	Opole	Likely
Ball pein hammer – small	—	27	27
Ball pein hammer – medium	40	45	45
Chipping hammer	—	39	39
Cold chisels × 3	27	27	27
Mason's square	Made	55	Made
Centre punch	2*	25	25
Measuring tape	—	49	—
Compasses	Made	150	Made
Tinsnips	45–80	140–200	140
Rail line	60	60	60
Flattening bar	10*	—	10
	184–219	617–677	373

* Manufactured in informal sector

There may be a cost for erecting a shed, but this is highly variable. At Shauri Moyo, no permanent buildings are erected. At Kiboye, the buildings are fairly permanent and would entail substantial costs in corrugated iron and building labour. At most other centres, buildings are fairly minimal because of council harassment and resulting insecurity. It is assumed anyway that most new fundis would operate at least initially out of existing sheds, and no capital cost is allowed for buildings.

Production costs

These costs have been gathered from Vitelus Okoth at Shauri Moyo, Monica Opole at Shauri Moyo, Bashir Mohammed at Mtwapa, and Julius Opolo at Nlenda. These costings are for a 10-inch KCJ.

| | Shauri Moyo | | Mtwapa | Nlenda |
	Okoth	Opole		
Drum (flattened)	60/–		85/–	60–120/–
Drum lids	2/50			
Metal (1)	5/–	11/–	17/–	12–24/–
Rivets	/75	1/–	1/–	1/–
Bars	1/33	—	5/42 (3)	2/–
Labour (piece rate)	5/–	5/–	5/–	4/–
Production costs	12/08	17/–	28/42	19–31/–
Surplus	7/92	3/–	(5/–) (2)	(5/–) (2)

Notes

(1) Okoth uses 2 drumlids per cladding. Other fundis use flattened drums and can make 5 10in claddings from one drum

(2) Hypothetical, since claddings are not sold separately.

(3) This seems excessively high since they are buying new ½in rods at Mtwapa. Buying scrap rods should bring this cost down to 2/–, giving a selling price of 30/–.

From these costings we can arrive at a number of maximum prices which can be paid to ensure a selling price of 30/– per cladding.

From these costings we can arrive at a number of maximum prices which can be paid to ensure a selling price of 30/- per cladding:

Item	Maximum Unit price	
Flattened drums	85/–	Each
Drumlids (if at all possible)	8/50	Each
Rivets	20/–	kg
Bars	6/–	kg
Labour	5/–	Piecework
Surplus	5/–	Each

It should be noted that drum lids are available in Nairobi at 2/50 each. If these are available or can be made available in other centres they should be used in preference to flattened drums as this can help to reduce costs substantially.

CHAPTER 11

The importance of marketing

Many people are suspicious of marketing and believe that it has no place in socially-orientated projects. This had often led to assumptions that if a product is socially useful – like an improved stove – it will 'sell itself'. This is very dangerous and has caused the downfall of many projects; while the project workers have known what a good product they have developed or what a valuable service they are offering, nobody succeeded in convincing the 'target market' of the fact.

Many projects also operate under more or less severe time restrictions (both from funders and also because of the acuteness of the deforestation problems facing many countries) and active marketing can help to speed up the process of adoption quite significantly.

This fact is true whether the product is something that is being manufactured and sold commercially – like a metal stove made by artisans – or something that is being distributed 'for free' – like a self-build mud stove. In fact, in certain ways, marketing can be even more important for a free good. Because people will not place a value on a free good (could you put a value on the air you breathe?) it is often difficult to persuade people to come and be trained, to spend the time necessary to build the stove and to use it properly. They will need convincing that the stove really will save time in cooking or collecting wood and – in the perverse way we humans work – people can take a lot more convincing over a free good than over one which they have paid for.

What, then, is marketing? It is the art of getting the right product or service at the right price at the right place at the right time to the right people. Advertising and promotion is part of this, but there is much more to it than that.

Identifying the market

Many stove projects set out with the aim of designing a stove for everyone. As we have seen in our early chapters, this is technically not always possible; people's cooking practices can vary substantially over quite small distances and this can require changes in design (different pot sizes, different foods, etc.) Similarly, people may have different needs for a stove: people living high up are likely to value space heating; elsewhere, perhaps, night-time lighting.

Over and above these differences are those caused by social and economic factors. A self-built mud stove is unlikely to appeal to better-off people. Similarly, a metal or metal-ceramic stove may appeal to all income groups but may only be affordable by wealthier sections of society.

It is important that you are clear about the market you are aiming at, and have a good idea how big that market is. This will determine your training and production plans, as well as any advertising you may need. For instance, there is not much point spending time getting publicity in an urban newspaper if your programme is aimed at rural people with a high rate of illiteracy.

The market you can aim at will be determined largely by the product's price, the type of fuel it uses, the amount of fuel it saves, its 'modern' look, and its ease of construction and use. Some of these factors can be changed to a certain extent, others cannot. You should have a very good idea of the potential market by the end of your field testing.

The size of that market can be more difficult to estimate. There is usually no shortage of government statistics in the capital, but they are often of dubious value and usually years out of date.

In the immediate area of the pilot project, you will probably have a good idea from talking to current users of the stove which sectors of society are most likely to adopt the stove. Talking to government officers and NGO fieldworkers will help you to guess how large those sectors are.

Do not try and set up large-scale market surveys. They can only be done with a lot of resources (both people and data-processing facilities) and you would probably learn little more than through your field testing. These big surveys are only justifiable within the context of national stoves programmes.

Ultimately, you will have to rely on the scant information you have. What is important to remember is that it is better to underestimate the market than to overestimate it. The reason is simple; if you spend a large amount of time training producers or stove builders and the results are small, the project will be jeopardized. producers will become disillusioned, prices will fall too fast to move excess stocks and the whole project could grind to a halt. With self-build stoves, the problem is less serious, but there could still be serious demoralization amongst staff when people fail to turn up to scheduled training courses.

There is another important question that needs to be answered: who will actually buy or build the stove? This can be more complicated than at first it appears. While in nearly all countries women do the vast majority of cooking and obviously stoves have to meet their needs primarily, the decision to invest in a new stove can be more complex. In many Asian countries, household decisions are made on a shared basis after discussion amongst members of the family. In much of Africa, money is controlled more strongly by the men and decisions tend to be taken more unilaterally.

Identifying who is going to make the purchase is vital; it determines the sort of outlets you should use – hardware stores, vegetable markets, itinerant sellers – and also the forms of advertising and promotion used. Encouraging men to buy a home improvement for their wives may be more effective in certain cases than stressing fuel-saving or ease-of-use aspects.

With self-build stoves, identifying the builder is important too, since that will determine not only your advertising but also the location and type of training you will offer. If women are the builders, it is unlikely that they could come to a centralized course and village-based training may be more appropriate.

Market segmentation

The overriding aim of most stove programmes is to reduce fuelwood consumption, and to do that as rapidly as possible. While it is likely that one model may meet the needs of a large segment of the population, a really effective programme needs to address every segment.

You should not, therefore, be looking simply for one overall best design, but instead for possibly two or three that best meet different people's needs and abilities to pay. Sometimes for example, urban markets will want improved charcoal stoves while rural markets will want better woodburning stoves. Wealthier people will want to purchase a stove; poorer people probably cannot, and will have to build their own.

All these 'market segments' are valuable within the overall aims of the programme. What must be remembered, though, is that any subsidies should be channelled towards the poorest people. Their options are the most severely limited and unless

Figure 11.1. The marketing mix.

they have access to and use improved stoves, the objective of saving fuelwood will always be constrained.

The Marketing Mix – the four P's

There are four key factors to be considered when working out how the stoves are going to be disseminated. These are often called the four P's: Product, Price, Place and Promotion. The combination of these four is called the 'Marketing Mix'. The relationships between the four and the target market are shown in Figure 11.1. We will consider each one in some detail.

PRODUCT

The stove has to deliver what it promises. That is, its quality must be good. Quality control has been a problem for many stove projects once production has moved away from the project's own work-shop. This has often led to stoves being produced that save little over a three-stone fire – there have even been cases of stoves that are less efficient. Also, durability has often fallen considerably over time, especially with ceramic stoves, where producers start using poorer clay bodies or try and make do with less clay.

Controlling quality is a problem. Registering a brand name which only approved producers can use can help. More important is to design the stove as simply as possible so that the key dimensions and details can be stressed. This is equally valid for artisan-/factory-built stoves as it is for self-built stoves. The dangers of producers or builders cutting corners or forgetting key dimensions are then reduced. A stove that is made using existing skills and production methods stands a much better chance than one that relies on new production methods or cooking practices.

Also, during training, it is important that dimensions and measures are given in units readily understandable to the people being trained. Some projects in Mali were using Bic pen widths and lengths to measure the critical dimensions of a user-built mud stove as they are ubiquitous there. Hand measurements (fists, fingers and palms) and tins (margarine, fat, meat, etc.) can also be useful. Simplicity holds the key to quality control.

Adoption of the stove will be further helped if the stove 'looks' improved, especially if people are going to pay for it. It should look different from existing models and 'worth the price'. A certain amount of styling can sometimes be introduced without adding to the cost. However, it should not look so different that people cannot recognize it as a stove!

Stoves can also be incorporated in a kitchen improvement 'package'. For example, in Sri Lanka, people are encouraged to build a wood/mud table to stand their new stove on rather than cooking on the floor. This gives the stove a stronger 'feeling' of being improved.

Guarantees can be offered to convince people that the stoves are good. The cost of this (some stoves are bound to fail) will have to be borne by the project as producers or sellers would refuse to bear it. Guarantees should only be offered during initial promotional phases, or things can get rather out of hand.

Packaging can also have a role to play in marketing purchased stoves. In Thailand, for example, improved stoves are marketed with a bright orange stick-on label to distinguish them. The Kenyan metal-ceramic charcoal stoves are painted to make the scrap metal look smarter.

PRICE
Price, of course, is unimportant for self-build stoves. However, an increasing number of self-build designs incorporate a ceramic liner which means that pricing of these can be important.

Prices have to be high enough to encourage producers to make the stoves and low enough to encourage consumers to buy them (see Chapter 10). What tends to happen is that prices are high initially to encourage production and then, as more producers become interested and competition increases, prices fall to more realistic levels.

This means that the initial purchasers of the stove will tend to be wealthier people. As long as prices subsequently come down, this is only a small problem. If the project wants to reach poorer people more quickly, then discounts may have to be offered (bearing in mind that wealthier people will demand the discounts too). This form of 'market skimming' (that is, targetting the wealthier

people first) does have one advantage though: should the stove not be as good as was hoped, it is wealthier people who have borne the risk and the cost, not the poor.

To reach poorer people, supposing the price remains too high for some of the poorest, payment terms can be devised. In Thailand, a ferro-cement drinking water jar programme established revolving loan funds in villages run by village committees to provide local people with finance to purchase materials to build their own jars. This money was then repaid over a number of months. Similar funds for stoves in poorer villages could be an option worth investigating. The problems are great, however; village committees have a habit of becoming taken over by wealthier people who then fail to repay the loans, leaving the poorer people with nothing. The range of excuses for not repaying loans can make interesting reading and project workers can waste a lot of time chasing repayments.

PLACE
'Place' refers to where and how the stoves will be made available to customers. Of all the parts of the marketing mix this is perhaps the most important, simply because it tends to get forgotten. In the early phases of projects, project vehicles are often used to deliver stoves or trainers or stove builders without any consideration being given as to what will happen when demand grows or the project ends. Consequently when project funding is terminated, it is not uncommon for stove production to end too because no one has the means of selling the stove.

For self-build stoves, 'place' is important to ensure that training and back-up are made available at the right place. This might be through village visits or more centralized training at market places. Mobile units to provide follow-up can also be very effective.

For purchased stoves, it is important that the stoves are on sale at places where your target market are used to shop, and preferably where they buy their fuel or existing stoves.

In a country or region where the new stove is replacing an existing stove which was already purchased, it is advisable to try and use the existing production and distribution network as much as possible. This ensures that people see the new stove in its right context and can readily compare it with existing models. It also avoids any danger of existing distributors trying to disrupt distribution because of a perceived threat to their own livelihood.

Investment costs are also minimized under this option since all facilities are already in place:

1 and 2: 'We used to collect our firewood near the village but now the women are spending a long time carrying loads of wood'

3, 4 and 5: 'Our traditional stoves have many disadvantages. They cause fires in the village, the smoke is bad for our eyes, and they burn people as accidents easily happen with these stoves'

6: 'As wood gets scarcer the price is going up all the time'

7 and 8: 'The new stoves use less wood, make less smoke, and are much more convenient to use'

Figure 11.2.   Awareness promotion. In Burkina Faso, a local artist was commissioned to produce a series of paintings on cloth which are used in teach-in sessions to 'sell' the stove to villagers.

wholesalers have stores and transport, shops have display space and market traders have stalls or ground space and some form of transport. It is thus well worth investigating traditional stove distribution networks first.

Even when there is no tradition of purchasing stoves, you should explore existing production and distribution systems for similar household goods such as cooking pots, kerosene lamps or washing bowls. These will tend to offer better long-term stability for a stove project than setting up some new network. If people are used to buying kitchen items direct from producers, then that system should form the basis for your marketing efforts.

Retailers and wholesalers (referred to collectively as distributors) are naturally conservative (as are artisans). They have very limited capital resources, at least the smaller ones in rural areas, and are unwilling to take risks. It will be necessary to convince them a market exists both through market demonstrations (to which they should be invited) and by offering them stoves on extended credit or on a sale-or return basis initially, to take the risk off them. In the same way, when a project is trying to build up stock levels prior to a promotion campaign, producers will require guaranteed orders and prices to get them to make more than a very few stoves.

If producers are used to selling direct to consumers, then placing guaranteed orders can actually be counterproductive. Producers will prefer selling to a project who do not haggle prices down and who place large orders. They may become unwilling to sell to consumers who will only ever place single orders and will try to barter prices down wherever possible. In these cases it will be important to minimize the number of stoves purchased and to concentrate on encouraging consumers to place orders direct with producers. The project could offer quality guarantees and itself bear the cost of replacing faulty stoves.

Where it appears that no existing system is suitable, other options can be explored. Sometimes there are existing government structures. In Sri Lanka stoves are disseminated using Special Service Officers who are village-based development 'facilitators', who earn a small commission for each stove installed. In Burkina Faso, large numbers of stoves have been disseminated using government structures. This system has the advantage of enabling rapid dissemination of stoves (especially self-built or mud/ceramic stoves) – but it does have dangers: there is the possibility of corruption, and government officers can always be given new priorities, leaving the stove distribution network in a very vulnerable position.

PROMOTION

What springs to mind when people talk of promotion is advertising. This is an important part, but not all of the picture. Demonstrations, point of sale material and publicity are all very important. Let us consider each one in turn.

Advertising can be very effective at raising people's awareness of the availability of a new product. Contrary to popular belief, it is unlikely that advertising on its own creates demand, but it certainly lays the foundations for that demand.

Advertising has to be treated very carefully. It is a potent instrument if you get it right, but an enormous waste of money for a small project if you do not. Whatever medium you choose (posters, hoardings, newspapers, cinema, radio, television) there are certain rules that must be followed. The simplest of these is to seek professional advice. This is fine for a national programme, but is unlikely to be a feasible option for a smaller one, especially if it is based in rural areas. In the latter case you should restrict yourself to the simplest (and usually the cheapest) media. In most cases, this will be posters, but local radio can also be very effective.

The second rule is to decide on the message you want to get across, which will depend on your target market and their perceived priorities for an improved stove. Each advertisement should concentrate on one aspect of the stove – on one message. Otherwise, advertisements easily get cluttered and boring. If you have a brand name for the stove (always a useful way of linking all parts of your marketing mix together and an effective way of getting the stove fixed in people's minds) make sure that all advertisements carry it.

Thirdly, only use those media which you know a substantial part of your target market have access to. Newspapers and television are little use in the rural areas of most countries, while radio is often listened to avidly, especially at certain times (often at cooking time). In Thailand, most villages are visited by mobile cinemas, so cinema advertising there can be very effective. Posters can also be useful, especially if they are wall-sited at places where people congregate, e.g. market places or the village meeting house.

Fourthly, make sure your advertising is not socially or culturally offensive. This is especially important if humour is introduced into advertising or if a country is divided between different religions, like sub-Saharan West Africa.

After you have done all this, look at the relative costs of the options left open to you and look at your budget. Your final decision will probably be

Figure 11.3. Car stickers. These stickers are available in many West African countries to promote stoves. They are seen on many public transport vehicles.

made for you! It should be remembered, however, that in many countries access to the radio can be free of charge and stove programmes can advertise for nothing if fuel conservation is a political priority.

Demonstrations can be a very effective promotional tool. People see the stove working and can satisfy any doubts they have. Demonstrations at markets are particularly valuable since people there tend to have money to spend. Invite wholesalers and retailers to watch the demonstrations; when they see people buying the stoves, they will be more willing to stock them themselves. This approach proved particularly successful in the Kenya National Stoves Programme.

Demonstrations at markets are also an effective way of training users on how to get the best out of their new stove, and to hear from users of any problems they may be having with their stoves.

Point-of-sale material helps to bring people's minds back to the product when they are in a 'purchasing mood'. Point-of-sale materials are such things as posters, free gifts if a stove is purchased, display stands and many other things to highlight the stove in the shop or market place. Posters are most likely to be effective, especially if posters are used as part of the advertising campaign. Point-of-sale material should be easily associated in consumers' minds with the advertising.

The most effective form of promotion is public-

ity. This consists of reports in the press or radio, and their effect is powerful because it is not advertising, which people often mistrust, but 'independent' reporting which 'must' be true. Thus, slots on radio programmes can be very powerful. KENGO, the NGO co-ordinating non-government fuelwood conservation activities in Kenya, has a weekly radio programme which enables it to publicize a wide range of activities.

It is crucial, of course, that all four 'P's', i.e. all four aspects of the marketing mix, complement each other. You must tailor what you plan to do to the price that will be charged and which you believe the target market will pay, and you must promote the stove in areas where it can be delivered to the people who need it.

How do you test the effectiveness of different parts of your marketing mix? It is important that you do this, so that any activities that are a waste of time and money are stopped as quickly as possible and the resources diverted to those things which appear to be working well.

When visiting households, you can ask them if they have heard of the new stove and if so, how they heard (friends, radio, market demonstrations). People purchasing the stove can be asked similarly. The reactions of producers and distributors to different marketing activities can also be gauged in a similar, fairly informal way.

Figure 11.4 Point of sale. This day-glo sticker is attached to all improved stoves produced by the Panomprai Eco Stove Factory in Thailand. It helps to single out the stove from the range of traditional stoves available.

Timing

Lastly, we need to examine the timing of your marketing activities. This is especially important in rural areas where incomes are highly seasonal. In Thailand, for example, all products are promoted in the rural areas from December to June when pockets are relatively full from the harvest. Virtually no promotional activity takes place for the rest of the year.

In urban areas, promotion may need to reflect monthly pay days. In Nairobi, over 50% of stoves are sold in the last week of any month when all private and public employees are paid.

Production can be similarly affected by seasons. In many countries, artisans stop production to go and help in the fields during planting and harvest. This can mean that production and stocks can be at their lowest when demand is approaching its highest. This may mean that the stove project will need to hold substantial stocks of stoves for a number of months to ensure they are available for purchase when the promotional campaign takes off.

Marketing campaigns do not necessarily have an immediate effect. Producers can get discouraged if orders do not start flowing quickly. Similarly, if demand grows faster than production, then potential buyers may get impatient.

The former is a bigger problem than the latter; if demand rises fast it is more likely that other artisans will copy the stove with or without training. But artisans will not sit around waiting for orders. It is important that projects grow at a manageable pace rather than making sudden quantum leaps through marketing activities which can raise expectations and threaten the project's future. Marketing should be seen within that context, not as an answer to all the problems of the world.

NEW MODEL COOKING STOVES
FURNO NOFLIE
ECONOMICAL • CONVENIENT

Stoves

Stoves are available from retailers in the Banjul, Serrekunda and Bakau urban areas. For an updated list of retailers, contact:

◗ Community Development, Stoves Project, Marina Parade, Banjul

Briquettes

Briquettes are available wholesale in 50kg sacks costing D4.00 with D1.00 deposit for the sack from GPMB at:

◗ Wellington Street Store (Banjul)
◗ HPS Plant Store (Kanifing)
◗ Denton Bridge Depot

If you have problems in obtaining stoves or briquettes, contact:

◗ Chief Depot Supervisor, GPMB, Denton Bridge

Figure 11.5.   Poster advertising. Posters in strategic places can be a valuable promotional tool.

CHAPTER 12

Stove production

Introduction

Field trails on a few hundred stoves made to the chosen stove design (or to a number of chosen designs) should be carried out before dissemination proceeds on a wide scale. Monitoring of the trials should reveal any design modifications necessary to improve the stoves when in large-scale production. In addition to the performance of the stoves in the field trials, a number of factors must be taken into account when considering the options for expanded production of the stove. For example:

- the adaptability of the stove to other cooking pots and cooking practices
- the 'consumer appeal' of the stove
- the cost of raw materials, construction, transport, and dissemination
- the number of stoves that can be produced
- the location of production
- the level of investment and external organization that will be necessary.

While the first few hundred stoves can usually be produced by a limited number of people using existing equipment, expanded production will involve and require the organization of artisans, owners of small-scale workshops and industries, retailers, and extension agents, who will have to take up new activities and changed sources of income. Of these groups, the artisans are crucial, and are often the most difficult to work with as they operate under a very different socio-economic framework than salaried industrial or office workers, shopkeepers or agriculturalists. For this reason, most of this chapter concentrates on different artisan production systems, either working as individuals or in small groups.

As with many products, there is potential for producing cheaper stoves in medium and large factories, but usually this requires a standardized product and a large market. It is probable that the production of improved stoves will go through an artisan stage, even if factory production later becomes dominant. The experience of successful projects based on artisan stove production, with which ITDG has collaborated, had shown a general strategy appropriate when working with artisans.

GENERAL STRATEGY FOR WORKING WITH ARTISANS
(1) Develop an understanding of the artisans, technicians in the industry, and entrepreneurs.
(2) Work with a limited number of carefully chosen artisans.
(3) Make the prototype stoves in conjunction with the artisans.
(4) Improve the stove production process by modifying the prototypes, as necessary, and using the artisans' skill to best advantage.
(5) Build up a steady demand for the stove wherever possible, for example, through channels such as the open market, or bulk purchases, so that artisans and entrepreneurs are willing to commit themselves to an expanding and economically-remunerative trade.
(6) Promote more organized and productive systems of manufacture, through more investment, job training, specialization and stronger management.

The continuing existence of informal-sector enterprises (artisans and small businesses) in most countries is the result of their ability to deliver needed goods and services that are of better quality than those which individuals could provide themselves, and in the case of goods, are still cheaper than factory-made items. To survive, they have to operate with low fixed, and working, capital, and be innovative in the types and quality of the goods they produce, in the procurement of raw materials and in the sale of their goods or services. They are often only part-time artisans, and low cash reserves will make them inherently conservative about taking risks, e.g. the risk of producing items which do not sell rapidly, and altering a steady, albeit low, income. Artisans often belong to a separate sector of society, e.g. metal workers in many urban African areas are often immigrants from other regions or even other countries; metal workers and potters in South Asia are usually of particular castes. Unless these factors are taken into account when developing financial and personal relationships with artisans, the chance of failure will be high.

The training of new people to become artisans in a short period is a difficult task, because of the complexities of covering all topics ranging from raw material procurement, to construction and production techniques, and to marketing. In all successful projects, whether they introduce mud, masonry, ceramic, or metal stoves, a great deal of training and follow-up has been necessary. In the case of mud stoves learning periods of six to twelve months are usually necessary before unskilled people accurately produce a durable product. It has been our experience that it is only the exceptional person who sets up a business or produces quality products after a short period of training.

The examples of stove production given in this chapter concentrate principally on the technical aspects because the organization will require modification for different areas. The examples nevertheless provide insights into how the production systems operate and compare with each other. For any type of material or stove the production options can be divided into three general categories:

(1) Individual artisans producing stoves as part of a range of activities.
(2) Small multi-person operations using traditional techniques and tools with limited job division.
(3) Multi-person operations with greater levels of investment, job division and output.

Typically, production systems for stoves become more advanced as the market grows; investment and increased specialization will pay off and will eventually become essential to maintain competitiveness in product price and quality. The existing pottery stove industry in Thailand which produces millions of stoves per year illustrates this development, even though the stove designs involved (described in earlier chapters) have considerable scope for improvement of performance. Most of the examples that follow are of small multi-person operations, but could be adapted to smaller, or larger, operations.

This chapter is organized into groupings of stoves according to the major material of construction, and not, as in the descriptive chapters, according to the number of pots and whether or not there is a chimney. A summary of the range of stove materials, in relation to their use in stove construction, has already been given in Chapter 4. This Chapter covers the physical characteristics of each material which are important in stove construction, before giving examples of production systems for stoves made from that material.

Mud-mix stoves

Throughout the world mud mixes are widely used for the construction of traditional stoves and newer designs. The promotion of improved mud-mix stoves began in India in the 1940's, and gained worldwide prominence in the 1970's and 1980's.

Unfortunately they have not proved as successful as hoped, and evaluations of a number of projects have highlighted several problems. It has been found that the usually large stoves did not meet the users' needs, and smaller, sometimes portable, designs were often more appropriate. On the other hand, basically satisfactory designs were often poorly built, and therefore did not function properly, or users did not understand the correct operation and maintenance requirements, or a relatively low production of stoves was achieved by each stove builder trained.

The most significant impact has been made by the increased development and promotion of smaller stoves made from materials other than mud mix, which in many cases has provided a cheaper, higher-quality stove. Where mud-mix stoves have nevertheless proved to be appropriate the promotion programmes have become more intensive. This situation is often found where large stoves were traditional and where mud-mix types provided greater convenience than traditional stoves or smaller new stoves (e.g. smokelessness, control of excess room heat, allowing the simultaneous use of many slow-cooking pots, provision of work space, etc). The programmes usually began to concentrate on giving more training and follow-up to a limited number of builders, who would then have the necessary skills to choose and prepare the proper materials, build quality stoves (often in a variety of designs) and give basic instructions on use and maintenance to future users. This shift to artisan, rather than owner-built stoves seems to be one of the keys to the continuing success of some mud-mix stove projects, although it has also required a greater level of organizational support in promotion, training and follow-up.

MATERIALS

Mud-mix stoves should be made from a mixture of materials that together have the strength and flexibility to withstand the thermal and mechanical stresses and retain their original shape.

Mud mix consists of 'binders' (usually clay, or an organic starch or glue) which hold together 'fillers' (usually sand, grain husks, brick dust, dung or fibres). Internal or external coatings to the stove are sometimes added for protection against heat, or abrasion and rain respectively. If the mix is not good the stove will often not last six months, but stoves made from good mixes can last up to five years.

The most readily available binder is clay, occurring naturally as a constituent of soil. Soils are composed of three principal inorganic ingredients – sand, silt and clay, together with rock fragments or stones, and small amounts of organic matter. *Sand* grains are visible to the naked eye and feel gritty between the fingers. Sand is valuable in a mud mix as the particles act as an 'anchor' for the finer clay particles, and it does not shrink when dry.

Silt particles are smaller, cannot be seen without a microscope, and feel smooth between the fingers. It is powdery when dry and the addition of water does not affect its characteristics. Silt is undesirable in mud-mix stoves because the particles are too small for many clay particles to bind to them, and it does not help the total strength of the mix.

Clay particles are the smallest and have the most unique characteristics of the major components of soil. They have a plate-like structure and attract and form chemical bonds with water molecules. It is the tightly-held water molecules that give clay its stickiness and strength.

The proportion of clay in different soils varies considerably, and it is therefore important to estimate how much is in a particular sample. A mix with too much clay will crack when it dries out, or is heated, whereas a mix with too little clay will crumble because of insufficient binding strength. Experience is necessary to make accurate assessments, but the following tests can be used for quick estimates (taken from Briggs, 1977):

'One particular [test] is to rub the thumb over the moist soil to determine whether it leaves a smooth, polished surface. This enables the distinction of soils with moderate amounts of clay (20% or more). Another useful test is to try to form a cube with the soil. Soils with about 5% or more clay form reasonably cohesive cubes. A further test is to roll the soil into a thread. Again this is only possible if clay is present in significant quantities (10–15% or more). Where clay is abundant (over 25%) the thread can be bent into a ring; the higher the clay content the firmer the ring.'

The amount of clay in a soil is important for agriculture, construction and small-scale clay industries (brick- and tile-making, pottery), so it is always wise to consult local people when seeking a source of clay for stove construction.

Cassava starch and *glues* from other plants are sometimes used as binders when there is not much clay available, but they usually require a significant amount of time and energy to prepare and often burn out on the inside walls of the stove, with a consequent loss of the strength they originally imparted.

There is a much greater variety in the type of *fillers* used in mud-mix stoves. As described earlier, *sand* is a much better filler than silt, because of its larger size. Large angular grains are better than

smaller, more rounded grains. If sea sand is used it should be washed to remove the salt which will otherwise weaken the bonding with the clay particles. *Crushed brick dust* can also be used but it is not usually available cheaply in large amounts. *Grain husks* are widely used in India and Indonesia, where they are available in large quantities. Grain husks mixed with wet clay and left in hot conditions will slowly rot, resulting in a strong mix. Short fibres, such as *coconut coir*, *sisal* and other *grasses*, and *pine needles*, are often added to mud mixes to stop cracking and increase the overall strength. They can be difficult to incorporate but the results are often worthwhile. Bundles of *long straw* mixed with mud were previously used in Europe and have been promoted in certain programmes, but problems have been experienced with cracking along the length of the bundles, and with straw adjacent to the firebox burning out.

CONSTRUCTION OF MUD-MIX STOVES

1. Preparation of the materials

Whatever materials are used it is critical that they are thoroughly mixed in the correct proportions to give the desired combination of strength and flexibility, that is, toughness. It is usually necessary to conduct tests with different proportions of materials to ensure that the stoves will last a number of years. The test pieces should not crack and should be strong both when dry, and after being exposed to hot fires.

The wet mix will generally require to be left to 'cure' for a certain period of time (from an hour to a week) and may also require to be tested in advance of stove construction.

2. Making the initial shape

The next step is to apply the mix in layers around moulds, in moulds, or in combination with pre-formed sections. The use of moulds can significantly increase the speed and accuracy with which the stoves can be built, but requires greater original investment and transport.

3. Carving the final shape

After the mix has hardened somewhat, and any mould used removed, the final shape can be made with hand tools such as knives, machetes, trowels, or spoons. During this step considerable accuracy is required if the stove is to perform properly. Each builder must develop or be taught consistent methods of checking all the critical dimensions at this stage. Internal coatings of special clay slurries, ash-clay slurries, etc., should be put on when the rest of the mix is still wet so that a good bond is formed.

4. Drying of the stove

The wet stove should then be slowly dried to

prevent cracks from forming which will grow larger during use. When it is first used it is best to start with small fires and gradually increase the size and duration. After the stove has dried and does not shrink any more, exterior coatings of cement or lime plasters, used engine oil, waxy plant substances, etc, can be applied for protection against abrasion and water.

LOUGA MUD STOVE (See Figure 12.1)

Prepare the mud mixture; mud used locally for building is usually suitable. Certain additives such as cow dung, sand and straw help to prevent cracking. Some experimentation into the ideal mix may be needed. The mixture should be sufficiently wet that it sticks but no wetter; use the driest possible mix. If the mixture is too wet it will sag as you build and then crack as it dries. (1)

(2)

(3)

Figure 12.1(1)

Have the cook set the most regularly-used cooking pot on the three stones, making sure it is level and that the distance below the pot is 12–15 cm (or width of hand with extended thumb, or height of a ballpoint pen). If the pot is too low, the fire will not light. (2)

Wet the stones and surrounding area. Build a mud wall around the pot and stones, up to the pot handles. The wall should be about 10cm wide (the width of a hand). If the wall is too thick, too much heat is lost to the mud; if the wall is too thin it will be fragile. (3)

Remove the pot carefully by twisting and lifting.

Smooth the inside wall of the stove and fill any holes around the stone. Leave the stove until it is dry enough to hold its form as it is cut.

Enlarge the pot hole with a knife until the pot will sit in it with a space of 6–8 mm (width of a pen, small finger) all round it. This space is to enable smoke to leave the fire; if it is too small the fire will not burn, if it is too large the hot smoke will not be held close to the pot and heat transfer will be less efficient. (4)

Using the knife, cut an arched doorway between two of the stones, approximately 15cm high and 15cm wide. If the door is too big, too much heat will escape; if the door is too small to accommodate two–three pieces of wood then the stove will be unusable.

A vertical slit can be cut above the door to enable the cook to see the fire and possibly prevent a crack forming in this position.

To make the stove more durable, the wall can be plastered with some mixture used locally to plaster the outside of mud buildings (often a mixture of

188

(4)

termite mud and cow dung).

The stove should be left to dry thoroughly for four–seven days. (5)

(5)

The stove will need regular maintenance as do other mud structures. Widen cracks with a knife, moisten and fill with fresh mud. Replaster the stove regularly.

Mud and rice-husk stoves
(See Figure 12.2)

One of the many traditional stoves of Java (Indonesia) is made with simple hand tools by artisans or villagers from a mix of mud and rice husks. The raw materials, preparation and tools needed are simple and widely available, and the stoves can be made cheaply and will last up to five years under heavy use, with very little maintenance. A finished two pot-hole stove weighs 15–20kg and is strong enough to be hand carried or transported on the back of a bicycle without damage. Production of the type of stove described below has been extended to other parts of Indonesia by emigrants from Java. Some of them have used their stove-building skills and have set up businesses selling large numbers of these stoves, which are an improvement over the existing traditional ones. Production cost of the stove (in Indonesia) is roughly equivalent to the wage paid for one day's agricultural labour.

The traditional design described below could be improved by making the stoves along the guidelines of examples described in the chapter on multi-pot chimneyless stoves.

A sandy clay that does not shrink much when it dries is selected, and mixed with rice husks at 2:1 by volume. The clay is usually obtained from rice paddies, and the husks collected from homes or small rice mills. A lot of water is added to give the mix the consistency of a wet mud mortar. One stove will require about 50kg of wet mix, which is left to rot for about one week, by which time it has a strong odour. During this 'maturing' the clay tends to break down into its constituent clay particles, and more bonds have been created within the mix rendering it stronger and less liable to crack during construction and use. Without this curing stage the stove would crumble within a few months. The large volume of rice husks also reduces the total shrinkage.

An internal mould for the firebox is used for this stove and this is placed in position where the stove is to be built. The mould is made of pre-cut wood pieces, banana stems, or some other packing. Mud is packed around the sides and at one end. After one day's drying, the mud for the top is laid on top of the mould. The walls and top are about 7cm thick. When banana stems are used, small bamboo pieces are placed across the stove to support the front arch, the middle arch and the rear, to prevent the top from sagging. The pot-holes are roughly shaped at this time. (1 and 2)

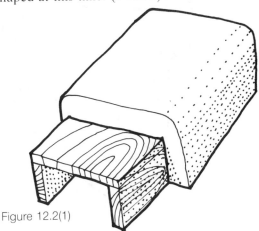

Figure 12.2(1)

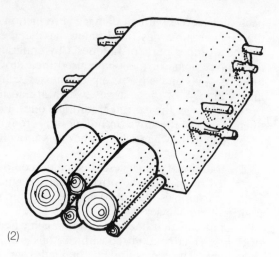

(2)

As the stove dries small cracks appear, and these are removed by gently beating the stove in its leather-hard state with a coconut frond or a bunch of twigs so that the clay spreads out and closes the cracks. At this stage the pot holes are finished off with bumps added to the second pot hole to enable exhaust gases to escape. (3)

After one or two more days the formwork is removed and the stove continues to dry. In the kitchens it dries in place, in the larger-scale operations the stoves are made outside and the stoves dried like bricks. They are dried flat, on one end, and then on the other to promote even drying. (4)

(3)

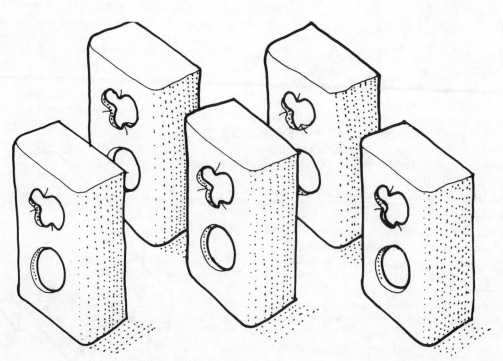

(4)

Cement stoves

Cement has often been used for improved stoves because it is relatively cheap, can be cast in nearly any shape, and does not need to be fired. However, a major drawback has been that cement degrades at the temperatures reached inside stoves, and will begin to crack and crumble after a few years of use. In some cases the relatively short lifetime of the stove (six months to four years) is not a problem if the cost per year is lower than that for stoves of other materials.

The commercial success of cement stoves in Thailand, India, Fiji and other countries is usually due to a quick and efficient production process using good-quality steel shuttering on large stoves, or casting the stove in a steel container for small stoves.

Cement top plates can be made in simple wood and brick moulds on the ground, but the finish is often rough and there is little scope for improving production.

In Fiji stoves are made from interlocking cement sections which are cast in the house. Steel shuttering, raw materials and skilled labour must be brought to the location. The interlocking sections allow for a variety of stove sizes, and for easy replacement of the sections that experience the greatest heat, particularly the top plates.

In Thailand, cement stoves made for burning rice husks have a number of advantages over essentially rectangular-shaped stoves. The pot sits on the stove walls rather than on a top plate, and a reinforcing wire skeleton is placed inside the cement. These changes take most of the tension off the top plate which is the weakest part of a cement stove, especially when heated, and increase the total strength of the stove. The stoves are also cast in a single piece in a central location which reduces the labour and fixed costs per stove considerably. They are mainly used in the flat, rice-growing plains of Thailand where the transport of these heavy stoves can be arranged cheaply and efficiently.

Another potential improvement that is promoted by the Royal Thai Forestry Department is the insulation of the inside of the cement stoves with a 3:1 mixture of rice-husk ash and clay (by volume), which should reduce the heat stress on the cement as well as improve the stove's performance.

Small cement stoves for charcoal burning can easily be cast directly into steel shells, but lightweight, heat-resistant additives such as vermiculite, perlite, or rice-husk ash should be added to decrease the total weight and increase the lifetime.

Pottery stoves

In many stove projects, especially those in Asia, a variety of pottery stove designs are being produced in large numbers and at low cost. Unlike metal, masonry and cement, which are relatively uniform, and are worked with the same techniques throughout the world, the quality of pottery stoves is governed by the materials used and the potters who make them. A good understanding of both materials and potters is necessary if a satisfactory production system is to be developed.

MATERIALS

Pottery has been made for many thousands of years and the traditions which go with its preparation, making and firing are many and varied. When working with local potters one must not forget that the methods they use have been handed down through the ages, and often have been specially developed to cope with the idiosyncrasies of the clay they use, and the wares sold. Talking with potters, and watching them work, from the digging of the clay to the pulling of a finished piece from the fire, will provide invaluable reference material when setting up a stove-making project.

In addition it is important to understand some of the technical aspects of the raw materials and the firing process. The following information should provide a basic knowledge; for more detailed information Michael Cardew's classic *Pioneer Pottery* (1969) is recommended reading.

Clay

The 'clays' that are used for the production of earthenware items rarely consists of pure clay as defined by its particle size and chemical composition. Pottery clays, like soils, usually contain significant amounts of sand and silt. The relative

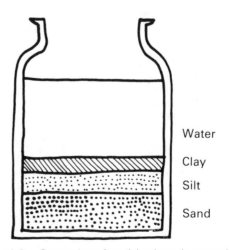

Figure 12.3. Separation of particles in a clay sample.

proportions of these three ingredients can be estimated by performing a simple test:

Mix a clay sample with three times as much water in a screw-top jar, and shake well, so that all the particles are in suspension. Allow to settle.

The relative proportions of the different materials can then be measured with a ruler. The longer the clay takes to settle the smaller the clay particles, and the more plastic (see page 193) the clay will be. For more accurate results measuring the rate of settling in a graduated cylinder is recommended. Experience with pottery stoves has shown that a significant amount of coarse material is needed for a body that will withstand cyclical heat and mechanical stress.

Pure clays are produced during geological weathering of the earth's surface when feldspathic rocks are slowly broken down in the presence of water to produce new minerals. Since this process is continuous there are clays all around the world, but their exact composition can vary greatly. Clays are classified into three different types, depending on how they were deposited – primary, secondary, and residual.

Primary clays are those created by erosion and chemical action, which remain as a deposit on the site of their formation. They often have irregular particle size but are usually chemically pure. The parent rock of this type of clay is often granite, which produces the whitest and purest clay – kaolin. Kaolin clays can be fired to very high temperatures before they melt (called a high firing clay), but are not very plastic and are difficult to form on a wheel.

Primary clays that are derived from plutonic rocks are slightly different in that they usually contain iron, which reduces the firing temperature and strength. The weathering of volcanic ash can produce bentonite, a very plastic clay that can absorb twenty times its weight in water. It is only used as an additive in clay mixes to improve the plasticity.

Primary clays are usually found deep below the ground in small deposits.

Secondary clays usually underwent the same original weathering process as primary clays, but were then transported by water and wind to their present location. During transportation the particle size was reduced due to abrasion and the plasticity of the clay was usually increased. The clay picked up minerals such as silica, limestone, dolomite, iron oxides and organic matter, which affect its chemical properties, and lower the temperatures at which the clay sinters and fuses. In addition, sand and silt are often mixed in which has the effect of lowering the plasticity of the mix, due to reducing the proportion of clay particles present. Unlike primary clays, secondary clays are generally found on or near the surface, are much easier to extract, and are therefore the most common type used in simple pottery works.

Residual clays. There is some disagreement concerning the use of this term, although Cardew describes a residual clay as being one (usually sedimentary) that has been deprived of some of its original impurities by weathering or by leaching. Many white or near-white plastic clays are residual, e.g. fire clays, from which most of the potassium, sodium and iron compounds have been removed by leaching.

The plasticity of clay

The term 'plasticity' used in the context of making an object in clay means that the material, when wetted with the proper amount of water, is easily shaped, almost elastic in quality, and will hold its shaped form as it dries.

Chemically, plasticity depends on three elements in the clay structure:

(1) Clay particles are microscopically small, plate shaped, elongated and thin; the smaller the particles, the more plastic the clay.
(2) Each particle is surrounded by a thin lubricating film of water (known as 'pore water') which allows smooth movement to take place within the mass, the plate-like particles sliding across one another. The plasticity is enhanced by the presence of ions in the pore water providing electro-chemical attraction between the particles which, whilst permitting the 'sliding' to take place, prevents complete separation.
(3) Bacteria and other tiny organisms within the clay also improve its 'workability' by releasing colloidal fluids into the pore water.

The degree of plasticity depends on uniformity of particle size, the degree of penetration of pore water into the clay, and its efficiency as a lubricating agent. A high proportion of organic material in a clay also increases plasticity, but the organic materials will burn out during firing, which will reduce the strength of the fired clay.

Plasticity can be improved by weathering or slaking the clay, requiring soaking in pits or containers. The clay particles gradually break down into even smaller particles, the quantity of organic compounds present increases (especially under hot conditions) and the heavier particles sink to the bottom.

Plasticity of a clay is qualitively determined using simple coil or snake tests, or by the same tests described for testing the clay content of soils.

The clay type for stove construction

The clay body used for stoves must usually be different from that used for pots, for a number of reasons. A stove shape is less spherical, and will have more openings and corners than a pot, which will reduce its structural strength. The stove must also withstand greater heat stress (expansion and contraction), knocks from firewood and pots, and the weight of heavy cooking pots. Water spilt on a hot stove surface can create a rapid cooling, or internal steam pressure, which can cause cracking.

However, unlike pots, stoves do not have to hold water, and can therefore be made of an open structured mix of different particle sizes held together with a plastic clay. When fired properly, this type of structure will be considerably tougher than a dense mix of uniform-sized particles. Unless local potters are already using a rough mix for their pottery wares (more common for hand-formed or large objects), they will probably have to add more large-sized particles to the base clay such as sand, crushed rock, crushed brick or broken pot dust (grog). For wheel-turned objects the amount of

rough material that can be added to the clay is limited because abrasion of the potter's hands makes it difficult to work.

The test results in Figure 12.4 for a number of independently-developed clay mixes used for wheel-turned stoves in various Asian countries show broad similarities in terms of the particle size distribution and the water requirement.

Clay used for stoves constructed from coils, sheets, or in moulds, can contain considerably more additives. Grain husks, which will burn out leaving open pores in the fired clay, are added to the clay mix for stove construction in some countries. In Thailand, clay is mixed with large quantitites of rice-husk ash to produce a mix that can only be moulded, but which has excellent strength.

Drying and firing

After construction, stoves must be dried and then fired. Special care must be taken with highly plastic mixes because they have the greatest amount of shrinkage. Differential shrinkage will often start cracks which greatly weaken or destroy the stoves,

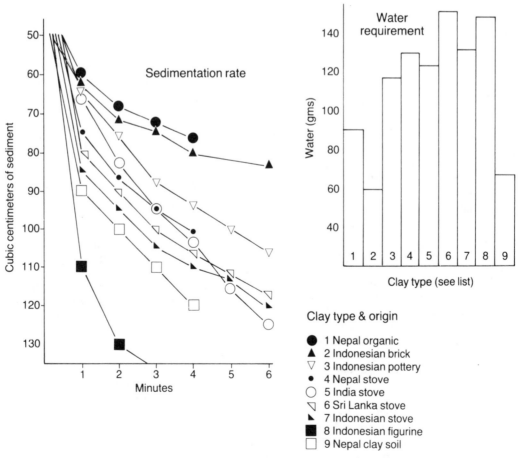

Figure 12.4.   Sedimentation rates and water requirements for a range of clays.

so slow controlled drying is a critical part of any production system.

When subjected to heat the composition of clay changes dramatically. the changes that occur are as follows:

15°C – 110°C   Any free water in the clay is evaporated.

190°C – 250°C   Clay losses absorbed and chemically-combined water.

550°C – 900°C   Pore size increases, and also total volume. Dry sintering begins.

900°C upwards   Sintering, contraction and then vitrification.

Up to 250°C pottery usually has to be heated gently. Too fast a temperature rise can turn any water present to steam and cause the pot or stove to crack. Smoking pottery before or at the beginning of a firing is a common practice to prevent cracking.

After this critical temperature (250°C) the final firing temperature can be reached quite rapidly without any damage to the wares. Care must be taken not to allow any sudden drop in temperature during firing, especially around 500°C as splitting and cracking will occur. Cooling should be controlled slowly, with pots not being removed above 200°C. Any draughts admitted during firing and cooling are liable to cause pots to crack.

Between 700°C and 900°C, depending on the type of clay, a clay body will develop considerable strength although it is still porous. This process is known as *sintering* which means that the clay particles have just started to melt and fuse together where they touch, but have not yet melted to a glassy state (this latter called *vitrification*). At this temperature many of the minerals present expand slightly, which increases the total strength while increasing the size of the pores. A well-fired stove or pot that has undergone sintering, but not vitrification, will have a good 'ring' when tapped with the knuckle. Under-fired, or cracked, stoves or pots will give a dull sound. Over-fired stoves or pots will be brittle and will be prone to early breakage. Different clay mixes will have different sintering and vitrifying temperatures, the heat released from different firing fuels will vary, and the temperatures will fluctuate through a kiln. It is therefore impossible to define the best firing method and schedule, but experience and constant attention are two critical ingredients.

THE POTTERS

There are advantages to using local potters for the production of improved stove designs. In many areas local skills and materials are available at relatively low cost; the potters are usually already producing kitchen wares; and production and marketing systems already exist for an extensive range of pottery wares. On the other hand, the skill of some potters is insufficient to produce stoves to specific standards, and this may be made worse in areas where potters only work part-time or seasonally at their trade, making it difficult to obtain a continuous, high-quality supply of the product. There may be problems with local production if the readily-available materials are of poor quality. In addition, difficulties may be found in persuading or convincing potters that making the stove will be worthwhile. Potters with a range of traditional items and long-standing market arrangements may be unwilling to try new products. Broken wares cannot be re-used, and many potters will be reluctant to go through the experimental stage necessary to change their clay preparation, construction and firing techniques.

It therefore follows that a close working relationship with the local potters will be necessary if correct technical choices are to be made, and if new designs or methods are required.

Steps must be taken to gather information about the local potters and pottery industry, and to assess the best method of approaching the subject of working with them.

Identifying suitable potters

One of the quickest ways is to go to markets and shops where pottery wares are sold and to find out where they were produced and how they were brought to market. Any significant difference in quality should be noted (e.g. the presence or absence of cracks, uniformity of size). From the type, range and quality of wares for sale some assessment can be made of the potential ability of the potters to make stoves or new designs of stoves. The innovativeness of the potter will be evident from his or her work, and the potter's willingness to attempt new items is important; a less competent but willing potter may be better for stove work than a very successful, and often very busy and meticulous, craftsperson.

After indentifying the active potters they should be visited and all aspects of their work as a potter discussed with them. The following topics should be covered:

Location

Is the potter or pottery near
- the organization implementing the stove project, and/or the area where the stoves will be distributed?
- the source of raw materials?
- a main road for easy transportation?
- markets?

Is the potter's location fixed?

Occupation

Does the potter make pots
- full-time?
- only in certain seasons e.g. the rainy season?
- only when the family needs pottery for their own use or to make extra money?

Does the potter work
- alone?
- in a family group?
- in a communal venture?

Are there any taboos which would prevent the potter making the proposed design of stove?

Has the potter enough time available to put the stove into production, or is he or she so successful that no extra work is needed?

Materials

Is the supply
- local?
- from a distance?
- only obtainable at certain times of year?

Are there any transport problems?

Is the cost of the clay, its transport, and of other materials
- free? (only requiring own labour)
- purchased?

Is the quality of the clay
- good, and plastic, just as it is dug?
- such that it requires –
  - soaking and maturing?
  - mixing with another type of clay to make it suitable for pots?
  - additional material(s)?

What is the availability of clay additions (for stove production)
- grog?
- sand?
- grain husks?
- dung?
- rice-husk ash?

Wares in current production

Cooking pots or storage jars – types and sizes

Decorative items

Stoves

Complexity
- simple rounded shapes?
- tall shapes?
- with handles?
- with cut-out holes?
- with clay shapes added on?
- decorated?
- glazed?

- are different mixes used for different items, if so why?

Production techniques and equipment available
- hand-formed shapes?
- simple wheel-thrown shapes beaten into forms?
- entirely wheel-thrown shapes?
- ability to join shapes?
- objects with lids?
- projection of uniform sizes?
- use of moulds?

Working and drying area
- ad hoc arrangement?
- small limited area?
- covered/uncovered?
- room for expansion?

Firings
- by potter, for own pots?
- by person solely responsible (and paid) for firings?
- communal firings?

Frequency of firings:
- regular e.g. once a month?
- only in certain seasons?
- only when very large number of pots available?

Method:
- bonfire?
- bonfire with small wall around?
- simple walled kiln?
- more sophisticated kiln (or has a sophisticated kiln been abandoned?)
- do potters know about sophisticated kilns?

Fuel:
- type?
- cost – purchased or collected?
- availability?
- do any of the above limit the length and number of firings?

Output

What percentage of pots are intact
- after drying?
- when removed from kiln? (NB. one low observed percentage may indicate a poor firing – several may need to be studied)
- what percentage crack in use?
- what is the average lifetime?

(NB. low percentages for all the above may indicate poor clay)

Breakage rate in transit.

Marketing

does the potter
- sell from the house?
- sell to a middleman?
- sell in the markets?

Marketing overheads:
- cost of transportation of products?
- commission to vendor?

Success

How successful is the potter, and if problems exist are these due to
- bad manufacture of pots?
- remote location?
- reduced demand for traditional pottery wares (e.g. resulting from the introduction of plastic or metal substitutes, in which case a new product line, such as a ceramic stove, may be especially welcome)?

By comparing the results of such a survey of potters, it should be possible to decide which potter or potters will be capable of producing the number of stoves that will be required and whether any assistance in equipment, skills, materials, etc. will be necessary. After choosing one or a few potters with which to work, the next step is to establish a good working relationship. The issues of payments and scheduling have often been shown to be crucial.

Payment

The first stoves made take up time and materials that could have been used to make marketable wares, and the potters may have to be paid a generous piece rate if the construction of the prototypes is slow and requires special care. Afterwards a lower price can often be agreed and it is important to understand why a potter may think a stove is worth much more than a number of pots requiring the same amount of labour and materials. It is often the case that they consider the production of these new products a risky venture and it may be necessary to pay an extra subsidy. On the other hand, excessive payments for the first stoves, especially if they are of poor quality, may prevent stoves later being sold at a price which the open market will bear.

Scheduling

Many potters only work part-time, or seasonally (e.g. cutting back production during periods of heavy agricultural work). It is best to start the new work when the potters are working full-time and to set reasonable deadlines for the completion of batches of new stoves.

The potter chosen from the survey will have been well observed. The stove design must initially bear some relation to current work, using techniques (especially for the prototypes) with which the potter is familiar, and bearing in mind the tools, equipment, space and firing method already in use.

Making the prototypes

A prototype stove can be shown to the potter and presented as an illustration of what is required. Alternatively, the basic shapes can be made by the potter, under instruction, and be cut out and the stove constructed as a joint effort with the stove promoter/designer. Potters usually cannot make a stove from a two-dimensional drawing, so active involvement in conveying the design concept to the potter is essential at the prototype stage.

The first stove should be simple, as too many structural innovations may weaken the stove and make it more difficult to reproduce with speed and accuracy.

Modifying the clay

The survey results will hopefully have eliminated potters working with unsuitable clays, such as those which are difficult to form, need an unacceptable amount of preparation, and still crack in the firing.

Good potters will know what is best to add to their clay to make their usual range of wares, but stoves will often require different additives, and the reasons for this should be explained to the potter.

Measurements and templates

Most potters work 'by eye'. It is unusual to see a potter using anything more than finger spans as a measure. However, stoves **must be accurate to be efficient**. Therefore a measuring system must be introduced which is accurate enough and yet is acceptable to the potter.

Consideration should be given to the following:
- rulers with notches
- sticks with notches
- metal templates for door and air-hole shapes, possible with wooden attachments for measuring heights, etc.

Shrinkage of the clay, and the difference between the straight and curved measurement on round sections, must be borne in mind.

For a successful relationship with the potter over the question of measurements, it must be made quite clear that only accurately-made stoves will be accepted, and therefore the potter must use the measuring system agreed upon. A centimetre short here and there will eventually mean that eight stoves can be made out of the clay originally meant for seven. The potter may gain but the stoves lose efficiency.

Firing and kilns

Pottery stoves can be fired to acceptable temperatures in traditional bonfires and updraft kilns (see

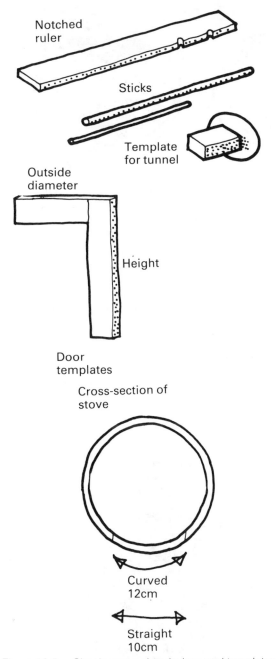

Notched ruler

Sticks

Template for tunnel

Outside diameter

Height

Door templates

Cross-section of stove

Curved
12cm

Straight
10cm

Figure 12.5. Simple measuring devices and templates.

page 207) but there are often problems with uneven firings, high cracking rates, and kilns that are too small to fire a reasonable number of pottery stoves. While traditional bonfires and kilns may appear crude, the firing practices required are often complex and the introduction of new kilns should be carefully considered. More consistent products and possibly some fuel savings can be achieved by introducing simple updraft kilns, but they will only be successful if the potters believe they will be an improvement and are willing to learn new firing techniques. The kilns used in the example production processes are illustrated at the end of each section.

Examples of pottery stove production

The following stoves have been selected to illustrate the production of pottery stoves under a wide range of conditions.

1. One-pot stove   Eastern Indonesia
2. Hand-formed stoves   South Asia (Sri Lanka, and South India)
3. Tungku Sae   Indonesia
4. T. Kallupatti version of the Magan Chulah   South India
5. Moulded stoves   Thailand

1. ONE-POT STOVE, ALOR ISLAND, EASTERN INDONESIA

The dry islands of Eastern Indonesia have a low, but steadily growing, population density with free-ranging animal herders maintaining a simple subsistence agriculture. Ecological degradation is severe in many parts because of the grazing and shifting cultivation activities of the growing population. Most rural households collect their own fuel, and fuelwood is sold in towns and villages. Unlike the more varied diet associated with traditional multi-pot stoves of the lush rice-producing islands of Indonesia, the staple is maize, which requires long simmering and is cooked along with simple side dishes over an open fire.

An American volunteer took up employment with Oxfam UK in Eastern Indonesia after having helped Yayasan Dian Desa establish its stove programme in Java (see Example 3 Tungku Sae stove). His observations of the local single-pot cooking practices and the rudimentary potting methods persuaded him that simplicity should be foremost in the design of any improved stove for the area. An Oxfam women's development field worker spent one month with the seasonal women potters in one village, before introducing the idea of a pottery stove and showing them how to make it. Prototypes were made and improved upon over a few months until the potters could consistently make good-quality stoves.

The simple production method used for the Alor Island stove is as follows.

An indent is made in a piece of clay placed on the potter's lap on a small pad, to make a dish-like base. This is put out in the sun to dry for two hours. After the base hardens more clay is added in coils and formed with a wooden paddle, on the outside, and a smooth stone, on the inside, to build up the walls and top lip. Templates are used to check the height, and the internal and external diameters of

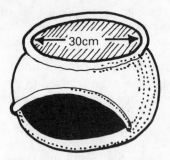

Figure 12.6. Templates used in construction of the Alor Island stove.

the top lip. The door is then carved using another template, and the pot rests added. When a batch of stoves are dry they are fired in a bonfire.

2. HAND-FORMED STOVES OF SOUTH ASIA

In Sri Lanka and South India the staple diet basically consists of rice with vegetable side dishes. It is very common to find two traditional fireplaces side by side, or one stove with two pot-holes. The cooking times are relatively short, and every day a wide variety of pots are used. Most potters are from pottery castes and work in family operations, usually full-time but with lowered production during the rainy season, or when working any fields they may own.

Most of the potters own large wheels – usually without bearings and not very steady. The preferred method of construction for items not spherical or cylindrical (and particularly for stoves) is hand-forming with coils. The following examples of stove production in Sri Lanka and South India illustrate two construction methods. In both cases the original design was modified to match the skills of the potters, and the major improvements have been directed at more continuous production and careful quality control, rather than significant technical changes. Both types of stove are bought wholesale by organizations which sell through their existing marketing systems rather than directly on the open market. The organizations are covering their marketing costs, but in the initial

The firebox is made by coiling

Figure 12.7. Construction of Sarvodaya pottery liner.

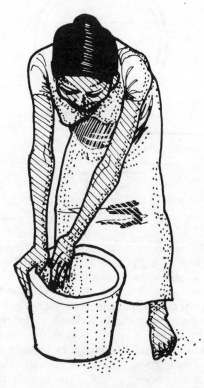

The coils are smoothed together

198

The second pot seat is made on a wheel

The tunnel is made

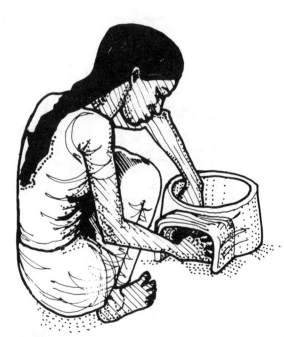

The door arch is coiled on to the firebox

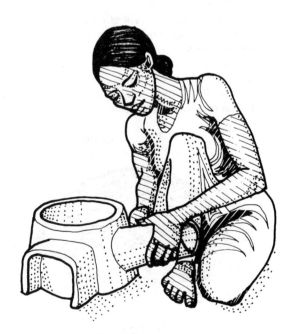

The tunnel is joined to the firebox

199

The firebox entrance is cut out

Pot rests are joined to the second pot seat and tunnel entrance removed

Figure 12.7.   Construction of Sarvodaya pottery liner (cont.).

stages the management costs were not fully covered by sales, which were therefore subsidized.

A. Sarvodaya pottery liner, Sri Lanka

The construction method for this stove is illustrated on pages 199–200.

Sand is added to pot clays to make them more suitable for the construction of these stoves. The combination of coiling and turning was found to be the best way to ensure dimensional accuracy for the specific stove design.

Also illustrated are a small Sri Lankan kiln, and a larger, co-operative kiln.

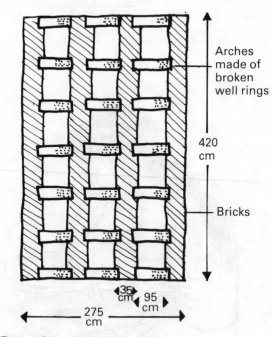

Figure 12.8.   Kochchikade co-operative kiln.

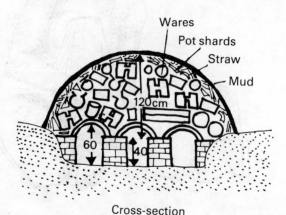

Cross-section

Figure 12.9.   Small Sri-Lankan kiln.

200

B. South Indian two-pot stove

In South India traditional two-pot stoves are made by coiling a clay/grain-husk mix (2:1 by volume). The grain husks prevent the stove from cracking during rapid drying in the sun and also reduce the total shrinkage. Sorghum husks are better to use, being softer and more absorbent than rice or wheat husks.

The construction sequence outlined below can be readily adapted for variations on the basic design.

The grain husks are thoroughly mixed with the clay.

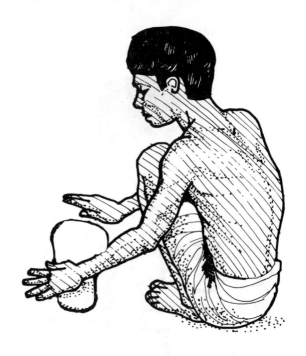

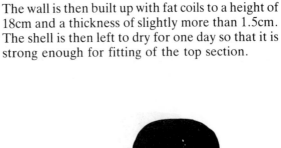

The wall is then built up with fat coils to a height of 18cm and a thickness of slightly more than 1.5cm. The shell is then left to dry for one day so that it is strong enough for fitting of the top section.

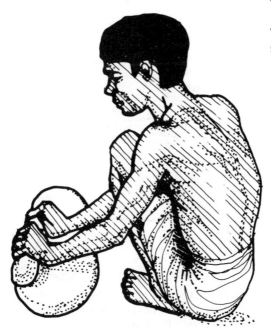

The shape of the stove base is drawn out on the ground and the mix is laid down on the outline.

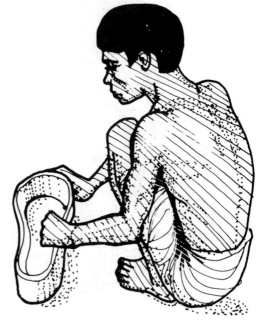

A bridge is placed between the two pot-holes.

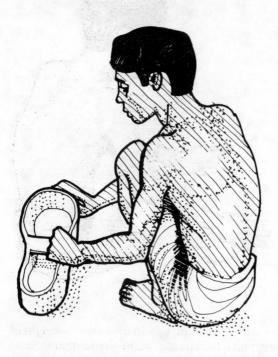

To support the baffle (fitted next), two strips of clay are attached to the inside walls, underneath the bridge, starting about 5cm from the first pot-hole and ending up in the middle of the second.

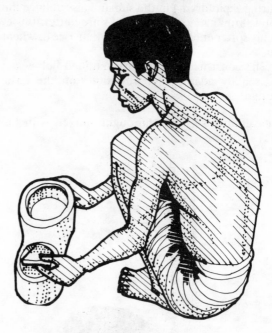

The first pot-hole (the one over the firebox) is reinforced with a ring of clay and smoothed into the walls of the stove.

The baffle is constructed from a piece of clay about 20cm long which is attached to the top side of the support strips.

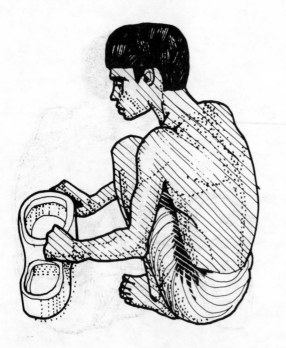

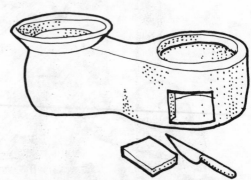

The rim of the second pot-hole is raised by 2cm and widened out, so that round-bottomed pots will be slightly inside the flame path.

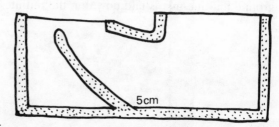

5cm

Figure 12.10.   Construction of South Indian two-pot stove.

202

The door opening (15cm × 12cm high) is marked out from a template and cut out with a knife. A 3cm ledge is placed above the door opening to support the insulation that will be placed on the stove later.

Three knobs are placed on the widened portion of the second pot-hole to raise the pot to allow smoke to escape. A good bond should be made so the knobs do not fall off, and they should be 1–1.5cm high.

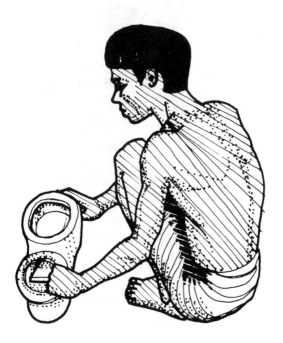

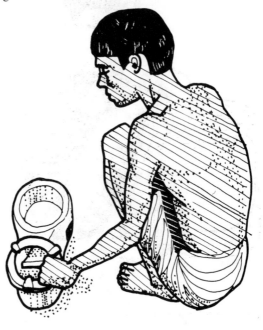

A round pot is twisted around in the first pot-hole to make a smooth fit. The whole stove is polished with water, and put aside to dry. Cracks occurring during drying are wetted and filled with wet clay.

Day 1   Potter makes two cylinders

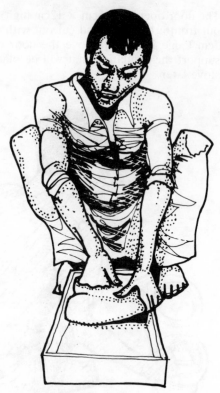

Stove fabricator makes connecting tunnel slabs in wooden former

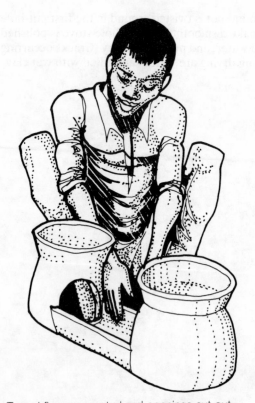

Tunnel floor connected and openings cut out

One side of the tunnel is attached

Figure 12.11.   Construction of Tungku Sae stove.

The other side is joined and smoothed together

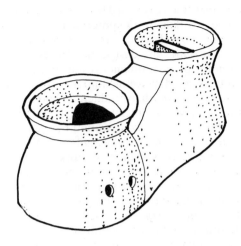

Baffle added in rear potseat. Air holes cut in firebox

The three pot rests are attached to allow smoke to escape

Reinforcing strip of clay placed around firebox entrance and door removed

3. TUNGKU SAE STOVE FACTORY, PAGOTAN, YOGYAKARTA, INDONESIA

Since 1980 the Yayasan Dian Desa organization has been working in the pottery village of Kasongan, near Yogyakarta, to make innovative pottery stoves. In 1981, one design, the Tungku Sae, was chosen for production and by mid 1982 a number of potters could make high-quality stoves. To increase and standardize production, and to give the workers greater financial security, a factory-like operation was organized around the best artisan, his wife, and a number of neighbours late in 1982. The production system was broken down into tasks and different people were made responsible for each. The stoves were marked with the trademark 'Gunung Api' ('mountain of fire'). The potters in this village are some of the most skilled in Indonesia, and had been involved throughout the development stages of the stove design, both factors favouring organization of a good production system.

However, in order to produce large numbers of improved stoves in Indonesia, production capability could not be limited just to one village. Dian Desa has therefore trained potters in a number of villages to produce the Tungku Sae. One village, Pagotan near Yogyakarta, has grown to become the largest producer in the country surpassing the original factory in Kasongan. The experience shows that it is possible to train and organize potters to produce improved stoves efficiently and accurately in a relatively short period of time if sufficient technical guidance is given.

The first step taken in Pagotan, in July 1982, was to show the Tungku Sae to three individual potters and to see if they could reproduce a facsimile. They were both able, and interested, so in August they and a fourth potter went to Kasongan for a week to see how the stove was made by potters experienced in stove construction. The potters (two men and two women) then went back to Pagotan and continued to make the stoves along with their other products. Two more potters considered the stoves to be a lucrative product and also started to produce them and sell to Dian Desa.

Unfortunately the quality of the stoves was not increasing with experience. There was still a fairly high rate of breakage and the measurements were often incorrect. By February 1983 all but two of the potters had given up producing the stoves because they felt they could not produce them up to standard. At this time the factory in Kasongan was going well and it was decided to try to set up a similar one in Pagotan. After numerous discussions with the potters it was agreed that Dian Desa would provide the money to buy the building materials for the factory, and would pay the workforce a monthly salary to produce stoves.

The four original potters, the two women potters' husbands, and two other young men, were hired. A suitable site was chosen at the home of two of the future employees, and the people collected and purchased the materials and started to build the factory.

A bamboo and thatch building, 16m × 6m was constructed and six wooden work tables built. Trial production began, with considerable assistance from Dian Desa staff, and from the leader of the Kasongan factory. As in Kasongan, different people were assigned responsibility for different stages in the production process.

To increase the quality of the stoves two other improvements were introduced. A metal, slab-making machine was made at the Dian Desa workshop and taken to Pagotan. Secondly, some of the men visited Kasongan to see the improved kiln. On their return they built a similar, slightly larger, kiln in Pagotan, to hold three layers of 25 stoves (the Kasongan kiln was built for four layers of 20 stoves, but only used for three layers per firing in practice). The fuel used on the traditional bonfire kilns was bundles of shrubs brought down from nearby mountains, and the fuel cost per stove was Rp50 (US cents 5). The new kiln increased fuel use because a higher temperature was achieved, fuel cost per stove being Rp65. These kilns are described below.

A note on Indonesian kilns

1. BONFIRE KILNS (PAGOTAN AND KASONGAN, NEAR YOGYAKARTA)

These kilns are usually fired with agricultural wastes such as sugar-cane stalks, rice straw, bamboo leaves, casuarina branches and shrubs. In none of the numerous firings observed in February-March 1983 was any hard round-wood used.

Four to six rows of old broken pots are laid down with 30–40cm gaps in between for the fuel channels. The kiln can be enlarged simply by increasing the number of pots. The front and rear openings of the fuel channels are spanned with broken lips from very large pots. Wares to be fired are piled in a hemisphere and covered with rice straw, sugar cane stalks, or leaves. After this top fuel is lit more fuel is pushed into all the ports over the next 1.5–2 hours, using long sticks. Care is taken to keep a 10–15cm layer of hot and carbonised fuel over the pile at all times. After the fuel is spent the pile is left with the still hot ashes covering it for a few hours. Sugar cane stalks and shrubs are the main fuel in Pagotan, bamboo leaves in Kasongan.

2. IMPROVED KILNS FOR TUNGKU SAE PRODUCTION AT KASONGAN AND PAGOTAN VILLAGES.

Kiln No. 1

Kasongan produces special pottery items such as

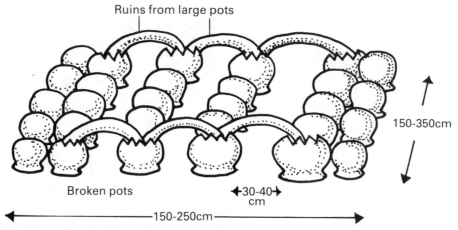

Figure 12.12.   Base of bonfire kiln.

Ruins from large pots

150-350cm

Broken pots

30-40 cm

150-250cm

figurines, savings pots, cooking pots, pottery stoves, water jugs and drainage pipes, as well as, more recently, the Tungku Sae stove. This small village industry attracted government attention a few years ago and government workers built a new kiln to replace the traditional bonfires in which differential heating often caused a high rate of breakage. Field surveys after one year have shown that kiln-fired stoves are much stronger than stoves fired in bonfires, and usually have no cracks, whereas bonfire-fired stoves often have many serious cracks.

The small updraft kiln (inside dimensions 130cm × 60cm × 60cm) was built by the government workers at one of the larger pottery production units. Pak Joyo, a drainage pipe producer who was already familiar with updraft kilns used in tile production, thought this type of kiln would be appropriate for firing his pipes and he built the kiln shown in Figure 12.14. This kiln is also used to fire Tungku Sae stoves. The kiln walls are of locally-produced double brick, and the whole kiln is protected from rain by a bamboo structure with a tile roof.

The door inlet area is approximately 3,300 sq cm (see Figure 12.13). The kiln inlet area above the fuel channels is approximately 4,700 sq cm. The outlet area is determined by the arrangement of tiles piled on top of the wares, and cannot be measured exactly. The total area is approximately 20,000sq cm. The walls are double brick except for the loading door which is repacked with single bricks each time. A number of spy holes are left in the door to check the progress of the firing. The bricks used in construction are 24cm × 12cm × 4cm.

Approximately 1 cubic metre of loosely stacked coconut wood is used to fire 50 stoves weighing 6kg each. The weight of fuel used per firing is about 100–200kg. A 5-hour firing cycle is used, usually starting around 3pm. Peak temperature is reached around 6pm, and by 6.30pm the fuel ports are partially closed and less fuel is put in. By 7pm no more fuel is added, but a large bed of charcoal still radiates considerable heat. At 8pm the fuel ports are totally blocked up and the kiln is left overnight and unloaded the following morning.

Kiln No. 2
With increased production the small kiln which held only 40 stoves was the major production bottleneck. Therefore in 1983 a larger 3.4 cu m kiln was built, to hold 80 stoves in four layers of 20. However, it was found that about 25% of the stoves broke, mostly on the bottom layer, so the kiln is now used to fire only three layers (a total of 60 stoves), and there is little breakage if the stoves have the correct moisture content when loaded into the kiln.

Three additional air-holes were made to allow in more air, to solve a problem of incomplete combustion in the centre of this long kiln.

Approximately 1.3 cu m of loosely stacked wood, costing Rp3,500 (US$3.50) is enough to fire 60 stoves, that is about 2.5kg of fuel costing Rp55 per stove. The stoves weigh about 6kg each.

3. Spider Kilns of Klaten (near Yogyakarta)
In a number of villages in Klaten the fuel used in pottery firing is the sheaths of sugar cane stalks that are left in the fields. This fuel can fire a large number of items in a unique kiln used in this area for over 50 years. Figure 12.14 shows a fairly large kiln, but the basic design is the same for smaller versions.

There are two fuel ports (34cm wide × 45cm high) on opposite sides of the outer wall. The fuel chamber is underneath the spider legs which support the pots or stoves. The legs are made of two

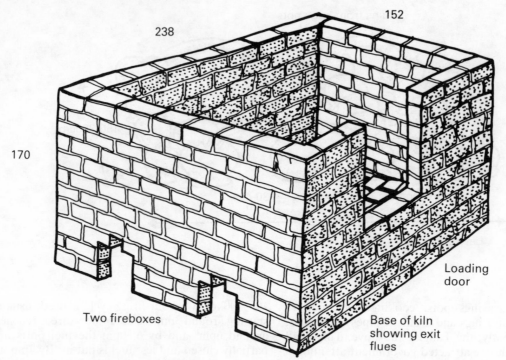

238

152

170

Loading
door

Two fireboxes

Base of kiln
showing exit
flues

Figure 12.13. Updraft kiln, Kasongan, Indonesia. Capacity 3m$_3$, average maximum temperature 750°C.

special-purpose straight bricks (45cm × 10cm × 10cm) which lean against each other at their apex. The wares are piled about 2m above the top of the kiln wall and are covered with straw. As the fuel burns, the ash is pushed down the circular channel so that more fuel can be fed in continuously. About 250 'Keren' (one-pot) stoves are fired at once. The total volume is aout 6 to 8 cu m. The firing cycle is 2.5 hours.

4. MAGAN CHULA STOVE PRODUCTION, T. KALLUPATTI, SOUTH INDIA

Production of the pottery Magan Chula can be undertaken at village level if a number of guidelines are followed:
- The clay should be matured and have sand added in excess of that added to clay when used for making pots.
- The stove measurements should be checked during production with measuring sticks; shrinkage must be taken into consideration.
- The stoves should be dried in a place protected from the sun, wind and rain.
- All cracks should be repaired during the construction process with wet clay and water.

- The stove is thicker than a pot so firing must be slightly longer to make sure the stove is fully fired.

The Magan Chula pottery stove production system described in the following pages is that used at the Ghandhiniketan Ashram (T. Kallupatti, Madurai District, Tamil Nadu, South India).

The raw materials (clays, and fuel – agricultural wastes and thorn branches) are delivered in bulk to the site by tractor; sand is collected nearby. About 90 sq m of covered space is used for production of 200–300 stoves per month. The firing is a major bottleneck preventing increased production, but there is no room to build another kiln.

The potter's wheel used in this production system is a design of the Khadi and Village Industries Commission, Type B wheel (Figure 12.15). The robust double-bearing design is well suited for work with large amounts of clay and is very stable at both high and low speeds. The wheels are made in Tamil Nadu according to KVIC blueprints, and are available at a retail cost of Rs340 (Rs 10 =

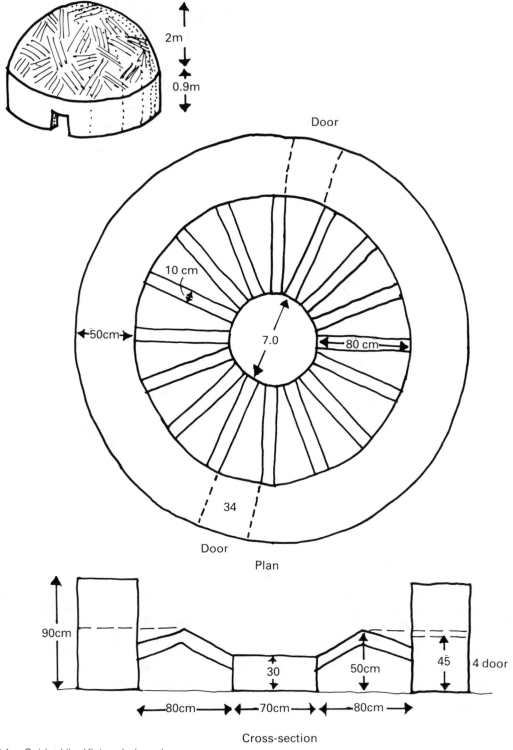

Figure 12.14.   Spider kiln, Klaten, Indonesia.

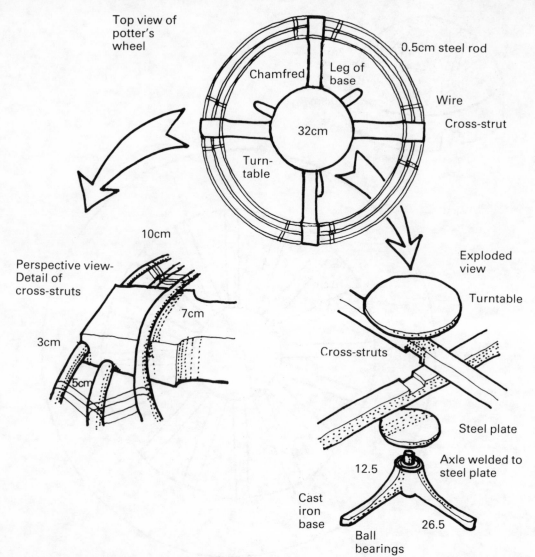

Top view of potter's wheel

0.5cm steel rod

Chamfred

Leg of base

Wire

Cross-strut

32cm

Turn-table

10cm

Perspective view-Detail of cross-struts

7cm

3cm

5cm

Exploded view

Turntable

Cross-struts

Steel plate

12.5

Axle welded to steel plate

Cast iron base

Ball bearings

26.5

Figure 12.15.   KVIC Type B potter's wheel. The steel rod perimeter is wrapped with a mud-straw mixture 22cm wide and 8cm thick, weighing approximately 100kg.

US$1), wholesale Rs315. The wholesale price of the cast-iron base, and the steel plate with the two heavy-duty ball bearings, is Rs215. Information on the availability of this wheel is obtainable from the Director, Village Pottery Industry, KVIC, 'Gramodaya', Irla Road, Vile Park (W), Bombay 400 056, India.

PRODUCTION SEQUENCE FOR THE MAGAN CHULA (See Figure 12.16)

Clay preparation
1. Two medium-plasticity earthenware clays are mixed together in settling tanks with a large quantity of water. After at least four days they are sieved though a screen with five wires per centimetre to remove rocks, sticks, and other impurities. The cleaned clay is matured for at least another four days. This soaking process breaks the clay particles down into smaller particles and improves the plasticity and workability of the clay. The excess water is scooped off to leave a thick slurry. (1)
2. To start the stove-making process enough clay for about ten stoves (120kg) is removed from the pit and spread on the ground in the afternoon sun.

In the monsoon season it is impossible to soak and dry the clay outside, so it is cleaned by hand and mixed with sand and enough water to make it workable. The mix is left to mature inside the workshop for at least four days.

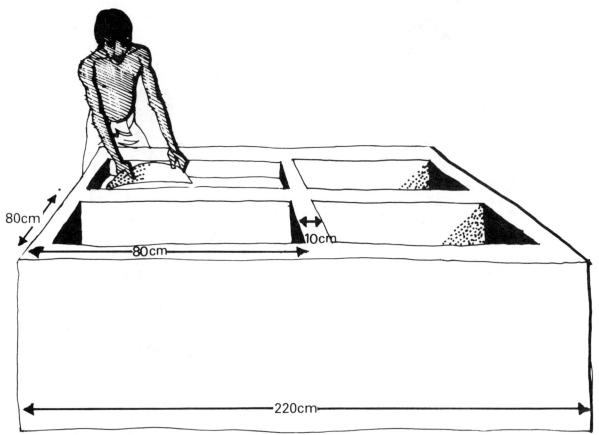

Figure 12.16. Construction of Magan Chula stove (1).

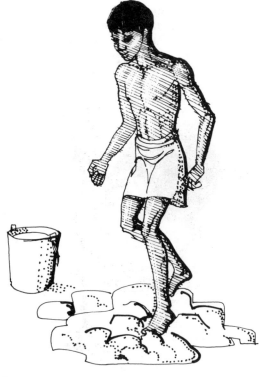

(2)

Stove construction
Day 1

3. After drying overnight the clay is brought inside and extra sand (previously sieved through a screen with eight wires per cm) is slowly kneaded into the clay (one part sand to every two parts clay). The principal role of the sand is to increase the strength of the stove by stopping cracks caused by heat or weight. The additional sand also reduces the shrinkage. (2)

4. 20 to 40kg of clay (enough for four to ten cylinders) is then placed on the potter's wheel – the KVIC Type B model. Its double-bearing design is important for the construction because it is stable at high and low speeds and during intermittent use, all of which are needed to construct the sections properly.

(3)

6. Both inside diameter and height are checked with pre-measured sticks. For a stove that will have a 17.5cm front pot-hole and be 22.5cm high the front cylinder should have a 20cm inside diameter and be 25cm tall. (5)

(5)

5. The front cylinders are thrown first. For a stove where the final inside diameter will be 17.5cm, a 20cm inside-diameter cylinder is made to allow for shrinkage. The top 2.5cm is cut off and put aside. The cylinder is pulled up until it is 25cm high. The top is turned out and around and smoothed down to make the top edge a double thickness. The top lip is bevelled inwards and flattened on top so that both round-bottom and flat-bottom pots will fit tightly. (3)(4)

7. The wheel is stopped and the 2.5cm thick strip that was removed from the top (step 5) is attached at one end, 17.5cm from the top. The wheel is turned slowly and a level ledge is put all the way around the inside of the cylinder. This will be the base of the firebox and will support the metal ash-collecting plate. (6)

(4)

(6)

8. After a number of front cylinders have been made, an equal number of second cylinders are made, with an internal diameter of about 16cm, if the final diameter is to be 14cm, and the same height as the front cylinders.

9. For each stove three smaller cylinders are made:
   - 21cm wide and 15cm high for the fuel entrance
   - 14cm wide and 14cm high for the connecting tunnel
   - 14cm wide and 17.5cm high for the air inlet.

10. At this time the cylinders are not rigid and must be handled carefully. The large cylinders are left out in the covered workshop to dry slightly, but the small cylinders are placed under plastic sheets and jute bags to keep them moist and flexible.

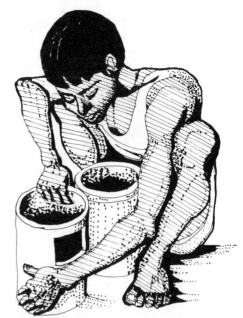

(7)

Day 2

11. On the following morning the large cylinders are put out in the sun for a few hours. They are turned over once to prevent uneven drying. If they are left out too long they will not dry evenly and will develop cracks.

12. By the afternoon the large cylinders are dry enough to hold their shape when handled, but can still be easily cut with a knife and are ready for assembly. The cylinders can be kept in this condition for a few days by putting them under plastic sheets and jute bags, out of the sun and wind.

13. The front cylinder is put on the potter's wheel upside down. The bottom, which is too thick, is scraped down and the cylinder is cut so that it is 23cm high. The front cylinder is taken off the wheel and put rightside up on the ground. The second cylinder is then turned upside down next to the front cylinder and trimmed to an equal height.

14. Rectangular holes for the connecting tunnel, 7.5cm wide and 5cm high, are cut in both cylinders with the hole on the second cylinder slightly above the one on the front. Wet clay is smeared around the two holes where the tunnel will be joined. (7)

15. The 14cm × 14cm cylinder that was kept moist is squeezed into an oval shape and the edges are thinned and flared out. It is then attached to the first cylinder and the joint strengthened and smoothed. The second cylinder is placed 6 – 7 cm away from the front cylinder at the closer point, and the connecting tunnel is attached, and the joints carefully smoothed and strengthened. (8)

(8)

16. On the inside the rectangular holes in the pot cylinders are enlarged to the oval shape of the tunnel, and properly smoothed.

17. A 3cm high and 7cm wide hole is cut out of the bottom edge of the front cylinder, on the opposite side from the connecting tunnel. Wet clay is smeared around the hole. (9)

(9)

The 14 cm wide and 17.5 cm high cylinder is cut like so. (10)

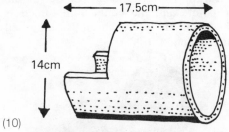

←—— 17.5cm ——→

14cm

(10)

and attached to the front cylinder.

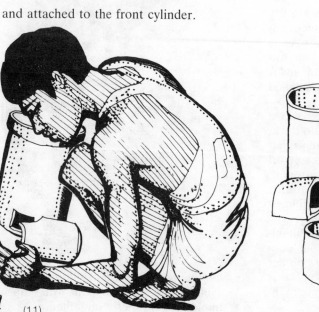

(11)

The connection is completed with soft clay on the top and with another piece on the rear to complete the curved tunnel. (12)

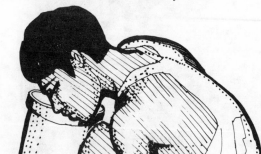

(12)

18. A 14cm wide by 10cm high rectangular hole is cut from the front cylinder starting right above the ledge for the grate, and wet clay is smeared around the opening. (13)

(13)

214

19. A brick to support the door structure is placed in front of the front cylinder on pieces of clay so that it is just slightly below the door opening.
20. The 21cm wide by 15cm high cylinder made for the fuel entrance, and kept moist (see step 9), is cut thus: (14)

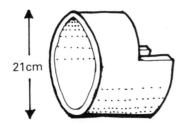

(14)

and squeezed into a rectangular section with the cutaway section of the top next to the cylinder. Extra clay is added to form a rectangular fuel entrance.
21. The connection between the door and the cylinder is made by smoothing the two sections together. (15)

(15)

22. The whole stove is now polished with water and left to sit in the covered workshop. In very dry weather the stoves are covered with jute bags to keep them from drying too quickly.

Day 3
23. On the following day the exit hole from the second cylinder to the chimney is cut; the hole is 6cm wide by 5cm high. Now that the fuel entrance has hardened it can be squared off and made to the proper shape. A strip of clay is placed across the second cylinder as a baffle guide to mark the position of the top of the mud baffle. A 10cm diameter chimney that is 2.5–3.5m tall should have a pot-to-baffle gap of 2–4cm. Since many pots have curved bottoms and will go down into the pot-hole, the baffle guide is placed 4cm from the top of the cylinder. (16)

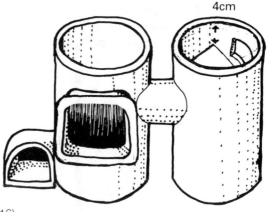

(16)

24. As the stove dries small cracks will sometimes appear where two pottery pieces have been joined. All the cracks should be moistened and filled with wet clay. It is important to make the joins as strong as possible, and that all cracks are patched before the stoves are fired. If there are too many cracks in a stove it will probably break during firing.

Making the chimney base and chimney

25. For the base of the chimney a cylinder 28cm high and 12cm inside diameter is made with the top lip going in so that the top opening is only 9cm inside. This will shrink down to a cylinder 25cm high that is 13cm wide on the outside with a 8cm top.

26. After the chimney base cylinder has hardened a hole 7cm wide and 6cm high is cut 14cm up from the bottom. A small cylinder is attached to make the tunnel between the second cylinder and the chimney base. The tunnel is cut so that it will fit flush to the second cylinder.

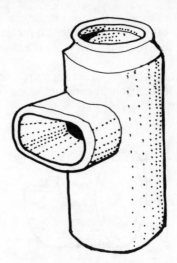

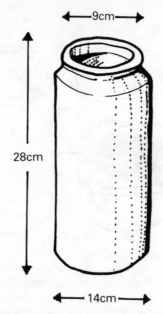

27. The chimney sections are 30cm high with a 10cm inside diameter when fired. They are made 10% bigger to allow for shrinkage.

Firing

28. After five days drying the stoves are ready to be put in the sun for full drying. When a whole batch is completed – about 130 – they are all put in the sun for two full days. On the second day all the cracks on all the stoves are filled in with wet clay and smoothed with water. The repairs take 2–5 minutes per stove. A red-coloured slip is applied to all the stoves, as is traditionally done with all pottery stoves.

29. The full batch of 130 stoves and over 100 chimney pipes are fired in one large bonfire kiln. The firing must be well controlled so that all the stoves get fired all the way through. The thicker walls of the stoves, as compared to pots, mean that they need more heat.

A cross section of the bonfire kiln is shown. The heating up of the stoves is controlled by the original layering of the fuel, the fuel added during the firing, the amount of air that is allowed into the bonfire, and the insulation provided from unburnt fuel, the mud covering and the ash.

Firing cycle
hours
0:00 kiln is lit at the edges; thick smoke given off
1:00 surface of mud is still wet; top has not burnt; holes near base are filled with more fuel
1:30 top fuel begins to burn.
1:45 bundles of fuel are tossed on the fire continuously; numerous cracks open in the mud coating
2:00 the mud coating is totally removed to allow air to reach all remaining fuel
2:30 the stoves stick out through the ashes on the top and the remaining carbonized fuel burns down.

30. On the following morning the stoves are all removed from the bonfire.

31. Metal grates are inserted into the stoves on the ledge at the base of the firebox. The grates are ordered from local metal workers and measure 17cm in diameter with holes covering 15–30% of the area.

32. The stove and chimney base are now wrapped in straw in a rectangular bundle so that they can be transported by cart, bicycle, or lorry without breaking.

5. MOULDED STOVES OF THAILAND

The most advanced production system for pottery stoves is the one that exists in Thailand, and to a lesser degree in neighbouring countries. In Thailand the stoves are made in production units rang-

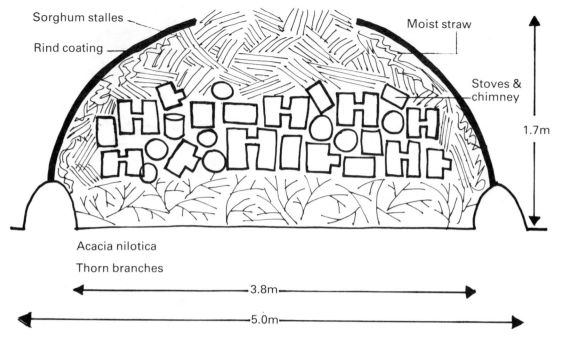

ing in size from one person and some part-time assistants, to units with up to 40 full-time workers. This system has been introduced in Kenya with a few modifications. For all the units the production process is basically the same.

Stage 1. Preparation of the raw materials
       2. Moulding the stoves
       3. Drying and cutting the stoves
       4. Making the grates
       5. Firing
       6. Inserting the ceramic stoves into metal buckets
       7. Firebox lining.

Preparation of the raw materials
The clay should be soaked in pits for a few days. In Thailand burnt rice-husk ash is added to the clay, usually in the ratio of 3:1, or 3:2, by volume of clay to husk ash. This can be added to the materials in the soaking pit, or wedged in later. In the larger scale units the raw materials are mixed with blungers or pugmills to get a consistent mix. In small operations buffaloes or people mix the raw materials with their feet.

Since mixing is easier with very wet materials, the final mix must be dried before it can be used. When it has reached the correct moisture content it is stored near the moulding area.

Moulding the stoves
The stoves are moulded in cement or wooden moulds that have the outside shape of the stove plus a percentage to make up for shrinkage. The bottomless moulds are placed on a table about 60cm high. A lump of the mix is measured out and kneaded to the proper consistency. The inside of the mould is wetted slightly and sprinkled liberally with ash to allow the finished piece to release easily. The clay is thrown into the base of the mould and forced up the sides with the fist, which is also used to reduce the floor thickness.

The moulder then uses his cupped hand to pull the clay up to the top of the mould all around, and to make a rough form of the inside. The stove must widen to allow the grate to fit in. A ledge is formed by the moulder on which to set the grate, and the inside is then finished to the proper shape. The mould is turned upside down on a board and the liner is tapped out. It is important that the stoves are consistently the correct size so that the grates will fit properly, and to reduce problems with cracking or warping.

Experienced moulders can mould a stove in this way every two or three minutes, but it takes time to develop speed, and quality control through the use of templates may be necessary in the early stages.

Drying and cutting
The liners are then stored in a shaded place to dry for two to three days. After that they can be put out in the sun, but they must be checked to make sure cracking does not occur.

When the liners are leather-hard, they can be cut and trimmed with a knife. Air openings and fuel doorways are cut with knives, and the top of the stove and pot-rests are smoothed and formed.

217

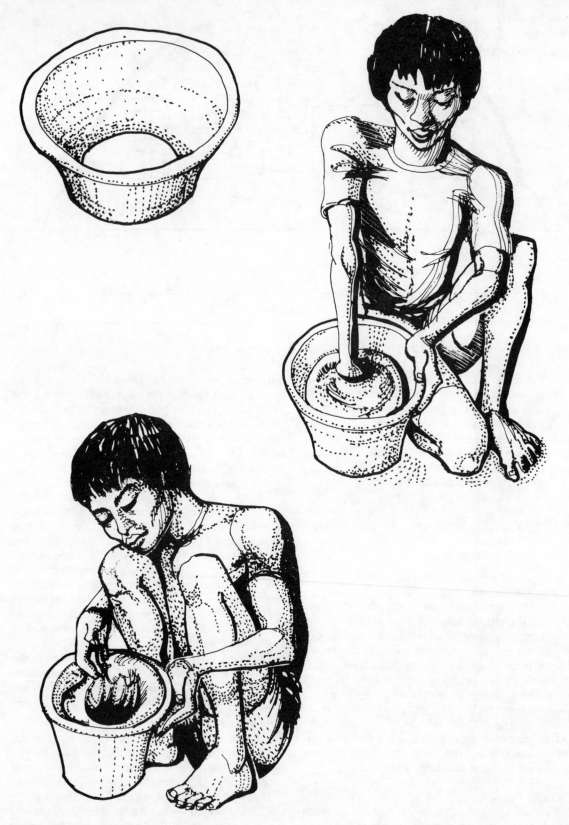

Figure 12.18.   Moulding Thai stove liners.

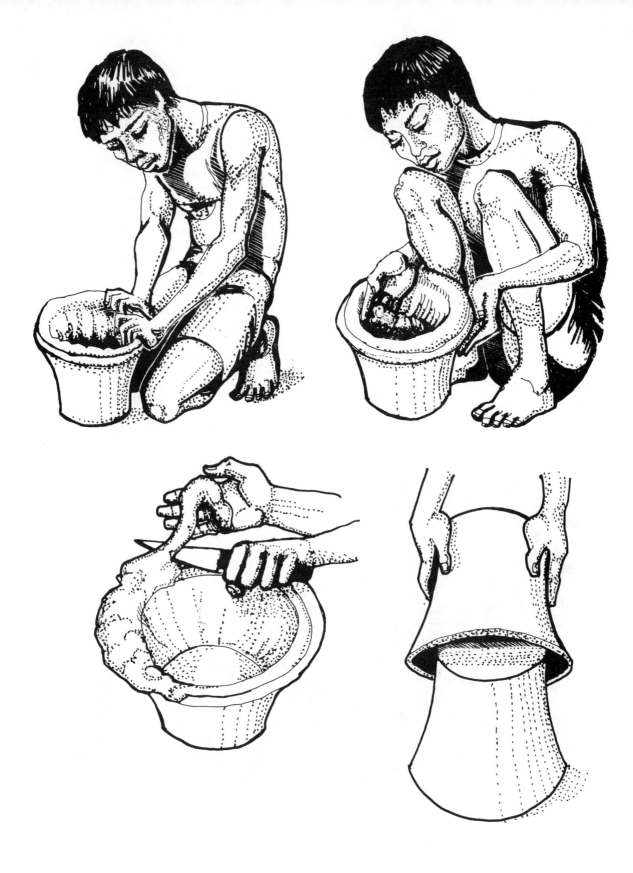

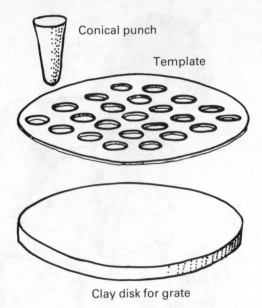

Conical punch

Template

Clay disk for grate

Figure 12.19. Making the grate.

For visual appeal, this is a most important step.

Making the grates

The grates take the greatest heat stress on the stoves and must be well made if they are to last. When a stove is designed so that uniform grates are used, the replacement of broken grates is greatly simplified.

The mix used for grates often has more rice-husk ash than that used for the stove body.

A piece of clay is formed into a circular disc. Average grates are 1.5cm thick after firing, but some improved designs use much thicker grates for greater insulation. If the final grate is to be 15cm in diameter, a 16.5cm template is used to allow for 10% shrinkage with this particular clay mix. A uniform pattern of holes is made by punching them out with a tapered tool through a template. The holes should be 1–1.5cm in diameter, and given an open area of 25–40% for charcoal and 12–35% for wood. The grates should be dried slowly and carefully so that they do not crack before or during firing. (See Figure 12.19).

Firing

For high volume production units large crossdraft kilns with a capacity of 29 cu m or more are used in Thailand. These are fired with wood. If the stoves are made along with other wares such as tiles, they can be fired in the same kiln. For smaller units, 2–6 cu m capacity updraft kilns will usually be sufficient as 30 to 60 stoves can be stacked in one cubic metre, depending on their size. For small firings the simple rice-husk kiln shown below will work

Figure 12.20.   Crossdraught kiln in a large Thai Bucket factory.

220

well and produce the ash needed for the construction process.

Figure 12.21. Simple walled kiln in Thailand (rice-husk fired). Note the stacking of liners. The door will be bricked up; air enters through ports on all sides. Rice husks are packed between the clay liners, ignited with a fire on top and left to smoulder. More fuel is added on top as needed.

Inserting the ceramic stove in a metal bucket
To protect the ceramic stove from mechanical shock and to make it easier to move around, it is usually fitted inside a metal bucket. The metal buckets are made by metal workers and can be straight-walled or tapered like a ceramic stove.

One to three centimetres of a low-density insulation like rice-husk ash is stuffed in between the bucket and the ceramic stove; the top rim and the primary air inlet are then sealed (usually with a cement/rice-husk ash mixture) to prevent the insulation from falling out. On some stoves no insulation is used, but these are more fragile.

Firebox lining
An optional final step is to coat the inside of the firebox with a thin mixture of rice-husk ash and clay (10:1 by volume) which probably improves the insulation and reduces the thermal shock to the ceramic stove.

Metal stoves

There are two types of production system for low-cost metal stoves. Medium to large factories produce relatively expensive gas and kerosene stoves from stamped and machine-cut pieces, and artisans working alone, or in small groups, produce a varied range of charcoal and wood-burning stoves. Artisans working at a small-scale level are often dominant producers; because they generally use cheaper (but non-uniform) re-cycled or scrap metal, they are available to do repairs, and they keep the retail mark-up low by selling direct from their place of production. Most traditional designs do not require the accuracy of construction neces-

sary for the proper functioning of kerosene or natural gas stoves, but improved stoves *must* be constructed accurately if they are to achieve a better performance. There is thus a need to promote higher quality production from individuals or small groups of artisans.

With high levels of production of standardized designs it is probable that medium to large workshops will take an increased share of the market, but this chapter is orientated towards the techniques and tools that would be used for small-scale operations. The examples are primarily drawn from metal workers in Kenya and The Gambia, but are applicable to most other countries.

RAW MATERIALS
The qualities of mild sheet steel – toughness, heat resistance and ductility – make it one of the best materials for stove fabrication. It can be purchased in a wide variety of thicknesses, new or used. The thickest in general use is that from oil barrels (1mm or 24 gauge) – this is easily worked with hand tools. Steel of 1.5mm or more thickness is difficult to work with hand tools, but is considerably stronger, more rigid, and lasts longer when subjected to high temperatures and to the corrosive compounds released by burning wood and charcoal.

Scrap mild sheet steel is a common raw material for artisans since its odd sizes, rust, or distortions, make it unsuitable for many formal engineering industries, and it is therefore considerably cheaper than new steel. Old oil barrels and scrap cars are two major sources of scrap sheet, and their systematic preparation for a new use can considerably quicken the production process.

Steel barrels are often cleaned by stacking and burning them in a bonfire to remove the oil or chemical residues. The next step is to open out the barrels and flatten them so that the steel can be marked out and cut.

A simple method is to lay the drum on its side and cut lengthwise with a hammer and chisel. The top and bottom plates are then cut out by chiselling around the inside of the rims. Then the top and bottom rims are cut by resting each rim on a section of railtrack and cutting through with a hammer and chisel. The drum wall will spring open slightly. The wall should then be stretched out and stamped as flat as possible so that the rims can be cut off, and the remaining metal can be flattened further with a large hammer. A typical oil barrel (90 cm tall and 55cm in diameter) will yield two 55cm circles and a 90 cm × 173cm rectangle giving a total of 2.7 sq m of sheet steel.

Old cars require considerably more work to release useful pieces of steel because of their irregular shape. Reclaiming sheet metal from cars

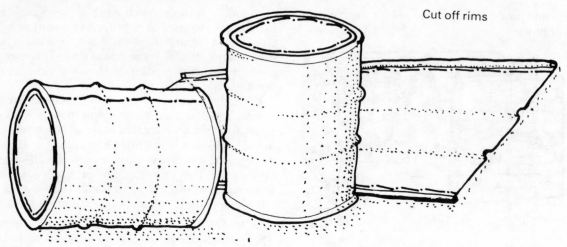

Cut off rims

Figure 12.22. Procedure for cutting up steel barrels.

is often done by independent artisans who then sell the flattened pieces. Systematic cutting up of cars will of course extract the greatest amount of steel, but this will be difficult with badly-wrecked vehicles. The roof, bonnet, boot lid, side wing panels and doors supply the sheet scrap. Unbolting, rather than chiselling off, the hinged parts is usually easier and quicker, and wastes less steel. Once the car is stripped to the frame it may be dismantled with a few strategically-placed cuts. Axes, or oxy-actylene cutting may be necessary for the thicker or inaccessible places.

CONSTRUCTION

Marking out
For a limited number of simple stoves the outline of the pieces can be drawn onto the steel with a nail or a sharpened hacksaw blade. For a larger number of stoves, especially if they involve complicated shapes, it is better to use templates, laid out on the sheet and re-arranged as necessary, to get the maximum number of pieces.

CUTTING
A *hammer* and *chisel* are the most versatile cutting tools, but *tinsnips* are more accurate. For greater leverage and control tinsnips can be modified by extending one handle by jamming a small length of pipe onto the end. The long end can then be lodged in the ground or on an anvil, allowing one hand to work the cutting blade and leaving the other free to support and manipulate the work piece.

Bench shears or *guillotines* are particularly useful for cutting thicker material up to 4mm, and can sometimes be made from used pieces. They are most applicable for medium to high levels of production and need a permanent place in the workshop.

Oxy-acetylene equipment can be used for cutting very thick metal (5–20mm) but it is usually not necessary for small-stove production. *Electrical* or *compressed-air powered devices* are available for cutting metals, varying from very thin to 3mm sheet, but require an even greater investment.

Holes can be punched, or drilled out. Drilling is more precise but requires more equipment and time, and hand-made *punches* and *dies* can be made for nearly all purposes. A *punch* is usually made from a bar of suitable diameter made of high tensile strength steel with a high carbon content. *Dies* can be a piece of pipe, or a hole in a piece of thick metal. The die is placed underneath the working piece, in the correct place. The punch is hammered through the material (resting on the die) to cut out a small disc leaving the required hole. The diameter of the die hole should be at least equal to the diameter of the required hole in the work piece, plus twice the thickness of the material. After a hole has been punched any slight flare can be removed by hammering the piece on an anvil. This can result in reducing the size of the hole, so it may be necessary to punch a hole slightly larger than the required finished diameter.

Small holes in thin steel for *rivets* can usually be made by simply hammering the rivet through each piece to be joined, or through both together.

Forming
The rolling of cones or cylinders is a skilled job without workshop equipment, but it is often done effectively using the following techniques.

A section of railtrack is placed on its side and the sheet to be rolled is placed at an angle to it, with one edge touching the ground. The sheet is struck with a hammer between the rail edge and the ground, whilst feeding the sheet slowly down-

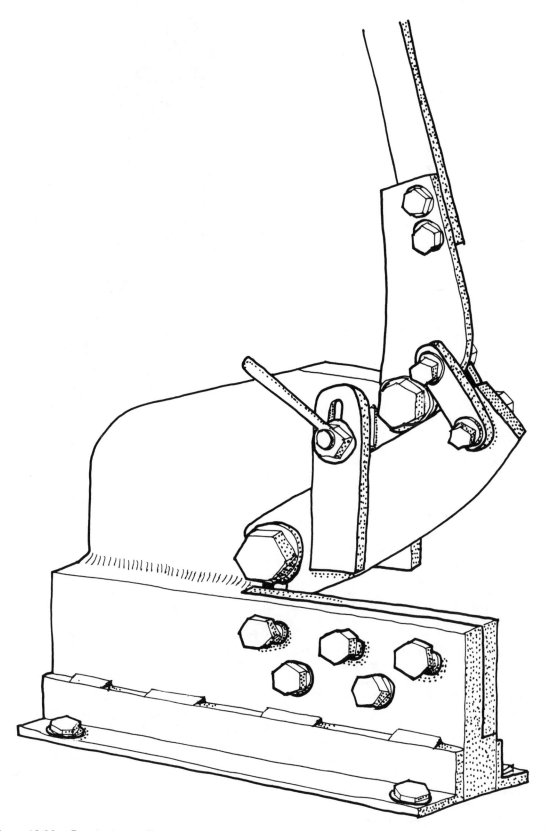

Figure 12.23.   Bench shears. These are mounted onto a concrete block for stability.

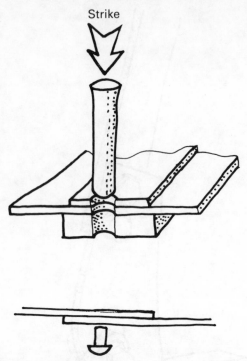

Figure 12.24. Punch and die. (Centre) Large holes in sheet metal can easily be made by striking a punch with a large hammer through sheet metal resting on a die.
D (Minimum) = diameter of punch + 2 × thickness of material (Bottom) Small holes may be made for rivet holes by resting the sheet metal on the rivet and striking it hard with a hammer. It may take several attempts to force the rivet through.

Section of rail

Figure 12.25. Finishing a rolled cone. Kenyan artisan using a flat bar made from a vehicle leaf-spring.

wards. When the piece is halfway rolled it is flipped over and the same method used on the other end to finish the cylinder or cone.

The cylinder or cone can be finished off by hammering with the inside on the flat side of the anvil.

Rolled or folded edges have greater rigidity, are aesthetically more appealing, and are less dangerous than unfinished edges.

Cylinders and cones can be made more easily with rolling machines, but unless large-volume production is being undertaken, investment in cheaper, more versatile tools and equipment may be the more appropriate option.

Joining

The technique for joining sheet metal depends to a certain extent on local traditions and skills, and on the availability and range of equipment. The most labour-intensive methods requiring the least investment, but considerable skill, are seaming and rivetting. Welding is simpler and quicker but requires expensive equipment.

Seam joints require considerable skill to complete accurately and quickly, but a well-made joint is extremely strong, air-tight and visually appealing. It is only used to join straight or curved lengths of sheet metal.

Rivets are used where seam joints are not possible, such as for fixing handles, pot supports and doors with hinges.

Rivets may be punched directly through metal less than 1mm thick. Thicker metal must be prepunched using a punch and die.

Welding is the most versatile method of joining because it only needs to be done in a few spots rather than along the whole edge. It can be done with oxy-acetylene equipment, or more cheaply with arc welders, or specialized spot welders. Oxy-acetylene welding is often necessary on thin metal

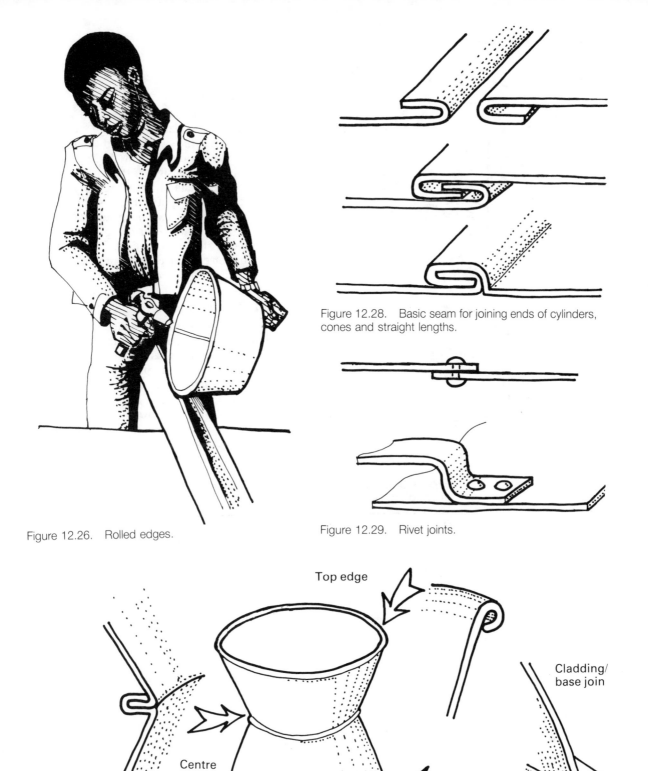

Figure 12.26.   Rolled edges.

Figure 12.28.   Basic seam for joining ends of cylinders, cones and straight lengths.

Figure 12.29.   Rivet joints.

Top edge

Cladding/ base join

Centre seam

Figure 12.27.   Typical folds and joints on the Kenyan ceramic Jiko.

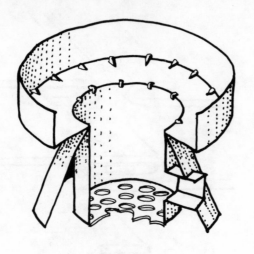

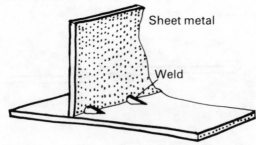

Sheet metal

Weld

Figure 12.30.   Spot – or track-welding sheet metal.

because arc welders can burn a hole.

The Gambian Noflie stove is joined entirely using spot welds.

Cast-iron stoves

Cast-iron stoves, and stove pieces such as grates and top plates, are made in a large number of countries around the world, and many other foundries could produce them if they had the proper moulds. The design of the moulds should be discussed beforehand with foundrymen and mould-makers to simplify the casting. Simple stoves or stove pieces can be produced in very small foundries, but large or complex stoves, or large numbers of stoves, are best produced in foundries better equipped and more experienced at large-size/scale production.

Cast-aluminium stoves

Cast-aluminium stoves are produced in a number of designs for burning charcoal and wood in the Philippines. Aluminium can be cast in small units using scrap metal, for example engine blocks. It is more expensive than cast-iron. Traditional artisans can make a wide range of designs if they have the proper moulds, but the low melting point and relatively high cost of aluminium will limit its use for stove production.

Typical accuracy and capacity of various types of weighing scales:

Market scales	1 to 5 g, to weigh up to 15kg
Laboratory scales	1 to 10g, various capacities depending on cost
Pendulum letter scales	5 to 10g, to weigh up to 1 kg
Kitchen scales	25 or 50g, to weigh up to 3 or 10kg

References

Page

9, 11, 13   Parker and Hurley, *Combustion of Vegetable Wastes in Relation to Power Production*, Conference Mundial Da Energia, World Power Conference, 1954

13   *Firewood Crops*, National Academy of Sciences, 1980 K.Openshaw, *Guidelines for woodfuel surveys*, FAO

17, 37   'Testing the Efficiency of Wood-burning Cookstoves – International Standards', VITA, 1985

52   M. Howes, 'The Sarvodaya Stoves Project: A Critical Review of Developments 1972–82; ITDG, 1983

57, 59, 61, 80   I. Evans and M. Boutette, *Lorena Stoves*, VIA, 1981

57   *Wood Conserving Cookstoves: A Design Guide*, VITA/ITDG, 1980

59   M. Sarin, 'Training Women as Trainers', *Boiling Point No. 8*, ITDG, 1985

61, 90   W. Micuta, *Modern Stoves for All*, IT Publications/Bellerive Foundation, 1985

60   P.G.M. Nievergeld, 'Wood-burning Tests on Two Metal Stoves', W.S.G., 1980

67   A. Bachmann, 'Less Smoky Rooms', UNICEF, 1984

67   G. Yameogo et al., 'Lab Tests of Fired Clay Stoves', CILSS/VITA, 1984

67   S. Prasad et al., 'Technical Aspects of Woodburning Cook-stoves', W.S.G., 1983

67, 113   S.F. Baldwin, 'Biomass Stoves: Engineering Design, Development and Dissemination', VITA, 1986

Page

75   S. Joseph and P. Hassrick, *Burning Issues*, UNICEF/IT Publications, 1984

77   M. Sarin/ITDG, *Boiling Point No. 7*, ITDG, 1984

79   A. Caceres, *Case Study – Dissemination of Woodstoves in Guatemala*, CEMAT, 1983

90   P. Young, 'Technical Notes: South India', ITDG, 1984

90, 128   'Improved Biomass Cooking Stove for Household Use', RTFD, 1984

108   C.R. Gupta, *Wood Heat for Cooking*, Indian Academy of Sciences, 1983

108, 128   S. Joseph and J. Loose, 'Testing a two-hole Indonesian Mud Stove', ITDG, 1982

111, 114, 128   S. Joseph and J. Loose, *Design and Laboratory Testing of Portable Metal Briquette Cooking Stoves in the Sahel*, UNSO/ITC, 1983

111, 128   K. Bennett, 'End of Mission Report: The Gambia National Improved Stoves Project', UNSO/ITC, 1984

112   S.F. Baldwin, 'New Directions in Woodstove Development', VITA News, 1984

112   F. Sulilatu, 'The Tamilnadu Metal Stove', WSG, 1983

141   Samootsakom, *Wood Heat for Cooking*, Indian Academy of Sciences, Bangalore, 1983

168   B. Herath, 'Standard Cooking Tests for Improved Stoves', CISIR, 1984

192   M. Cardew, *Pioneer Pottery*, Longman, 1979

Further Reading

Cookstove Technology, Tata, 1985

K. Darrow, K. Keller, R. Pam, *AT Sourcebook*, VIA, 1986

M.T. Feuerstein, *Partners in Evaluation*, Macmillan, London, 1986

Firewood Crops, National Academy of Sciences, 1980

G. Foley, P. Moss and L. Timberlake, *Stoves and Trees*, Earthscan, 1984

G. Foley and P. Moss, *Improved Cookstoves in Developing Countries*, Earthscan, 1983

Fuel Saving Cookstoves, Aprovecho, 1984

M.K. Garg, *Development of an Appropriate Technology for Decentralized Pottery in Rural India*, ATDA

D.O. Hall, G.W. Barnard, P.A. Moss, *Biomass for Energy in the Developing Countries*, Pergamon Press, 1982

M. Harper, *Consultancy for Small Businesses*, IT Publications, 1977

M. Harper, *Small Business in the Third World*, J. Wiley/IT Publications, 1984

International Directory of New and Renewable Energy, UNESCO, 1980

A.L. Little Jnr., *Common Fuelwood Crops*, Communi-tech Associates, Morgantown West Virginia, 1983

G.F.C. Rogers and Y.R. Mayhew, *Engineering Thermodynamics, Work and Heat Transfer*, Longman, 1967

Y. Shanahan and S. Joseph, *The Stove Project Manual: Planning and Implementation*, IT Publications, 1985

S.K. Sharma, *Dynamics of Development* (2 vols), Concept Publishing Company, Delhi, 1978

E.L. Struening, M. Guttentag, *Handbook of Evaluation Research*, Sage, 1975

Technical Aspects of Woodburning Cookstoves, Eindhoven, 1983

D.A. Tillman et al., *Wood Combustion*, Academic Press, 1981

Newsletters are published by all regional centres and also by:

ITDG – *Boiling Point*

Bois de Feu – *Bois de Feu*

FAO (Bangkok) – *Newsletter*

Approvecho – *Cookstove News*

Who to Contact for Further Support

'Northern' organizations providing technical advice

ITDG
Myson House
Railway Terrace
Rugby CV21 3HT
United Kingdom

Bellerive Foundation
Case Postale 6
1211 Geneve 3
Switzerland

Woodenergy Systems Group
Korte Jansstraat 7
3512 GM Utrecht
The Netherlands

GTZ/Gate
Postfach 5180
Dag Hammerskjold Weg 1
D6236 Eschborn 1
BRD
West Germany

Aprovecho Institute
80574 Hazelton Road
Cottage Grove
OR 97424
USA

Association Bois de Feu
28 Bde De La Republique
13100 Aix en Provence
France

VITA
1815 North Lynn Street
Arlington
Virginia 22209
USA

FAO
Documentation Office
Via Terme di Caracalla
00100 Rome
Italy

A.T. International
1331 H. Street NW, Suite 1200
Washington DC 20005
USA

Regional activities are co-ordinated by the Foundation for Woodstove Dissemination (FWD), located at:

Korte Jansstraat 7
3512 GM Utrecht
The Netherlands

The FWD regional centres are located at:

Central and South American Region
Centro De Estudios Mesoamericano Sobre
   Technologia Apropiada
(CEMAT)
Apartado Postal 1160
Guatamala City, Guatamala C.A.

East African Region
Kenyan Energy Non-Governmental
   Organizations Association
(KENGO)
P.O. Box 48917
Nairobi, Kenya

West African Region
Comité Interétat Permanent de Lutte Contre la
   Sécheresse dans le Sahel
(CILSS)
B.P. 7049
Ouagadougou, Burkino Faso

Indian Region
Consortium on Rural Technology
(CORT)
E-350, Nirman Vihar
Delhi 110092, India

South-east Asian Region
Yayasan Dian Desa
P.O. Box 19, Bulaksumur
Yogyakarta, Indonesia

Pacific
Contact F.W.D., Netherlands

In addition the FAO Regional Office in Bangkok is a valuable contact:

Maliwan Mansion
Phra Atit Road
Bangkok 10200
Thailand